Shakespeare

Shakespeare,

Annotated Bibliographies
and Media Guide for Teachers.

Andrew M. McLean, *1941-*
University of Wisconsin—Parkside

National Council of Teachers of English
1111 Kenyon Road, Urbana, Illinois 61801

For my nephews Lee, Andy, Chris, and Keith Duval

Grateful acknowledgment is made for permission to reprint the following material. Descriptions from the *NICEM Indexes*. Copyright © 1977. Reprinted by permission of the National Information Center for Educational Media. From *Teaching Shakespeare,* edited by Walter Edens *et al* (copyright © 1977 by Princeton University Press): "Annotated Bibliography," by Andrew M. McLean. Reprinted by permission of Princeton University Press.

Book Design: Tom Kovacs

NCTE Stock Number 43776

Library of Congress Cataloging in Publication Data

McLean, Andrew M   1941–
    Shakespeare, annotated bibliographies and media guide for teachers.

    1. Shakespeare, William, 1564–1616—Bibliography.
    2. Shakespeare, William, 1564–1616—Study and teaching.   3. Shakespeare, William, 1564–1616—Film adaptations.   I. Title.
Z8813.M32   [PR2987]   016.8223'3   80-13603
ISBN 0-8141-4377-6

Contents

.

Preface

These bibliographies and guide began as a search of the literature to determine how I could improve my college sophomore Shakespeare course, expanded when I could not answer a student-teacher's questions about teaching *Julius Caesar* in high school, and coincided with my growing interest in Shakespeare on film. It soon became clear that while Shakespeare is taught in every school and college in America, there has been only piecemeal public discussion of that teaching. Within the last few years, however, *teaching* Shakespeare has been discussed at meetings of the National Council of Teachers of English, the Modern Language Association of America, the Shakespeare Association of America and has been the subject of special issues of the *Shakespeare Quarterly, Shakespeare Newsletter,* and a 1977 book published by Princeton University Press. At the same time, growing interest in teaching Shakespeare on film has established this as an exciting new area of study; while an old strategy, teaching through performance, has been revived as a challenging way to encounter Shakespearean drama. Yet, because there is no one way or method to teach Shakespeare, it is important for teachers to share their experiences. What works well for one teacher may not work at all for another, but there are many approaches or techniques that might work if tried.

The primary purpose of this book is to identify resources for the variety of approaches that teachers might use. If the teacher finds something here which helps the student to understand and enjoy Shakespeare better, then this project has been worthwhile. In this regard, the high school teacher and college professor share many common problems in introducing students to Shakespeare's language, poetry, dramatic structure, portrayal of character, and to those universal themes that make teaching Shakespeare so rewarding. Perhaps the difference in teaching Shakespeare to high school students and to college undergraduates is less one of kind than degree; the division of bibliographies between secondary school and college teaching is one of convenience. I hope those using the book view it as a whole, gleaning useful suggestions from all parts and not just from one section.

Part One of this book offers annotated bibliographies for teaching

Shakespeare in school and college as dramatic literature, through performance, and with other authors. For the few entries where no annotation appears, either the title is self-explanatory or for some reason I was unable to secure a copy or verify the entry. My annotations are meant to indicate the essay or book's substance and relative usefulness. The general sections list materials that broadly discuss teaching Shakespeare in the school or college. These are both immediately followed by materials focused on the individual Shakespeare plays. Items concerned with Shakespeare's non-dramatic poetry follow materials for individual plays in the college section. These deal less with theoretical matters than with explication of the texts; and they are, of course, useful for teachers at all levels. I have, with some exceptions, excluded traditional literary criticism, unless the essay would serve some particular pedagogical purpose. This, obviously, is often a hard decision to make, but those seeking a bibliography of recent Shakespearean criticism should consult the annual bibliographies found in *PMLA* and *Shakespeare Quarterly* and the convenient Goldentree Bibliography compiled by David Bevington, *Shakespeare* (AHM Publishing Corp., 1979). In the bibliography of materials for teaching Shakespeare through performance, I have tried to provide a generous sampling of classroom-related suggestions for enactments of various kinds. The last section of Part One provides a checklist of books and articles for teachers who like to demonstrate Shakespeare's influence or popularity by comparing his work to that of other authors.

Part Two presents the first substantive bibliography to the growing body of criticism of Shakespearean films. Discussions of the filming of Shakespeare and of teaching Shakespeare on film are listed together in the general section. Then follows a bibliography of the criticism of twenty-six feature-length Shakespeare films. This material will complement Jack Jorgens and Christine Egloff's *Shakespeare on Stage and Screen: A Bibliography of Criticism* (Indiana University Press, 1979), the annual *Shakespeare Quarterly* bibliography, and checklists appearing in the *Shakespeare on Film Newsletter.* The short section on Shakespeare on television is not meant to be as comprehensive as that on film, but it does sample the critical reception of Shakespeare on television. While critics have not yet tackled the theoretical or practical differences between filming Shakespeare for television as opposed to the cinema, the present BBC/Time-Life series, which will televise all of Shakespeare's plays over the next several years, will certainly generate such discussion. The entries listed may provide the background for future criticism, and suggest to the teacher ways of using the BBC/Time-Life productions in the classroom.

Part Three is a guide to available media resources for the classroom. The audio-visual section is divided into Shakespeare's Life and Times, Shakespeare's Theater, and Shakespeare's Plays. It lists filmstrips, films, audio-cassette tapes, and transparencies. The general format of these media entries gives the title, number of parts, grade level (J,H, and/or C), number of frames (if a filmstrip) or running time (if a film or tape), if color or black and white, producer, year, distributors (including educational AV centers), titles of parts, a brief description taken from the distributor's catalog, any reviews, and my comment (if viewed or heard). Even distributors' catalogs do not always provide this information, so some entries will not contain all of this information. A key to abbreviations together with the name and address of distributors is found in the appendix. Users should request catalogs from distributors or from the nearest state educational media center to determine costs. In addition to consulting distributors' catalogs, I have consulted the Library of Congress *Film Catalogue,* the *National Union Catalogues of Motion Pictures and Filmstrips,* and have found helpful the various educational media indexes, especially those on films and filmstrips, published by the National Information Center for Educational Media (NICEM) at the University of Southern California. NICEM indexes are periodically updated and should be consulted together with the *Educational Film Locator of the Consortium of University Film Centers* (Bowker, 1978). The final sections of Part Three provide a listing of available Shakespeare play recordings, with no attempt to evaluate them, and a list of rental sources for feature-length sound films.

I have attempted to make these bibliographies and the guide as complete as possible through 1978, although a bibliographer's work is never done nor is it ever as complete as he might wish. My thanks to Louis Marder, editor of the *Shakespeare Newsletter,* and to Princeton University Press for permission to use material which first appeared in *Shakespeare Newsletter* 25 (April 1975) and in Walter Edens, et al., eds., *Teaching Shakespeare* (Princeton University Press, 1977), pp. 317–33. I hope to update, correct, and amend this work through frequent contributions in the *Shakespeare Newsletter,* and I ask authors and teachers at all levels to inform me of omissions and additions.

In preparing these materials I have incurred obligations to University of Wisconsin-Parkside librarians Linda Piele, Judy Pryor, and especially Larry Crumb (now at the University of Oregon); to the resources of the Wisconsin Interlibrary Loan System; to my indefatigable student assistant, Gregg Hermann; and to UW-Parkside's Center for Teaching Excellence for a small grant which helped to prepare earlier versions of these materials. I would also like to extend my appreciation for the invaluable assistance of Becky Buschak, Nicky Kroll, Darlene Safransky, Tracy Pavela, and Kathy Kennedy, and to Beatrice McLean, who helped get this project underway.

A.M.
Kenosha, Wisconsin
23 April 1979

Part One

Title Abbreviations

Ado: Much Ado About Nothing
Ant: Antony and Cleopatra
AWW: All's Well That Ends Well
AYL: As You Like It
Cor: Coriolanus
Cym: Cymbeline
Err: Comedy of Errors
Hamlet: Hamlet
1H4: 1 Henry IV
2H4: 2 Henry IV
H5: Henry V
1-3H6: 1-3 Henry VI
H8: Henry VIII
JC: Julius Caesar
John: King John
LLL: Love's Labor's Lost
Lear: King Lear
Macbeth: Macbeth

MM: Measure for Measure
MND: Midsummer Night's Dream
MV: Merchant of Venice
Othello: Othello
Per: Pericles
R2: Richard II
R3: Richard III
Rom: Romeo and Juliet
Shr: Taming of the Shrew
Temp: The Tempest
TGV: Two Gentlemen of Verona
Tim: Timon of Athens
Tit: Titus Andronicus
TN: Twelfth Night
TNK: Two Noble Kinsmen
Tro: Troilus and Cressida
Wiv: Merry Wives of Windsor
WT: Winter's Tale

Teaching Shakespeare in the Schools

General

Adland, David E. **Group Drama. Teacher's Book . . . A Companion to the Group Drama Approach to Shakespeare, pupil books 1–4.** London: Longman, 1964.

Ahrens, Rüdiger, ed. **Anglistik & Englischunterricht** (Trier) 3 (1978).

"Shakespeare im Unterricht" issue. Includes the following essays: R. Ahrens, "Die Tradition der Shakespeare-Behandlung im Englischunterricht," pp. 12–38; W. Habicht, "Zum Shakespeare-Bild heute—Tendenzen und Impulse neuerer Shakespeare-Forschung," pp. 39–52; T. Finkenstaedt, "Shakespeare zwischen Wissenschaft und Unterricht—Sechs Fragen an die Schule," pp. 53–61; R. von Ledebur, "Die Shakespeare-Lektüre in den Curricula der reformierten Oberstufe," pp. 63–76; E. Hombitzer, "Shakespeare-Lektüre in der reformierten gymnasialen Oberstufe—unter besonderer Berücksichtigung von Grundkursen," pp. 77–91; E. Häublein, "Shakespeare und die hermeneutische Erziehung," pp. 93–99; W. Hortmann, "Shakespeare-Unterricht zwischen Text und Theater," pp. 101–131; V. Schulz, "*Ado*—Ein Unterrichtsmodell," pp. 133–160; W. Hortmann, "Shakespeare made in Duisburg," pp. 161–172; W. Clemen, "Die Fortbildungsseminare für Gymnasiallehrer an der Shakespeare-Bibliothek München," pp. 173-179; and I. Boltz, "Bibliographie zu 'Shakespeare im Unterricht'," pp. 181–189.

Alexander, A. G. **"English Stones."** *Peabody Journal of Education* 17 (1939): 35–41.

Relates how a colleague ruined a Shakespeare course by dwelling on trivial details instead of concentrating on Shakespeare's concern with the entire human condition.

Allen, R. T. **"How a Teen-ager's Dream Came True at Stratford."** *Maclean's Magazine* (Toronto), 12 October 1957, pp. 28–29, 75–79.

Angoff, Charles. **"Was Shakespeare 'Shakespeare'?"** *Clearing House* 31 (September 1956): 23–25.

Argues that students should be told about "the grave doubts" of Shakespeare's authorship.

Arndt, Reinhold. **"Shakespeare-Lektüre in der Schule. Rückblick u. Neubesinnung."** *Praxis des neusprachlichen Unterrichts* (Dortmund) 5 (1958): 35–42.

Arnold, Elizabeth. **"No More Hurly-Burly."** *English Journal* 41 (January 1952): 37–38.

The teacher abandons traditional lectures on *Macbeth* and lets students imagine the staging of the play, including casting their favorite actors in each role.

Ayer, Coburn H. **"Shakespeare Festival."** *English Journal* 43 (May 1954): 259–60.

Neighboring schools and an actor take Shakespeare out of the classroom and put "the show on the road."

Bailey, Margery. **"Shakespeare in Action."** *English Journal* 43 (March 1954): 111–18, 141.

Use of the Tudor stage restores the vital action and original interpretation of *MV* and *Hamlet*.

Baker, Franklin Thomas. **"Shakespeare in the Schools."** In *Shakespearean Studies,* edited by Brander Matthews, and Ashley H. Thorndike, pp. 31–41. New York: Russell & Russell, 1962. (Originally published by Columbia University Press, 1916.)

A brief survey which ends by asking "Do we really know what our pupils are getting from their study of Shakespeare?"

Baker, H. T. **"Should Shakespeare Be Expurgated?"** *English Journal* (College edition) 22 (February 1933): 127–31.

Contends that since Shakespeare combines frankness with good taste, he is safe for the young to read.

Ball, Bona W. **"Shakespeare's Language in Appalachia."** *Kentucky English Bulletin* 18 (Fall 1968): 26–30.

Catalogs unusual expressions of Appalachia "which would sound pleasant to the ear of Shakespeare."

Ballet, Arthur. **[Shakespeare Unit.]** In *The English Language Arts in the Secondary School,* prepared by the Commission on the English Curriculum of the National Council of Teachers of English, pp. 234–36.

New York: Appleton-Century-Crofts, 1956.

A twelfth grade unit on Shakespeare (following study of ancient and medieval drama) to give "mature students an understanding of the elements which combined to make Shakespeare a major playwright."

Bannerman, Andres. **"Approach to Shakespeare."** *Use of English* (London) 20 (Spring 1969): 239–41.

Benelli, Peter. **"Oh, Noble Fool!"** *English Leaflet* 57 (February 1958): 1–6.

Surveys comedies to show how "the criticizer becomes the criticized."

Bennett, R. C. **"Oral Tradition and the Teaching of Shakespeare."** *English Language Teaching* (London) 23 (October 1968): 56–59.

Teachers should first encourage students to read Shakespeare's finest lines aloud to experience the joy of the language; then give brief and uncomplicated explanations of sentence structure and vocabulary. Shakespeare should not be translated word by word.

Bensley, Gordon E. **"Use of Shakespearean Films at Phillips Academy."** *Educational Screen* 22 (April 1956): 35.

Describes experiment in regarding films of Shakespeare's plays as works of art independent of text.

Bernstein, Abraham. **"Humanizing Shakespeare."** Paper presented at the New York State English Council meeting, 4 May 1974. (Available from EDRS; ED 092 986.)

Suggests the use of bulletin boards, signs, maps, etc. to arouse attention; and, if possible, the choice of a play in performance locally or scheduled for TV.

Bernstein, Abraham. **"The Shakespearean Play."** In his *Teaching English in High School,* pp. 190–229. New York: Random House, 1961.

The teacher should (1) know the play thoroughly, (2) be prepared to act the play, and (3) have questions ready that intensify interest. Discusses eight plays.

Bildersee, Max U. **"Shakespeare, Living Literature."** *Educational Screen and Audio Visual Guide* 45 (March 1966): 45–46, 58.

Suggests use of recordings of plays and scheduling a brief Shakespeare season with the cooperation of school libraries.

Blaisdell, Thomas C. **"Teaching Drama."** In his *Ways to Teach English,* pp. 454–70. New York: Doubleday and Doran, 1930.

Focuses on Shakespeare and how the teacher must "transport the pupils from the schoolroom to the scene of action." The teacher reads play aloud, substitutes synonyms for difficult words, places emphasis on character portrayal and development, encourages memorization of lines, and avoids discussion of sources or grammar.

Blakely, Gilbert S. **Teacher's Outlines for Studies in English.** New York: American Book, 1908.

Supplies outlines for the study of *MV, AYL, JC,* and *Macbeth.* A four step method is proposed: (1) preparation by initial presentation to arouse interest, (2) a first reading to get the main facts of the play and the progress of each scene, (3) a second reading, more careful, to interpret Shakespeare's thought, (4) study of the play as a whole, the form (meter and style) and content (setting, plot, and character), as well as study of Shakespeare's life and character.

Bliss, Laurence E. **"Reply to Mr. Loveall."** *English Journal* 37 (January 1948): 39–40.

Argues that study of Shakespeare and other literature contributes to the development of mature, critical thinking by adolescents. See also, in this section, Loveall.

Boas, F. S., et al. **"Shakespeare and the School."** Conference of Educational Associations: Report, 1929, pp. 44–45.

Bolenius, Emma M. **Teaching Literature in the Grammar Grades and High School.** Boston: Houghton Mifflin, 1915.

Suggestions for teaching drama include initial rapid reading of a play for the story, followed by a second reading "to study characters, development of plot, descriptions and fine lines." Students should make plot charts. Specific suggestions for teaching *AYL, TN, Macbeth, Hamlet, MV,* and *JC* with more emphasis given latter two plays, pp. 175–86.

Bolle, W. **"Shakespeare im Rahmen der Bildungsarbeit der höh Schüle."** *Neuphilologische Monatsschrift* (Leipzig) 4 (October 1933): 362–79.

Borgwardt, P. **"Shakespeare und seine Behandlung im heutigen Klassen-unterricht."** *Die Neueren Sprachen* (Marburg) 44 (May 1936): 197–212.

Bose, Amalendu. **"Teaching of Shakespeare."** *Indian Literature* (New Delhi) 9 (1966): 77–84.

Teachers must generate in student's mind a sense of the drama of Shakespeare to counter lack of available theater.

Branscombe, Fred. **"Third Way to Shakespeare."** *Audiovisual Instruction* 12 (June/July 1967): 606–07.

Mentions videotape of selected items from 400th Anniversary Shakespeare Exhibition in Stratford-on-Avon acquired by East Detroit Public Schools.

Brichto, Mira P. **"Shakespearean Drama as It Is Taught and Learned in Three Urban Secondary Schools."** Ph.D. dissertation, University of Cincinnati, 1977. *Dissertation Abstracts* 38 (1977): 2135 A.

Describes classroom study of *Othello, JC,* and *Hamlet,* and discusses student literacy levels and teacher preparation.

Bridge, G. F. **"Shakespeare in Schools."** *Journal of Education* (London) 68 (August 1936): 525–28.

Because schools have not created a widespread interest in Shakespeare, advocates teaching school children from cut versions of the plays in order to eliminate "the dull and incomprehensible." Suggests cuts for *AYL, H5,* and *Macbeth.*

Briggs, A. **"Grade Four in a Public School Hailed Shakespeare as a Contemporary."** *Instructor* 74 (November 1964): 109, 112.

Teacher reads *Taming of the Shrew* during story-time and pupils want to put on their own production.

Brignoli, H. **"Suggestions for a Trip to Stratford."** *High Points* 42 (January 1960): 57–58.

Bring, Rose. **"A Shakespearean Project."** *High Points* 12 (March 1930): 61–62.

Shows how high school pupils can devote a week to compiling a background book covering ten topics to prepare them for study of the plays.

Bromberg, Murray. **"If Shakespeare Were a Supervisor."** *High Points* 45 (May 1963): 46–50.

Offers a series of humorous quotes from Shakespeare.

Burton, H. M. **Shakespeare and His Plays.** Illustrated by Richard G. Robinson. London: Methuen, 1958.

General introduction for children, with reproductions of manuscript pages and pictures of Stratford-on-Avon buildings.

Butler, E. H. **"Shakespeare Through the Imaginative Writers."** *English Journal* 30 (November 1941): 749-53.

Presents comments of famous writers on Shakespeare suitable for school.

Carroll, Sydney. **"The Teaching of Shakespeare in Schools."** In *Conference of Educational Associations . . . 24th Annual Report,* pp. 61–67. London, 1936.

Teachers should inculcate pupils with "Shakespeare's spirit as an Englishman."

Chaplin, C. H. **"Third-Graders in a Parochial School Did** *Midsummer Night's Dream* **in Costume."** *Instructor* 74 (November 1964): 109, 112–13.

Chapman, Mary E. **"English Classes Live in Merrie Olde England."** *Virginia Journal of Education* 59 (May 1966): 16.

Report on a senior class study of English literature and culture.

Chubb, Edwin W. **"Common-Sense Interpretations of Shakespeare."** *Elementary School Teacher* 5 (March 1905): 420–27.

Attacks critics who try to gain a reputation by constructing a system for interpreting and explaining all of Shakespeare. Shakespeare took great pains to make himself understood, and those who try to see more than is really there are lost in their own pedantry.

Chubb, Percival. **The Teaching of English in the Elementary and Secondary School.** New York: Macmillan, 1924.

The first year *Julius Caesar* is read to the class by the teacher with minimum comment, followed by a second reading by the class and the memorization and presentation of selected scenes. *Macbeth* is read in the fourth year with emphasis on diagramming plot and character analysis.

Colijn, I. **An Introduction to Shakespeare: For Secondary Schools.** Zutphen, Netherlands: Thieme, 1958.

Craig, Hardin. **"In the Teaching of Shakespeare Avoid Avoidance."** *Shakespeare Newsletter* 10 (December 1960): 45.

Teachers wrong Shakespeare when they occupy class time with background studies. Experiencing the plays themselves is the only way for students to learn to appreciate Shakespeare.

Craig, Virginia J. **The Teaching of High School English.** New York: Longmans, Green, 1930.

The class should dramatize parts of Shakespearean plays, especially those scenes with intense feeling, natural movements, and quick repartee. Students prefer the tragedies because of their powerful excitement and suspense.

Crawford, John W. **"Shakespeare: A Lesson in Communications."** *Clearing House* 47 (April 1973): 509–10.

Shakespeare can be made relevant to youth by focusing on such themes as the communication problems in *Rom* and *JC.*

Crompton, Donald W. **"Shakespeare in the Sixth Form: The Problem of Modern Criticism."** *Use of English* (London) 10 (Spring 1959): 171–80.

Modern critics have made Shakespeare more difficult: "(1) by demanding much closer study of the poetry as poetry, (2) by talking in terms of abstract associations rather than in terms of concrete characteristics, (3) by virtually demanding that *all* the plays be read if one is to appreciate fully the Shakespearean experience."

Cross, E. A., and Carney, Elizabeth. **"The Reading of Plays."** In their *Teaching English in High Schools,* pp. 468–92. Rev. ed. New York: Macmillan, 1950.

Includes reference to various Shakespearean plays in discussions of overcoming difficulties that students meet in reading drama, making the characters live, visualizing stage settings and effects, etc.

Crowl, Samuel. **"The Arm'd Rhinoceros and Other Creatures: Shakespeare's Language and the Reluctant Reader."** *FOCUS: Teaching English in Southeastern Ohio* 2 (May 1976): 19–25.

"Mocking the language, playing with it, simply listening to its sounds and rhythms . . . may prove a way of bringing the students closer to the poetry's living textures than treating their resistance to its power and beauty as sacrilege." Encourages memorization and use of motion pictures when possible.

Dakin, Dorothy. **"Drama."** In her *Talks to Beginning Teachers of English.* New York: Heath, 1937. Reprinted in her *How to Teach High School English,* pp. 260–79. Boston: Heath, 1947.

Focuses on teaching Shakespeare's plays from the *acting* point of view, i.e., visualizing the scene. Suggests each play be introduced by reading with the students and preparing questions to ask pupils (samples provided for *Macbeth* I.ii and I.iii). Stresses importance of the first scene since Shakespeare often strikes the keynote there. Advocates avoiding bardology, and spending no more than three weeks on any one play.

Davis, James E., ed. **FOCUS: Teaching English in Southeastern Ohio** 2 (May 1976).

"Teaching Shakespeare" issue. Contains eight essays.

Davis, James E. **"Pluck out the Heart of My Mystery: How to Bring Shakespeare to the Boondocks, and Other Places."** *FOCUS: Teaching English in Southeastern Ohio* 2 (May 1976): 3–12.

Summarizes pertinent articles from *English Journal.* See also, in this section, Greene, Simmons.

Daws, Roberta. **"Why Shakespeare?"** *Peabody Journal of Education* 33 (May 1956): 332–33.

"The literature of Shakespeare forms a great reservoir from which both students and teacher can draw in the process of developing 'the kingdom within'."

DeBoer, John J.; Kaulfers, W. V.; and Miller, H. R. **Teaching Secondary English.** New York: McGraw-Hill, 1951. Reprint. Westport, Conn.: Greenwood Press, 1970.

The Shakespearean play "is not a vocabulary workbook"; teachers must introduce characters and plot before developing exercises with Shakespeare's language. Uses *JC* and *Macbeth* to exemplify suggestions, pp. 222–26, 340–42.

DeJulio, A., and Bikle, P. W. **"Group of Grope; or, Shakespeare's Seven Ages of Man and Group Dynamics: An Informal Discussion."** *Educational Forum* 23 (1959): 351–56.

Diesman, Florence M. **"Shakespeare in High School Today."** *Journal of Secondary Education* 40 (March 1965): 131–33.

After visiting twenty-two high schools in Washington and Colorado, reports the following plays are being taught: *Err, Shr, MND, 1&2H4, H5, Rom, MV, AYL, JC, Hamlet, Othello, Lear, Macbeth,* and *TN.*

Dieterich, Daniel J. **"On Teaching Shakespeare: An ERIC/RCS Review."** *Illinois English Bulletin* 61 (January 1974): 7–9.

Notice of recent Shakespeare items of pedagogical interest.

Dieterich, Daniel J. **"An ERIC/RCS Review: On Teaching Shakespeare."** *The Leaflet* 72 (May 1973): 31–34.

Reviews briefly fourteen books and essays.

Diltz, B. C. **"Shakespeare: Stage or Study?"** *School* (Toronto) 18 (September 1929): 4–11.

Donald, Louise. **"Shakespeare in the Schoolroom."** *Aberdeen University Review* 32 (1948): 272-75.

Suggests different plays for each school age group.

Downing, E. Estelle. **"International Good Will Through the Teaching of English."** *English Journal* 14 (November 1925): 675-85.

Drabeck, Bernard A. **"Ban Shakespeare."** In *Structures for Composition,* edited by Bernard Drabeck, et al., pp. 215-19. Boston: Houghton Mifflin, 1974.

Ban Shakespeare from the high school curriculum because of his difficult vocabulary, the problem students have with poetry, and the students' lack of maturity and experience which prevents them from appreciating Shakespeare's "revelations about life."

Driggs, Howard R. **"Seeing Classics as a Whole."** *English Journal* 7 (January 1918): 7–14.

Duke, Charles R. **"Shakespearean Drama."** In *Creative Approaches to the Teaching of English,* edited by Robert B. Shuman, pp. 63-71. Itasca, Ill.: Peacock, 1974.

Sensible focus on problems of language and background.

Dunn, Esther Cloudman. **"Shakespeare Enters the American Consciousness by Way of the Schools and Colleges."** In her *Shakespeare in America,* pp. 219-48. New York: Macmillan, 1939. Reprint. New York: B. Blom, 1968.

Essentially a recounting of H. W. Simon, *The Reading of Shakespeare in American Schools and Colleges.* See also, in this section, Simon.

Dunning, Stephen, and Sams, H. W., eds. **Scholarly Appraisals of Literary Works Taught in High Schools.** Champaign, Ill.: National Council of Teachers of English, 1965.

Reprints parts of essays on *JC* by G. B. Harrison and L. F. Dean, and on *Macbeth* by L. C. Knights and G. W. Knight.

Eagleson, R. D. **"'Propertied as all the tuned spheres': Aspects of Shakespeare's Language."** *Teaching of English* 20 (1971): 4-15.

Edgerly, Lydia. **"Shakespeare in 1951."** *English Journal* 40 (December 1951): 573-74.

Films, records, and texts lead students to a greater appreciation of Shakespeare.

Edwards, Rev. Mark. **"Shakespeare in High School with an Assist from A-V."** *Catholic Educator* 27 (April 1957): 546–49.

Practical and graded approach to the teaching of five Shakespearean plays in the twelfth grade, combining analysis, composition, and the use of specific audio-visual aids.

Evans, Bertrand. **Teaching Shakespeare in the High School.** New York: Macmillan, 1966.

Chapters 1–8 defend choice of Shakespearean plays for study, discuss the best method for presentation, and suggest which editions to use. Chapters 9–11 give notes on teaching fourteen plays and Chapter 12 discusses teaching the sonnets. A controversial book; see review by G. Veidemanis in *English Journal* 56 (April 1967): 626–28.

"Family Movie Guide: Should Children See the Tragedies of Wm. Shakespeare?" *Parents Magazine and Better Family Living,* 23 September 1948, p. 13.

Feeney, Helen M. **"The Lovely Worlds of Shakespeare."** *Girl Scout Leader,* June 1964, pp. 15, 25.

Suggestion for introducing Shakespeare to growing girls.

Felsher, Roy L. **"Two Shakespearean History Plays: *Richard III, Henry V.*"** In *Teaching Literature in Grades Seven Through Nine,* edited by Edward Jenkinson and Jane Stouder Hawley, pp. 117–43. Bloomington: Indiana University Press, 1967.

An excellent, succinct discussion.

Finch, Hardy R. **"Unbury the Bard."** *Scholastic Teacher,* 7 April 1954, pp. 36T–37T, 42T.

Describes different ways teachers have made Shakespeare come alive, such as using T.V. productions in private homes and bringing current films, filmstrips and slides, records and dramatizations into the classroom. Other techniques mentioned are writing a diary recording the motivations, fears and hopes of a main character, paraphrasing soliloquies in modern English, and rewriting a scene as a modern incident.

Finlay-Johnson, Harriet. **"The Shakespearean Play."** In *Dramatic Method of Teaching,* edited by Ellen M. Cyr, pp. 77–108. Boston: Ginn, 1912.

Recounts how pupils abridged and enacted *H5, MND, AYL, MV, John, JC,* and *H6.*

Fisher, Mildred. **"Shakespeare: Why Ignore the Comedies and the Histories?"** *English Journal* 60 (May 1971): 587–90.

An overview of a successful Shakespeare unit that emphasizes some little-used plays. Shakespeare as drama comes first; as literature, second. Students read aloud in class. Some Shakespearean films are used and panels discuss and dramatize different plays.

Flecke, J. M. **"Shakespeare in Elementary School? Fifth-Graders Did Macbeth."** *Instructor* 73 (January 1964): 34–35.

Fleege, Urban H. **"Streamlining Shakespeare."** *English Journal* 30 (May 1941): 408–11.

The way to get students to enjoy Shakespeare is to let them rewrite the play in modern English, slang included.

Flower, Archibald. **"Making Shakespeare Live."** *New Era in Home and School* (Cambridge) 12 (March 1931): 81–83.

Emphasizes getting students interested first in "the very human individuality of the boy and the man Shakespeare" by biographical and historical background. Most important, however, is to see the plays performed well.

Force, William. **"Plays Should Be Heard in the Classroom."** *English Journal* 52 (March 1963): 206–08.

Frank, Maude M. **"A Shakespeare Course in the High School."** *High Points* 2 (June 1920): 27.

Fränkel, Ludwig. **"Shakespeare an den deutschen Hochschulen der Gegenwart."** *Jahrbuch der deutschen Shakespeare-Gesellschaft* (Berlin) 32 (1896): 87–108.

Fränkel, Ludwig. **"Die gegenwärtige Beschäftigung der akademisch-neuphilologischen Vereine Deutschlands mit Shakespeare."** *Jahrbuch der deutschen Shakespeare-Gesellschaft* (Berlin) 26 (1891): 120–30.

French, Richard. **"Student Recommendations for Teaching Shakespeare in High School."** *English Journal* 57 (March 1968): 350–55.

Summarizes college students' recollections of their experience of Shakespeare in high school. Because of their generally poor exposure—having the plays read to them and having to memorize lines—they recommend discussion method, the importance of motivation, knowledge of background material, analysis of character, and the use of visual aids.

French, William W. **"Shakespeare in West Virginia High Schools."** *Dialogue: For English Teachers in West Virginia* 9 (Fall 1976): 2–3, 7–8. Abstracted in *Shakespeare Newsletter* 27 (September 1977): 27, 31.

The most popular plays are *Rom, Macbeth, JC,* and *Hamlet.* County boards of education often decide which play is taught; but large numbers of teachers teach the plays because they "ought" to be read and because of their universal themes. Reading the play aloud was most widely used teaching method; the use of records and audio tapes the second most popular technique; then the use of visual aids and class discussion. Most teachers thought the teaching of Shakespeare had changed since they were students.

Fries, Charles C.; Hanford, James; and Steeves, H. R. **The Teaching of Literature.** New York: Silver, Burdett, 1926.

The neophyte teacher soon learns that "it is not his knowledge of the technique of drama which will best aid him in interesting his class in Shakespeare but his personal fund of wit and of wisdom, imagination, feeling, and experience in life." Before the tenth year, "the attempt to grapple at all fully with an Elizabethan play is all but hopeless."

Garrett, John. **Talking of Shakespeare.** London: Hodder & Stroughton, 1954.

General thoughts on the teaching of Shakespeare in "Introduction."

Gelhard, J. **"Shakespeare in der deutschen höheren Schule."** *Neue Sprache* 43 (1935): 174–82.

Gibson, Christine M. **"Teaching Shakespeare."** *English Journal* 31 (September 1942): 548–51.

Develops Renz's suggestion to give interpretive reading of play because students cannot read. See also, in this section, Renz, Wonnberger.

Ginsberg, Walter. **"How Helpful Are Shakespeare Recordings?"** *English Journal* 29 (April 1940): 296.

Glicker, Frank J. **"Shakespeare Made a Hit with My Sixth Grade."** *Instructor* 58 (March 1959): 64, 66.

Comedy of Errors rewritten and adapted for the class by students.

Golding, William. **"Shakespeare's Birthplace."** *Holiday,* May 1962, pp. 82–83.

A view of Stratford-on-Avon for the tourist.

Graham, Virginia. **"Unwillingly to School."** *Spectator* (London), 9 March 1951, p. 306.

Suggests that Shakespeare is like religion and that the young react to both the same way, i.e., with boredom. Students should be given Shakespeare in small doses and left to discover him themselves (as the author did) and thereby come to appreciate him more. Suggests, tongue-in-cheek, that the real way to arouse interest in Shakespeare is to ban his works. (See *Spectator,* 16 March 1951, p. 344 for a letter in agreement, and *Spectator,* 23 March 1951, p. 384 for a letter in dispute.)

Greene, J. Gordon. **"Motivating Students to Study Shakespeare: A Creative-Notebook Approach."** *English Journal* 61 (April 1972): 504–07.

Students condense action of scene into one sentence summary in notebooks. They are given the option of writing their sentence summaries in plain modern diction, in the style of the King James version of the Bible, or in current language jargon.

Greene, Jay E. **"Memorizing Shakespeare for Fun."** *High Points* 26 (September 1944): 78–79.

Students memorize Shakespearean lines in order to quote them on appropriate occasions.

Greer, M. C. **"Shakespeare in the Senior High School."** *Schoolmen's Week University of Pennsylvania* (1956): 99–110.

Gribble, Dorothy Rose. **"Our Hope's 'Bove, Wisdom, Grace, and Fear: An Account of a Tour of *Macbeth.*"** *Shakespeare Quarterly* 5 (1954): 403–07.

Techniques of Plantagenet Productions' tour of English Schools.

Gunter, John, and Ohlendorf, H. **"Die Behandlung von Shakespeare in der Sekundarstufe II: Ein Erfahrungsbericht über einen Versuch."** (Mimeographed report.) Braunschweig: Institut für Anglistik und Amerikanistik, TU-Braunschweig, 1979.

Reports on experiment with *Romeo and Juliet* as a text for English as a Foreign Language.

Guth, Hans P. **"The Teaching of English: Objectives."** In his *English*

Today and Tomorrow: A Guide for Teachers of English, pp. 326–27. Englewood Cliffs, N.J.: Prentice-Hall, 1964.

"The complexities and ambiguities of Shakespeare's work tend to upset the preliminary generalizations about literature that students in the early years of high schools should just be attempting."

Guthrie, Tyrone. **"Why Bother with the Bard?"** *Seventeen* 23 (September 1964): 148–49, 210, 212, 214.

Discusses for teenagers why Shakespeare has such a good reputation and encourages them (and teachers) to see plays performed.

Halliday, E. M. **"The Man Who Cleaned Up Shakespeare."** *Horizon* 5 (September 1962): 68–71.

On Thomas Bowdler and his lasting influence on texts for schools.

Hamil, Louise Knudsen. **"Try Shakespeare—It's Fun."** *Alabama School Journal* 56 (October 1938): 9.

Dramatics teacher has pupils revise and rework scenes and speeches as dramatic exercises.

Hancock, A. S. **"One Way to Teach Shakespeare."** *English Journal* 23 (September 1934): 592–93.

Pupils memorize a dramatic part of a particularly powerful scene, then act it out together in small groups.

Handwerker, B. **"When Should Shakespeare First Be Taught in the Schools?"** *High Points* 43 (March 1961): 69–71.

Julius Caesar should be the introductory play no earlier than the ninth grade. Recommends oral reading of the play with students assigned parts.

Hankins, Gretchen. **Shakespeare Tragedies: English.** Miami, Fla.: Dade County Public Schools, 1971.

Focuses on the tragic hero.

Harrison, G. B. **"A Shakespeare Shelf."** *Sunday Herald Tribune Book Week,* 26 April 1964, pp. 4–5, 12.

Bibliography for the nonspecialist.

Harrison, G. B. **"The Teaching of Shakespeare."** *English Journal* 52 (September 1963): 411–19. Reprinted as *The Teaching of Shakespeare* (Lincoln, Neb.: Cliff's Notes, 1963) and as "The Teaching of *Julius*

Caesar" in *Scholarly Appraisals of Literary Works Taught in High Schools,* edited by Stephen Dunning and Henry W. Sams, pp. 22–28. Champaign, Ill.: National Council of Teachers of English, 1965.

Approaches the play in terms of Shakespeare's craftsmanship with emphasis on the plot, characterization, and diction.

Haselmayer, Louis A. **"Shakespeare Workshop."** *Shakespeare Newsletter* 4 (November 1954): 38.

Describes workshop planned to stimulate high school teaching of Shakespeare's plays. One session dealt with Elizabethan staging and another with the use of audio-visual aids as supplements to teaching.

Hayden, Howard. **The Immortal Memory: A New Approach to the Teaching of Shakespeare.** London: Dent, 1936.

Discusses using the "dramatic form" method for teaching Shakespeare to students aged fourteen to sixteen: episodes from Shakespearean plays are so worded as to present "a living picture of Shakespeare." Suggests that "first each scene should be treated as a form-room play to be produced as simply or as elaborately as may be convenient." Also contains suggestions for "follow-up" lessons.

Hays, Edna. **College Entrance Requirements in English: Their Effects on the High Schools. An Historical Survey.** Contributions to Education, No. 675. New York: Teachers College, Columbia University, 1936.

Includes Shakespeare as an integral part of the school curriculum.

Heavey, Regina. **"Goodbye, William Shakespeare."** *English Journal* 38 (November 1949): 512–15.

To delete Shakespeare from the program is to lose "the exaltation of mind and spirit so essential to great literature."

Heeden, B. **"Shakespeare in the First Grade."** *The Grade Teacher* 82 (October 1964): 91–92.

Hill, Roger, and Welles, Orson. **"William Shakespeare (Biography No. 1,000,999)."** *Scholastic,* 14 April 1941, pp. 17–18, 24.

A general biographical sketch written for *The Mercury Shakespeare.*

Hipple, Theodore W. **Teaching English in Secondary School.** New York: Macmillan, 1973.

"For the uninitiated the language of Shakespeare is too difficult for them to read an entire play on their own. An act-by-act progression makes sense, as it permits teachers to keep on top of the comprehension problems students may be having."

Hirai, Masaho. **"Shakespeare and Students."** *Shakespeare News* (Tokyo) 1 (1961): 4.

Hook, Frank S. **"So You're Going to Teach Shakespeare?"** *English Journal* 56 (November 1967): 1120–26.

An informative description of what a teacher should know about the historical, intellectual, and social background of Shakespeare's works.

Hopkins, Lee B. **"No Sighs for Shakespeare!"** *Catholic School Journal* 68 (February 1968): 52–53.

Fifth graders rewrite *Macbeth* for outdoor performance.

Hovelaque, Émile. **"Comment Faire Connaître Shakespeare aux Petits Francais."** In *A Book of Homage to Shakespeare,* edited by Israel Gollancz, pp. 392–98.

Suggestions for having French pupils appreciate Shakespeare.

Hübner, Walter. **"Shakespeare."** In his *Die englische Dichtung in der Schule. Grundzüge einer Interpretationslehre,* pp. 31–82. Leipzig: Quelle & Meyer, 1940.

Hudson, Arthur K., comp. **Shakespeare and the Classroom.** London: Heinemann, 1954, 1966.

Study of Shakespeare should be stage centered: "The *average* pupil has to be introduced first to the dramatic quality of one of Shakespeare's plays if his interest is to be aroused. . . ." Pupil should come to think of class-time "as a rehearsal, not as a lesson." Suggests lessons for pupils eleven to thirteen on *MND* and *MV,* for pupils thirteen to fifteen on *AYL, JC, H5,* and for pupils sixteen to eighteen a discussion of *Macbeth* III.ii. Lists films, filmstrips, slides, and recordings available for classroom use. Reviewed by R. Mayhead in *Use of English* (London) 6 (1954): 126–27.

Huffman, C. H. **"Omission of Important Incidents from Shakespeare's Historical Plays."** *Virginia Teacher* 10 (January 1929): 24–28.

Illsley, W. A. **A Shakespeare Manual for Schools.** Cambridge: Univesity Press, 1957.

An introduction to Shakespearean plays for Nigerian secondary school students which "is intended primarily for use as a class-book to help both pupils, and teachers who have no qualifications in English literature." Discusses the problems of paraphrasing and gives model examination papers for *Macbeth, JC, R2, H5, AYL,* and *TN.*

"Improvising an Elizabethan Stage." *High Points* 4 (October 1922): 33–34.

A cardboard box becomes a model stage.

Jacobs, Ida T. **"A Shakespearean Banquet."** In *Conducting Experiences in English,* edited by A. M. Broening, pp. 49–50. New York: Appleton-Century-Crofts, 1939.

Describes how student committees can organize diverse aspects of a Christmas season festival with guests drawn from Shakespeare's contemporaries and the characters of his plays.

Jensen, James H. **"On Teaching Shakespeare."** In *Teaching Literature in Grades Ten Through Twelve,* edited by Edward B. Jenkinson and Philip B. Daghlian, pp. 231-32. Bloomington: Indiana University Press, 1968.

Suggests choosing from among *Ado, MND, AYL, TN, Shr, Rom, JC, Macbeth, Othello,* and *Hamlet* for grades ten through twelve.

Johnson, William. **"Shakespeare . . . Still Modern After 400 Years."** *Senior Scholastic,* 24 April 1964, pp. 4–5, 18.

An appreciation.

Jones, Helen C. **"Shakespeare: Elementary Style."** *Audiovisual Instruction* Supplement. 18 (April 1973): 14–15.

Jones, John D. **"Shakespeare in English Schools."** *Jahrbuch der deutschen Shakespeare-Gesellschaft* (Berlin) 42 (1906): 113-26.

Jones, Martha Howard. **"Shakespeare for Superior High School Sophomores."** *School and Community* 46 (January 1960): 16–17.

Explains how a very advanced group of students began with *Julius Caesar* and then broke into small groups to read additional plays and give panel presentations. Gives seven assignments for sophomores which are nearly college level.

Jones, Patracia. **"A Slanguage of Shakespeare."** *Clearing House* 39 (December 1964): 247–49.

On using slang to help high school students appreciate *As You Like It.*

Jones, Whitney. **"Teaching Shakespeare Conference."** *Shakespeare Newsletter* 25 (April 1975): 12.

Four high school teachers discuss use of audio-visual materials, use of professional actors in the classroom, etc. The greatest problem for students is Shakespeare's language.

Jones, William M. **"Teaching Shakespeare's Insubstantial Pageant."** *English Record* 21 (1970): 4–10.

Keller, I. C. **"Shakespeare for Pleasure."** *Shakespeare Association Bulletin* 15 (1940): 249–53.

Discusses "the pleasurable" approach to Shakespeare as distinct from "the scholarly" approach.

Kellogg, Brainerd, ed. *The Tempest.* New York: Maynard, Merrill & Co., 1882.

His "Plan of Study for Perfect Possession" (pp. viii–ix) is an early example of methodology for teaching Shakespeare. See also, in this section, Mersand.

Kerman, Gertrude L. *"Midsummer Night's Dream."* In her *Plays and Creative Ways with Children,* pp. 255–73. Irvington-on-Hudson, N.Y.: Harver House, 1961.

A twenty minute adaptation for young players (ten to fourteen years old) including "staging suggestions."

Klein, M. **"Shakespeares Dramatisches Formgesetz in seiner Bedeutung für die Schule. Ein neuer Weg zu *Macbeth* und *Hamlet.*"** *Neuphilologische Monatsschrift* (Leipzig) 6 (1936): 487–98.

Klemola, Jeannette. **"Taking the Spinach Out of Shakespeare."** *Illinois English Bulletin* 34 (January 1947): 13–18.

Names three schools of teaching Shakespeare: Spinach School ("It's good for you"); Bronze Pedastal School ("There is no other playwright before him—nor after"); Detective School ("The plays are mines of hidden information"). Suggests adopting the "Archie School," i.e., Shakespeare's plays were written for the common man and are still good entertainment.

Klug, Nancy. **"Teaching Seminars."** *Shakespeare Newsletter* 25 (April 1975): 12.

Reports on an in-service seminar for secondary school teachers with emphasis on the tragedies.

Knapton, James, and Evans, B. **Teaching Literature—Centered English Program.** New York: Random House, 1967.

Suggests that the teacher read the play aloud, interspersing the reading with historical, critical, and interpretive comment.

Lapp, Charles E., Jr. **"Appreciation through Understanding."** *Illinois Education* 50 (April 1962): 350–51.

Techniques to make Shakespeare more appealing in the junior high schools.

Lasser, M. L. **"Shakespeare: Finding and Teaching the Comic Vision."** *English Record* 20 (December 1969): 4–17.

The Shakespearean comic vision uniquely heightens rather than relieves tension, as in *Rom* with the death of Mercutio, and in *AC* with the diminution of Antony.

Lazar, Bernard. **"How to Sound Out Your Shakespeare."** *Scholastic Teacher,* 1 March 1956, pp. 7T–8T.

Advocates student interpretation of important scenes and comparison with the Old Vic Company's interpretation on records.

Lease, Ruth, and Siks, Geraldine B. **"Use of Shakespeare's Plays."** In their *Creative Dramatics in Home, School, and Community,* pp. 96–98. New York: Harper & Bros., 1952.

Use of scenes from *MND* and *Shr* in junior high school.

Leonard, Pauline W. **"Comparative Literature Methods in High Schools."** *School and Society,* 10 September 1932, pp. 336–37.

Through Shakespeare the teacher can introduce high school pupils "not only to great literature but also to a peculiarly interesting and significant period of the world's history."

Leonard, Sterling Andrus. **"Class Help in the Understanding of Literature."** In his *Essential Principles of Teaching Reading and Literature in the Intermediate Grades and High School,* pp. 200–261. Philadelphia: Lippincott, 1922.

"The usual study of plot organization and development on the lines of the Freytag drama-triangle or by means of analyzing plots and sub-plots is no subject for high school classes." Suggests more simplified structural study which focuses on central idea or purpose, as in *Julius Caesar* where students can "align the forces for and against the conspirators, and discuss what bearing each had on the issue." An important question eighth and ninth graders can answer for themselves is, "Why call the play after Caesar when he dies before the middle of it?"

"Literature or Language?" *Times Literary Supplement* (London), 17 July 1962, p. 541.

Such classics as Shakespeare require "tailoring" if allowed a place in curricula where English is being taught as a foreign language. D. A. N. Jones protests (21 September 1962, p. 725) citing the success of Shakespeare in Nigeria.

Lloyd, F. V. **"Shakespeare in Junior High."** *English Journal* 32 (June 1943): 337–38.

Experience producing Pyamus and Thisbe suggests Wonnberger's contention that Shakespeare is too difficult for an audience is wrong. See also, in this section, Wonnberger.

Loveall, James. **"Shakespeare Is for Adults."** *English Journal* 36 (September 1947): 363–66.

The author is not convinced that all students should read Shakespeare; a certain maturity and experience are necessary to appreciate the element of human dignity central to Shakespearean drama. See also, in this section, Bliss.

Lückemeier, Renate. **"Shakespeare im Deutschunterricht."** *Wirkendes Wort* (Düsseldorf) 17 (1967): 186–98.

Lüder, A. **"Shakespeare in den oberen Klassen des Realgymnasiums."** *Neue Sprache* 18 (1910): 129–44.

Lynch, James J., and Evans, Bertrand. **High School English Textbooks: A Critical Examination.** Boston: Little, Brown, 1963.

Discusses excerpts and abridgements from various editions. Recommends reading of a Shakespearean play in each of the four high school years and avoiding excerpts of the plays.

Lytle, Clyde F. **"The Effectiveness of Stage Presentation as a Supplement to Classroom Instruction in Shakespearean Drama in the Secondary Schools."** Ph.D. dissertation, New York University, 1943.

MacIsaac, Warren J. **"Viva Voce: On Speaking and Hearing Shakespeare's Sentences."** *Shakespeare Quarterly* 25 (1974): 172–87.

Argues that the analogy between conversation habits and our experiences of invented speeches for all characters in the plays lies at the heart of our teaching of drama. The teacher should have Kokeritz's pronunciation phonograph records as well as, say, a record of selections from the Houseman-Mankiewicz film of *Julius Caesar*. Suggests how students ought to read plays aloud.

McCaul, R. L. **"A Worksheet for a Shakespearean Drama."** *Education* 58 (February 1938): 325–29.

McBride, Otis. **"Progressive Shakespeare in the High School."** *Peabody Journal of Education* 15 (July 1937): 23–24.

McCarthy, Helen. **"One Teacher's Shakespeare."** *Arizona English Bulletin* 7 (1964): 7–9.

McGraw, H. Ward. **"The Plays of Shakespeare."** In his *The Teaching of Literature in High School: A Manual for Teachers,* pp. 87–109. New York: Charles Merrill, 1929.

Discussion of *MND, AYL, MV, JC,* and *Macbeth.*

McLean, Andrew. **"Selected Bibliography for Shakespeare and The Media."** In *New Approaches to Shakespeare in the Classroom: A Workshop for High School English Teachers,* pp. 9–13. Laurinburg, N.C.: St. Andrews College, 1975. (Bulletin for workshop).

McLean, Andrew. **"Shakespeare—Media Symposium."** *Shakespeare Newsletter* 25 (April 1975): 12.

Multiple workshops on Shakespeare in the secondary school discuss audio-visual materials, *Hamlet,* and *JC.*

MacLeod, M. **"Shakespeare Assignments."** *English Journal* 21 (December 1932): 822–25.

A teacher's outline for a one month study (three classes per week) of a Shakespearean play.

MacPartland, John. **"A Day with Shakespeare."** *English Journal* 32 (November 1943): 512–14.

Describes a successful experiment allowing one teacher to remain with a class throughout the day to dramatize a whole play in one continuous session.

Mallay, Miriam. **"The Winch: If the Pupil Is Short, S-t-r-e-t-c-h Him!"** *Clearing House* 22 (September 1947): 11–14.

Students able to understand Shakespeare should have the opportunity; while those who find Shakespeare difficult should read other good literature.

Marder, Louis. **"Do's and Don'ts of Shakespeare Teaching."** In *Shakespeare in the Classroom: Resources and Media Aids,* edited by A. McLean, pp. 51–55. Kenosha: UW-Parkside's Center for Teaching Excellence, 1977.

Lists seventy-two tidbits of advice.

Marder, Louis. **"The Responsibility of the Shakespeare Teacher."** *Oklahoma English Bulletin* 1 (1964): 1–7.

Marder, Louis. **"Un-willingly to School."** In his *His Exits and His Entrances: The Story of Shakespeare's Reputation,* pp. 272–93. Philadelphia: Lippincott, 1963.

Brief history of the introduction and teaching of Shakespeare in schools and colleges.

Marsh, George L. **A Teacher's Manual for the Study of English Classics.** Chicago: Scott, Foresman, 1912. Revised 1921.

Discusses *MV,* and *MND,* for first year students; *AYL, H5, JC, TN, Temp,* and *Rom,* for second year; and *Macbeth* and *Hamlet* for the fourth year.

Marsh, Philip M. **How to Teach English in High School and College.** New York: Bookman Associates, 1956.

A frank discussion of how to teach literature (pp. 77–102) includes mock dialogue of teacher presenting *1 Henry 4,* suggestions for class playacting, and a sample Shakespeare test combining the essay and objective test.

Martin, Martha Wing. **"Shakespeare in Today's Classroom."** *English Journal* 44 (April 1955): 228–29.

Reports results of California survey of secondary schools which shows *JC* and *Macbeth* are the plays most often taught; teachers utilize "any technique which might add to the students' enjoyment and comprehension of Shakespeare." The biggest barrier for students is Shakespeare's language but often the teachers themselves lack enthusiasm for Shakespearean plays.

Mary Barbara, Sister. **"Play's the Thing!"** *Catholic School Journal* 68 (February 1968): 62–63.

A presentation of background materials for stimulating interest in *Hamlet.*

Mary Helen, Sister. **"Living Shakespeare."** *English Journal* 54 (January 1956): 48–51.

Describes a four-week Shakespeare festival (unit) that culminates in a school-wide drama competition.

Mary Louis, C. P. S., Sister. **"Does Shakespeare Present a Challenge?"** *Peabody Journal of Education* 42 (September 1964): 109–13.

Offers suggestions for increasing appreciation of Shakespeare in secondary schools. Exhorts teachers to "cull every possible resource to set her stage" to enhance the dramatic qualities of the plays.

Mary Sylvia, S. S. J., Sister. **"Learning About Shakespeare in His Hometown."** *Scholastic Teacher,* 28 February 1964, pp. 8T–9T.

Describes Stratford-on-Avon, its institute, and 1963 productions.

Mary Theophane, Sister. **"Shakespeare's Allusions to Education."** *Journal of Teacher Education* 16 (1965): 226–28.

Mersand, Joseph. **Teaching Drama in the Secondary School, 1880–1937.** Metuchen, N.J.: Scarecrow Press, 1969.

Contains a useful survey of important educators' suggestions for teaching Shakespeare in the schools.

Mersand, Joseph. **"The Teaching of Literature in American High Schools, 1865–1900."** In *Perspectives on English,* edited by Robert C. Pooley, pp. 271–302. New York: Appleton-Century-Crofts, 1960.

Traces the teaching of literature from 1865, often using the earlier period's emphasis on Shakespeare to illustrate the place of literature in the secondary school curriculum.

Mirrieless, Lucia B. **Teaching Composition and Literature in Junior and Senior High School.** New York: Harcourt, Brace, 1937. Revised ed. 1952.

Certain stage conventions must be taught, but the teacher is cautioned not to attempt too much too early with students; the main thing is to keep a play a play.

Mizener, Arthur, ed. **Teaching Shakespeare: A Guide to the Teaching of** *Macbeth, Julius Caesar, Merchant of Venice, Romeo and Juliet, Hamlet, Midsummer Night's Dream, Othello, As You Like It, Twelfth Night, Richard II, 1 Henry IV, The Tempest.* New York: New American Library, 1969.

For each play there is an introduction to its general character, followed by an act and scene description of the action—"a discussion that represents as closely as possible the actual teaching of the play." Sample short-answer and discussion questions and sample tests are provided.

Monson, Leland H. **"Shakespeare in Utah (1847–1900)."** Ph.D. dissertation, University of Utah, 1956. *Dissertation Abstracts* 17 (1957): 848–49.

Surveys the part played by Shakespeare in shaping the culture of Utah and discusses Shakespeare courses in schools.

Morgan, Charles. **"To the Young—*Macbeth*. Philosophical Note on an Audience of Children at the Theatre."** *New York Times,* 4 June 1939.

Points out that many children are unaware of what a theatre really is because they are brought up on films. For them to go to the theatre means to be entertained and they react very vocally.

Mueller, Richard J. **"A Groundling's Approach to Shakespeare."** *English Journal* 53 (November 1964): 584–88.

Discusses the "spectacle of the groundlings" and their reactions to Shakespeare's plays as a means to motivating students, who might otherwise respond reluctantly or negatively, to an actual study of the plays.

Müller, J. **"Shakespeare im Deutschunterricht."** *Zeitschrift für Deutschkunde* (Leipzig) 52 (1939): 497–517.

Münch, Wilhelm. **"Shakespeare-Lektüre auf deutschen Schulen."** *Shakespeare Jahrbuch* (Berlin) 38 (1902): 118–43.

Mussoff, Lewis. **"Enriching a Literary Survey of Renaissance England."** *English Journal* 51 (May 1962): 337–39.

Considers the question: "Why not set the stage for Shakespeare with more study in depth of the great literary artists who preceded and were contemporary with Shakespeare?"

Myresko, M. **Shakespeare in the Elementary Grades.** Schenectady, N.Y.: Hugo Press, 1967.

Neumeyer, Peter F. **"Teaching Shakespeare: An Anti-Method."** *Clearing House* 38 (April 1964): 478–80.

Offers a smorgasbord of twenty-one approaches to teaching Shakespeare.

Nye, R. A. **"Shakespeare in the Seventies: ERIC Report."** *Speech Teacher* 22 (1973): 348–55.

A review of twelve works on Shakespeare and Education.

Ohlmarks, Ake. **"Shakespeare skolmästarekomplex."** *Aftonbladet* (Stockholm) (April 1960): 10.

Schools and teachers on Shakespeare.

Ommanney, Katharine Anne. **"Living the Drama with Shakespeare."** In her *The Stage and the School,* pp. 258–76. New York: Harper & Bros., 1939. Rev. ed.

Introduces pupils to Shakespeare emphasizing his modern tone, characters, the use of Welles's *Mercury Shakespeare,* and provides list of scenes to practice. "The lover of the drama must be a lover of Shakespeare; the actor, an actor of his roles; the student of the drama, a student of his plays."

Ornstein, J. A. **"Th' Art a Knowing Cookie, Will."** *High Points* 37 (November 1955): 65–69.

Thirty-eight Shakespearean quotations applied to the pedagogical situation.

Palmer, Dora E. **"The Play's the Thing."** *English Journal* 38 (December 1949): 568–71.

JC, H4, and *Rom* became, with the help of the teacher's stimulating questions, a popular and successful unit. Lists preparation materials for panels on Shakespearean plays.

Parker, Carolyn. **"Shakespeare in Swing Time."** *Clearing House* 8 (April 1939): 462–63.

Ushers in Shakespeare unit with popular songs of the 16th century, comparing them with popular songs of today.

Parry, John. **A Guide to Shakespeare for Malayan Students.** London: Harrap, 1956.

Patterson, T. **"Stratford and Education."** *Food for Thought* (Toronto) 17 (1957): 169–73.

Pearson, F. B. **"On Teaching Shakespeare."** *Ohio Schools* 8 (February 1930): 48.

Peat, R. C. **Presenting Shakespeare.** London: Harrap, 1947.

Perks, D. M. **"Paperbacks Preferred: Shakespeariana."** *High Points* 47 (May 1965): 72.

Perle, Friedrich. **"Die Auswahl der Shakespeare-Lektüre."** *Lehrproben und Lehrgänge* 13 (1887): 26–37.

Peters, William H. **"Implications from Johnsonian Criticism for the Teaching of Shakespeare on the Secondary Level."** *Kentucky English Bulletin* 19 (Fall 1969): 3–10.

Uses Johnsonian notes to *Macbeth* and *Hamlet* to illustrate how Johnson's criticism of Shakespeare provides insights into Shakespeare as "the poet of nature."

Phase-Elective English: An Experimental Program for Grades Eleven and Twelve. Jefferson County Board of Education of Louisville, Kentucky. 170. (Available from EDRS; ED 037 458.)

Describes a 12-week phase-elective Shakespeare course.

Phillips, A. L. **"Letting Shakespeare Live Again."** *Education* 58 (February 1938): 321–24.

Urges careful cutting of a play to make Shakespeare more readable before acting it out in class.

Piper, Laurence F. **"Shakespeare and the Younger Generation."** *English Record* 15 (December 1964): 9–14.

Discusses Shakespeare's potential appeal to high school students.

"The Play's the Thing." *Scholastic Teacher,* 25 February 1965, 4T.

Reports on National Shakespeare Company performing in high schools.

Poethen, Wilhelm Von. **"Shakespeare und die Jugend."** *Wirkendes Wort* (Düsseldorf) 17 (1967): 132–37.

Poethen, Wilhelm Von. **"Shakespeare im Deutschunterricht."** *Wirkendes Wort* (Düsseldorf) 9 (1958): 43–56.

Provides suggestions on what plays to teach and when, with lesson plans for *JC, Lear, R3, Macbeth,* and *Temp.*

Poethen, Wilhelm Von. **"Shakespeares Bildersprache im Unterricht."** *Lebenden Fremdsprachen* (Braunschweig) 2 (1950): 260–66.

Poley, Irvin C. **"Drama in the Classroom."** *English Journal* 44 (March 1955): 148–51.

Poley, Irvin C. **"Keeping Out of Hamlet's Way: Some Notes on the Teaching of Drama."** *English Journal* 30 (September 1941): 538–49.

Potter, Rachel. **"Shakespeare in School."** *Praxis des neusprachlichen Unterrichts* (Dortmund) 4 (1957): 77–79.

Price, George R. **Reading Shakespeare's Plays. A Guide for College Students.** Great Neck, N.Y.: Barron's Educational Series, 1962.

Chapters include "Suggestions for Study," "Shakespeare's Theater and Co.," "Some Elizabethan Attitudes Reflected in Drama," "Shakespeare's Career," "Canon, Chronology, and Text," and "A Chronology of Literature and Events, 1557–1616." Reviewed in *English Journal* 16 (1964): 185.

Purves, Alan C. **"You Can't Teach *Hamlet,* He's Dead."** *English Journal* 57 (September 1968): 832–36.

In view of the nature of reading literature, suggests we "start with the response of the whole poem" and focus on "the consciousness that is dealing with the text." No special Shakespearean emphasis in this article.

Ratliff, John. **"A Shakespearean Bibliography."** *Arizona English Bulletin* 7 (1964): 15–19.

Annotated bibliography for high school teachers.

Rehfeldt, W. **"Die Shakespeare-Lektüre im Englischunterricht der Oberschulen."** *Fremdsprachenunterricht* (Berlin) 1 (1957): 83–88.

Reising, R. W. **"Keeping Shakespeare Alive and Well in the Seventies."** *English in Texas* 3 (Fall 1971): 8–9.

Suggests matching a picture of a contemporary athlete or politician from a newspaper or magazine with a character from the play being studied; then writing an essay to defend the comparison.

Renz, B. **"Teaching Shakespeare."** *English Journal* 31 (January 1942): 56–59.

"An interpretive reading of the play by a skillful reader contributes much to visualizing it." Suggests a method of presentation. See also, in this section, Gibson, Wonnberger.

Richardson, Lorabel. **"Making Shakespeare Enjoyable."** *Iowa English Bulletin* 1, No. 1; and in *Illinois English Bulletin* 39 (October 1951): 15–17.

Recommends *Twelfth Night* as an introduction for sophomores, and suggests moving through play quickly.

Rider, Maurice L. **"'In Glorious Titles He Excels'."** *English Journal* 54 (January 1965): 52–55.

Examines how many authors owe their titles to Shakespeare.

Riley, Roberta. **"Five or Six Plays are Better Than One."** *California English Journal* 9 (1973): 27–30.

Rodes, David. **"They Don't Loathe Shakespeare."** *High Points* 35 (April 1953): 47–55.

Advocates an approach with ninth graders reading *JC* and *Macbeth* that mixes graphic narration, direct play reading, class discussion, questioning, and a 'foreshadowing' chart for key characters.

Roland, Barbara. **"Debates to Clarify Ideas in Shakespeare."** *FOCUS: Teaching English in Southeastern Ohio* 2 (May 1976): 57.

For advanced students, searching out quotes to support pro and con debate topics sends pupils back to the play for a second reading of important scenes.

Rolfe, William J. **Shakespeare's Tragedy of Romeo and Juliet.** New York: American Book Co., 1879, 1898, 1907.

Contains introduction, history of play, plot sources, critical comments, text, and notes. (An example of one of Rolfe's many school editions of Shakespeare.)

Rollo, J. C. **"Teaching Shakespeare in India."** *Literary Criterion* (Bombay) 6 (1963): 75–78.

A plea for reading several plays rapidly instead of one or two with the distraction of pseudo-scholarship.

Rosinger, Lawrence. **"The 'Class Answer' as a Teaching Device."** *English Journal* 57 (October 1958): 1032–35.

Suggests "pooling the knowledge of the members of the class" to bolster student confidence and understanding. "Class answers" to questions on *Hamlet* illustrate the method.

Rostron, David. **"Some Approaches to Teaching Shakespeare."** *Use of English* (London) 26 (Spring 1975): 222–28.

Suggests discussing background and varying approaches to text as means of sustaining interest.

Rowan, Mary H. **"Do-It-Yourself Kit: Ninth Graders Run the English Class."** *Clearing House* 38 (February 1964): 373–75.

Pupils plan their own six week Shakespeare unit.

Royster, Salibelle. **"More About Shakespeare."** *Education* 75 (November 1954): 193–94.

Offers pupils plays not often read in high school with tragedies preferred to comedies, the histories least popular, and audio-visual aids used to facilitate appreciation. The teacher should stress understanding of plot, themes, and character.

Royster, Salibelle. **"Classics in the Early High School Years."** *English Journal* 41 (April 1952): 206–07.

Streamline Shakespeare: "Let us give our underclassmen the classics . . . but in a form easily understood."

Royster, Salibelle. **"Shakespeare for the Superior."** *English Journal* 36 (January 1947): 34–37.

A semester's unit on Shakespeare for a superior class included *Cym, Err, TGV.*

Royster, Salibelle. **"What! More Shakespeare!"** *Journal of Education* (London) 197 (January 1944): 13–14.

Superior junior high girls read *MND, JC,* and *MV* in six weeks.

Royster, Salibelle. **"After the Convention: Two Ways of Teaching Shakespeare."** *English Journal* 31 (September 1942): 559.

The two ways discussed are either spending four weeks on *Macbeth* and requiring the memorization of a scene, or spending three to four days without any memorization.

Rust, Dorothy Ann. **"Give Shakespeare a Break."** *Journal of Education* (London) 122 (February 1939): 48–50.

Sager, Olof. **"Shakespeare-Lasning Pa Gymasiet."** *Moderna Sprak* (Saltsjo-Duvnas) 55 (1961): 128–30.

Salingar, L. G. **"Shakespeare in School."** *Use of English* (London) 1 (Winter 1950): 64–71.

Suggests "the single scene as the natural unit of study . . . and concentration on scenes and their sequence, rather than events, is in keeping with Shakespeare's methods of construction."

Sauer, E. H. **"New Methods of Teaching Shakespeare."** *Ohio Schools* 18 (April 1940): 162–63.

Savanyu, Jean. **"Curl Up and Read."** *Seventeen* 22 (April 1964): 94, 96.

A teenager recommends Shakespeare.

Schäfer, Jürgen. **"Was ist 'Englishe' Literatur? Wissenschaftstheoretische Probleme und Curriculare Herausforderung."** *Die Neueren Sprachen* (Marburg) 25 (1976): 512–24.

References to Shakespeare throughout.

Schevill, James. **"Bright Enigma, All Thy Puzzles Glitter."** *Teachers College Record* 65 (April 1964): 591–602.

Discusses balance, rhythm, and lyrical technique, as illustrated especially by use of songs (*TN*), "poetry of soliloquy" (*Othello* V.), and treatment of Falstaff.

Shakespeare I. Language Arts Mini-Course. Lampeter-Strasburg School District, Pa. 1973. (Available from EDRS; ED 105 503.)

Contains topical outline for a beginning Shakespeare course, including twenty-four course objectives and suggestions for AV materials.

"Shakespeare in Harlem." *America* 102 (1960): 747.

"Shakespeare in Primary Schools." *Times Educational Supplement* (London), 10 June 1939, p. 229.

Contends that children can learn much about poise and grace of movement and can form new standards of speech from the study of Shakespeare.

"Shakespeare in School." *Times Educational Supplement* (London), 23 November 1929, p. 515.

Discusses changes in examinations which move away from the "picky" to establishing an overview; 30 November 1929, p. 527, urges acting text out, beginning at age fourteen, and using modernized texts; 7 December 1929, p. 541, recommends two year program for Shakespeare study, moving to more difficult material and encouraging reading aloud; 21 December 1929, p. 559, tells how to make Shakespeare an acceptable part of examinations.

"Shakespearean Lovers in the Classroom." *Times Educational Supplement* (London), 11 March 1966, p. 717.

"Shakespeare Projects." *High Points* 8 (December 1926): 27–28.

Female pupils create set of books about historical background for the study of Shakespeare.

"Shakespeare's Theatre at Washington Irving." *High Points* 8 (December 1926): 35.

Committees of five pupils each work on seven projects outside of class and write reports.

Sharov, E. L. **"A Conference on Shakespeare Conducted in English (at a Moscow School)."** *Literatura v shkole* (Moscow) no. 5 (1963): 72–75. English version in *Soviet Education* 6 (March 1964): 39–42.

Sherman, Lucius Adelno. **"The Art of Shakespeare."** In his *Analytics of Literature. A Manual for the Objective Study of English Prose and Poetry,* pp. 144–89. Boston: Ginn & Co., 1893.

Advocates minute and searching questions upon every detail with an especially close analysis of *Macbeth,* and discussions of *Hamlet* and *Othello.*

Sikeston, Martha H. **"Shakespeare for Superior High School Sophomores."** *School and Community* 46 (January 1960): 16–17.

Simmons, John S. **"Shakespeare and the Boondocks."** *English Journal* 57 (October 1968): 972–76.

Teacher can reinforce ninth grader's silent reading of Shakespeare by constant attention to difficult words, using model stage, preparing oral readings, using media resources, interrupting frequently during oral readings by students, and assigning students to write summary statements of long and important speeches.

Simon, Henry W. **"Why Shakespeare?"** *English Journal* 23 (May 1934): 363–68.

A list of "bad" practices in the study of Shakespeare's plays.

Simon, Henry W. **The Reading of Shakespeare in American Schools and Colleges. An Historical Survey.** New York: Simon & Schuster, 1932.

Simons, Sarah E. **English Problems in the Solving for the Junior and Senior High Schools.** Chicago: Scott, Foresman, 1920.

While no text study should be made, obscure passages should be clarified and strange words and allusions explained. Plays should be read aloud in class in character, memorization should be required. Frequent dramatizations from *MND, JC,* or *AYL* are recommended for grades seven, eight, and nine respectively. High school pupils should "dramatize the age of Shakespeare"; *TN, H5,* and *Macbeth* are suggested for grades ten, eleven, and twelve.

Smith, Milton. **"Shakespeare in the Schools."** *Shakespeare Association Bulletin* 6 (1931): 38–47.

Complains that few students know how to read a play and that Shakespeare is too often presented as "a philosopher, or a writer of texts for philological study."

[Smith, Reed.] Cross, Tom P.; Smith, R.; and Stauffer, E. C., eds. **Good Reading for High Schools.** Boston: Ginn, 1931.

Admits that Shakespeare is difficult for high school students, but suggests teachers use good scholarly edition of the play, discuss it as performance, read aloud, and require memorization. The teacher should also stress the importance of characterization, give the plot beforehand, and substitute simpler synonyms for more difficult words.

Smith, Winifred. **"Teaching Shakespeare in the School."** *English Journal* 11 (June 1922): 361–64.

A college teacher's plea for changes in secondary school's approach to Shakespeare.

Söderwall, Margreta. **"Shakespeare i engleska och svenska skolor."** (Shakespeare in English and Swedish Schools.) *Aktuellt fran Skolöverstyrelsen* (Stockholm), 8 August 1954, pp. 180–86.

"Sri Lanka Prohibits the Study of Shakespeare." *Asian Student* 25 (September 1976): 1.

Shakespeare is not "linguistically within the reach of our students" say government officials.

Stambusky, A. **"More Shakespeare on the High School Stage."** *Illinois Education* 50 (1961): 162–63.

Suggests that if Shakespeare is to be taught at all in high school, the production of one play a year should be a "whole school project."

Stephenson, Henry T. **The Study of Shakespeare.** New York: Holt, 1915.

A handbook for students which suggests the "eye, ear, and mind" must all be at work in reading a play. Emphasizes familiarity with the text, reading play in stages. Contains act and scene study notes for *R3, R2, H5, Rom, Shr, MV, JC, Hamlet, Lear, Macbeth,* and *Temp.*

Steppat, Margaret. **Shakespeare in the Classroom: With an Account of Preparatory Study and Exercises in Dramatic Work Leading Up to the Reading of the Play.** London: Allen & Unwin, 1933.

Stock, Dennis. **"Shakespeare: A Photographic Tribute on Shakespeare's**

400th Anniversary." *Look,* 7 April 1964, pp. 750–58.

Photographs accompanied by appropriate Shakespearean quotations.

Stoller, L. **"We Learn, See, and Play Shakespeare."** *School Activities* 31 (1960): 205–07.

Stratton, Clarence. **"Drama."** In his *The Teaching of English in the High School,* pp. 103–26. New York: Harcourt, Brace, 1923.

Teacher should explain meaning of play's title, cast of characters, discuss place of action as well as the initial appearance and development of characters. Students should read out loud.

Stroud, Ruth. **"Learning to Read Shakespeare."** *Illinois English Bulletin* 39 (October 1951): 1–6.

The teacher is urged to provide an overview as students begin the study of Shakespeare.

Sunday, Daniel M. **"Modern Shakespeare."** *English Journal* 19 (February 1930): 160–61.

The student can be interested in Shakespeare's language by searching for "wisecracks," or better, by seeing a dramatized play in modern dress.

Süssman, Irving. **"Honorificabilitudinitatibus."** *English Journal* 54 (September 1965): 530–32.

Gives an account of students' overzealous searches for puns in Shakespeare to uncover proof of non-Shakespearean authorship.

Tannebaum, Samuel A. **"Shakespeare's Verse."** *Shakespeare Association Bulletin* 14 (1939): 60–61.

Lists nine aspects of Shakespeare's verse and provides examples for students.

Tannebaum, Samuel A. **"Exit Shakespeare."** *Shakespeare Association Bulletin* 12 (1937): 191.

Reacts to the suggestion that Shakespeare be removed from the high school curriculum.

Tartacoff, Henry A. **"The Project Method in Shakespeare."** *High Points* 5 (September 1923): 24–26.

Provides list of projects and seventeen questions to be answered with the title of Shakespearean plays.

Taylor, Richard V., ed. **Shakespeare for Secondary Schools.** London: Macmillan, 1961; New York: St. Martin's Press, 1964.

Includes adaptations of *R2, MND, MV, H5, AYL, JC,* and *Temp.*

Teaching Shakespeare: Resource Units in Language Arts for Secondary Schools. New York: New York City Board of Education, 1970. (Available from EDRS; ED 053 127.)

First step in teaching Shakespeare is to acquaint class with the meaning of words. Suggests reading with a colleague, student dramatization, and choral reading, as well as use of audio-visual materials.

Terkelson, Care; Perona, Sue; and Manker, Wendy. **"Feelin' Free with Shakespeare."** *English Review* 7 (Winter 1977): 2–4.

Fourth through sixth grade students are introduced to Shakespeare through total immersion.

Terman, Lewis. **"Cake With 400 Candles On It."** *Mademoiselle,* February 1964, pp. 76–80.

Theatre's Different Demand: An Approach to the Classroom Teaching of Plays. Hartford: Connecticut State Department of Education, 1970.

Emphasizes Shakespeare.

Thomas, Charles Swain. **"The Teaching of Drama with Particular Reference to Shakespeare."** In his *The Teaching of English in the Secondary School,* pp. 282–311. Boston: Houghton Mifflin, 1917; rev. ed. 1927.

Assuming familiarity with *Macbeth* and *AC,* discusses sensualizing the scene, clarifying allusions, poetic appeal, memorization assignments, dramatic presentation, Shakespearean humor, plot structure (in terms of introduction, rising action, turning point, falling action and catastrophe), and character study.

Thomas, Charles Swain. **How to Teach English Classics.** Boston: Houghton Mifflin, 1910.

Suggests that "the keenest enjoyment and appreciation of a Shakespearean play will come with its study."

Tisdel, Frederick M. **"The Drama."** In his *Studies in Literature,* pp. 38–74. New York: Macmillan, 1913.

Gives suggestions for the study of *H5, JC, Macbeth, TN, MND* (while pp. 223–37 survey Renaissance drama).

Tough, A. J. **"Introducing Shakespeare."** *Use of English* (London) 11 (Autumn 1959): 23–25.

Begin with an explanation of blackboard diagram of Shakespearean stage; describe the behavior of spectators; then proceed to an explanation of plot and reading selections.

Townsend, C. L. **"Shakespeare and the Wide, Wide World."** *English Journal* 19 (February 1930): 117–27.

Records parallels "in the world of fact to the incidents and to the psychological phenomena in the world of Shakespeare."

Townsend, C. L. **"Shakespeare in the High School."** *Peabody Journal of Education* 6 (March 1929): 268–77.

Because both have good plots, *JC* and *MND* are "ideal plays" for introducing Shakespeare to high school pupils. Argues against using historical or linguistic (philological) methodology, and cautions teacher not to get lost in sources and not to be the voice of authority. Suggests having students find out why they like or dislike a Shakespearean play.

Toyama, Shigehiko. **"Shakespeare for a School Text."** *English Teachers Magazine* 13 (1964): 8–10.

Trent, William P.; Hanson, Charles L.; and Brewster, William T. **"Dramatic Poetry."** In their *An Introduction to the English Classics,* pp. 148–86. Boston: Ginn, 1911.

Suggests pupil reads Shakespeare play for story outline and familiarity with text, which is more important than knowledge of introduction or footnotes. Pupils should memorize passages and act out simple scenes in class. Discusses *Macbeth* (pp. 150–57), *AYL* (pp. 157–61), *JC* (pp. 161–66), *TN* (pp. 167–71), *H5* (pp. 171–77), *MV* (pp. 177–82), *MND* (pp. 183–86).

Turner, David A. **"Shakespeare and the Status Seekers."** *English Journal* 49 (December 1960): 634–36.

Sees Charles Bartling's suggestions as symptomatic of high school emphasis on famous books badly taught rather than on education. If Shakespeare is really too hard, teach simpler authors.

Tyson, Ivernia. **"Shakespeare—When?"** *Shakespeare Association Bulletin* 15 (1940): 57–59.

Fifth graders progress from Lamb's *Tales from Shakespeare* to enacting short scenes from *Temp* and *John*.

Uhlig, H. **"Zur Behandlung Shakespeares in der 10. Klasse der allgemein-bildenden polytechninischen Oberschule."** *Deutschunterricht* (Stuttgart) 93 (1960): 195–202.

Van Cleve, Charles. **The Teaching of Shakespeare in American Secondary Schools: A Survey of Methods Employed by 363 Superior Teachers**

(1962). (Research Study No. 1.) Indiana Council of Teachers of English, 1970.

Reports on ten of the most used techniques: six are teacher initiated, four are pupil activities.

Van Cleve, Charles. **"The Teaching of Shakespeare in American Secondary Schools."** *Peabody Journal of Education* 15 (May 1938): 333–50.

Provides an historical survey of the methods used in teaching Shakespeare in American high schools 1877–1936, reviews discussion in periodicals on methods of teaching and current pedagogical techniques.

Vandiver, Edward P., Jr. **Highlights of Shakespeare's Plays: With Explanation Summary, Comment, and Emphasis on Famous Quotations.** 2nd ed., rev. and enl. Woodbury, N.Y.: Barron's Educational Series, 1976.

Selections from twenty-six Shakespeare plays compiled for high school or college students. Includes summaries, discussion topics, definitions of Elizabethan words and phrases, etc.

Veidemanis, Gladys. **"Special Techniques in Teaching a Shakespeare Play."** In *Literature in the High Schools,* edited by Dwight L. Burton, pp. 152–54. New York: Holt, Rinehart & Winston, 1970.

Suggests three to four weeks to study play, focus on inner conflicts of characteris and the consequences of their actions; also concerned with problems of attention, verse, and emphasis.

Veidemanis, Gladys. **"Shakespeare in the High School Classroom."** *English Journal* 53 (April 1964): 240–47. Reprinted in *Shakespeare in School and College,* pp. 55–62. Champaign, Ill.: National Council of Teachers of English, 1964.

An excellent discussion of problems of attention, verse, emphasis, and gives practical considerations.

Veselukhina, K. V.; Kovaleva, L. I.; and Razgovorova, T. I., eds. **William Shakespeare: Materials for the 400th Anniversary of His Birth. An Aid for Teachers of the English Language.** Perm': Permskii obl. in-tusover-shenstvovaniia uchitelei, 1964.

Simple discussion in Russian and English of Shakespeare's biography with attention to sonnets 2, 30, 33, 60, 66, 91, and 116.

Vogel, Alfred T. **"Take This from This."** *English Journal* 57 (December 1968): 1316–20.

Argues for the value of close textual examination of poetry, illustrated by reading of passages from *Macbeth.*

Walker, Brenda. **Teaching Creative Drama Age Group 9 to 15 Years.** London: Batsford, 1970.

Macbeth and *Cor* illustrate approaches to the scripted scene. Also has discussion of the "Era Approach: The Elizabethans."

Walker, Reginald F. **"Making the Most Shakespeare."** *Catholic Educator* 28 (1958): 539–41.

Presents a synthesis of principles for teaching which "show that a total view of life gradually forces itself out of the constant reading of Shakespeare's plays."

Wallace, S. A. **"Getting the Fun Out of Shakespeare's Comedy."** *English Journal* 20 (September 1931): 562–65.

Argues that pupils' "earliest impression of the comedy should be that it was a lark, great fun, and so jolly that he laughs and wants to do it all over." Uses *As You Like It* to illustrate how students can act out parts.

Walsh, William. **"Shakespeare in the Classroom: An Approach."** *Journal of Education* (London) 84 (January 1952): 16, 18.

Because "the life of the plays resides in the words themselves" no introduction or account of plot or character should occur "which is not anchored precisely in specific places in the text. Because the plays are essentially dramatic poems they are concerned with feelings, attitudes, and experiences which are not susceptible in any valuable way to prose paraphrase."

Walter, J. H. **"Shakespeare in Schools."** *Shakespeare Survey* (Cambridge) 10 (1957): 107–10.

Answers critics who don't want Shakespeare taught in (British) grammar schools and proposes means of improving instruction.

Ward, Winifred. **"Shakespearean Stories."** In her *Playmaking with Children from Kindergarten through Junior High School.* 2nd ed., pp. 111–13. New York: Appleton-Century-Crofts, 1957.

"In schools where children are prepared by a considerable amount of preliminary work in dramatics, they look forward to Shakespeare as being the most interesting material they can use."

Ward, Winifred. **"Creative Dramatics as a Medium for Teaching Literature."** *Elementary English Review* 10 (February 1933): 40–44.

Includes Shakespeare in eighth grade in a discussion of the value of creative dramatics in the teaching of literature.

Watt, Herman; Holzknecht, Karl J.; and Ross, Raymond. **Outlines of Shakespeare's Plays.** New York: Barnes & Noble, 1934.

Welles, Orson, and Hill, Roger. **"On Teaching Shakespeare and Other Great Literatures."** *English Journal* 27 (June 1938): 464–68.

A plea for an enjoyable approach to Shakespeare through the use of records.

Wells, Mary. **"A Musical Term Paper."** *English Journal* 38 (November 1949): 526.

Short account of eleventh grade research paper entitled "Music in Shakespeare's Time."

Wells, Mary Alice. **"Appreciation Follows Understanding."** *NEA Journal* 47 (November 1958): 545.

Six Shakespeare plays are included in a drama course required of students at Minneapolis high school.

"Who Wrote What? And How?" *High Points* 37 (October 1955): 72–73.

Wight, John G. **"The Pleasures of Reading Shakespeare."** *English Leaflet* 4 (January 1904): 1–2.

Pleasures are found in quotable lines and in Shakespeare's characterizations.

Williams, Deborah A. **"Shakespeare in the High School Classroom."** *Shakespeare Quarterly* 25 (1974): 263–64.

Reports on a three-day unit developed by the Folger Shakespeare Library for use with urban minority-group students. Actors present scenes from the plays the first day, slides are shown on the second day, and all discuss the play the third day.

Willy, Margaret. **"School Shakespeare."** *Drama* (London) 42 (Autumn 1956): 58.

Contends that the plays are better when women's parts are acted by young boys as they were in Elizabethan era.

Wilson, Robert F. **"Shakespeare Enters the American Schools."** *Shakespeare Newsletter* 25 (April 1975): 17.

Brief survey of Shakespeare in early America.

Wolfe, E. **"Shakespeare in Elementary School? Sixth-Graders Gave** *Julius Caesar.*" *Instructor* 73 (January 1964): 34–35.

Wonnberger, Carl G. **"Meat Not Mete for Babes."** *English Journal* 32 (May 1943): 275–77.

Takes issue with C. M. Gibson and sides with B. Renz "that Shakespeare if he belongs in the secondary school, must be presented for drama and not as a linguistic exercise." See also, in this section, Gibson, Renz.

Wonnberger, Carl G. **"Choosing the Right Play for the J.H.S."** *English Journal* 32 (March 1943): 150–54.

"Shakespeare is too difficult, and an audience is likely to receive its performance too critically." See also, in this section, Lloyd.

Wood, Stanley. **The New Teaching of Shakespeare in Schools (with illustrations from the plays** *Julius Caesar* **and** *Midsummer Night's Dream*). London: Gill, 1947.

"New Teaching" emphasizes everything centers in the child; gives lessons on *JC* (pp. 13–20) and *MND* (pp. 20–26) with tips on how not to teach (pp. 33–34).

Individual Plays

Antony and Cleopatra

"Antony and Cleopatra." *Senior Scholastic,* 19 April 1948, pp. 15–18.

Introductory version of the play.

See also, in General section, Lasser.

As You Like It

Elledge, Scott, **"As You Like It."** In *Teaching Shakespeare,* edited by Arthur Mizener, pp. 215–42. New York: New American Library, 1969.

Includes analysis of the play by act and scene, short-answer and discussion questions, and a sample test.

Emslie, MacDonald. **"Set Books: 6.** *As You Like It.*" *Use of English* (London) 6 (Winter 1954): 99–104.

"What the play has to say is to be found in the way 'characters' move from one world to another within the play, in the way they behave in these different worlds, and in the remarks which relate one world to another."

Evans, Bertrand. *"As You Like It* (Grade 9 or 10)."* In his *Teaching Shakespeare in the High School,* pp. 207–22. New York: Macmillan, 1966.

Hartinger, Elizabeth A. **"As We Like It."** *English Journal* 20 (November 1931): 764–66.

The class acted parts of *As You Like It,* then worked out programs for class presentation (e.g., songs, puppet shows, and miniature stages).

Henry, George H. **"Escaping *As You Like It."*** *English Journal* 30 (June 1941): 443–49.

A listless and bored class came to life after reading the portion of *As You Like It* describing the Forest of Arden. Students related to the description because they were all day-dreaming about someplace similar.

Kobayashi, Shyozo. **"How to Read Shakespeare's *As You Like It* with the Aid of Gramaphone Records."** In *Memoirs of the Osaka Institute of Technology,* vol. 5, no. 1, 1–12.

Powell, Neil. **"Liking It."** *Use of English* (London) 26 (Autumn 1974): 3–8.

Teaching *As You Like It* for 0-level fifth-form boys.

Scott, Richard E. **"Shakespeare for Beginners."** *English Journal* 42 (December 1953): 504–06.

Eighth graders are introduced to *As You Like It.*

See also, in General section, Blakely, Bolenius, Bridge, Hudson, Illsley, Jones, P., McGraw, Marsh, G., Simons, Taylor, Trent, Wallace.

Comedy of Errors

Richeson, Emily. **"Shakespeare for Fun."** *Dramatics* 27 (April 1956): 8, 30–31.

Comedy of Errors, the "immortal slapstick," works with students who are conscious of cast and humor.

Hamlet

Baldwin, Louis. **"Shakespeare: To Be or Not to Be?"** *Illinois English Bulletin* 39 (October 1951): 7–14.

Excerpts from *Hamlet* in modern idiom.

Bernardete, Doris. **"An Experiment in Primary Research."** *English Journal* 51 (October 1962): 487–89.

Hamlet is used as a source for papers in primary research; cites subjects of best papers.

Boyer, Leonard. **"Shakespeare a la Mode."** *High Points* 29 (November 1947): 74–75.

Hamlet is staged in ninety minutes in the classroom for evening adult students by combining recordings with teacher-narrator role.

Danker, Frederick E. **"Composition Themes from *Hamlet.*"** *English Journal* 51 (November 1962): 571–73.

College preparatory class paraphrases soliloquies, comments on critical observations, and writes character sketches, among other things.

Dean, James S. **"What's the Matter with *Hamlet* in the Schools."** In *Shakespeare in the Classroom: Resources and Media Aids,* edited by A. McLean, pp. 16–30. Kenosha: UW-Parkside's Center for Teaching Excellence, 1977.

Recommends: *Hamlet* best introduced in the theatre; in classroom maintain pace used in actual productions; students can grasp that Hamlet is in love with Ophelia, but not much of his introspection; do not depend only on text analysis.

Drew, E. **"Alas, Poor Hamlet!"** *Living Age* 355 (1938): 150-52.

A compilation of student remarks from examination papers.

Ducharme, E. R. **"M.A.T.S. Meet Hamlet."** *Record* 71 (September 1969): 65–69.

Fidone, William. **"An Above-Average Class Studies *Hamlet.*"** *English Journal* 45 (November 1956): 470–76.

Describes variety and depth of responses to the play and post-reading activities.

Frenkel, R. V. **"Studying Shakespeare's *Hamlet* During Literature Lessons in Schools."** *Archangel. Gosudarstvennyi pedagogicheskii inst. Uchenye zapiski* no. 5 (1969): 58–77.

Goba, Ronald. **"*Hamlet* and 'The Emperor's New Clothes'."** *English Journal* 56 (December 1967): 1263–68.

Argues *Hamlet* is outside of the high school student's experience.

Grumette, Jesse. **"A Plan for the Teaching of *Hamlet.*"** *High Points* 17 (October 1935): 11–17.

Presents plan for sixteen lesson units, a plot quiz of twenty-five questions, and a very good fifty questions, short answer, open book test on the whole play.

Hefling, Selma Eda. **"Shakespeare in Brownsville."** *High Points* 42 (October 1960): 27–30.

Reports on taking high school pupils to see *Hamlet.*

Holt, Ben Edward. **"A Modular Approach for Teaching Classical Literature in Inner-City High Schools."** Ph.D. dissertation, University of Massachusetts, 1975. *Dissertation Abstracts* 36 (1975): 3355A–3356.

Using *Hamlet* as exemplar, "the study combines a prose adaptation of *Hamlet* (pp. 54–104) with a student learning plan (pp. 105–47) to develop a teaching model for teachers to use to successfully teach grade-level literature to low achievers."

Howes, Alan B. *"Hamlet."* In his *Teaching Literature to Adolescents: Plays,* pp. 49–54. Glenview, Ill.: Scott, Foresman, 1968.

Important to discuss dramatic issues with students. "Students must be led to an appreciation of the part that inner discoveries play in shaping the action as the effects of these discoveries intertwine with those of the discoveries of external fact."

Kitzhaber, Albert R. *"Hamlet."* *Literature Curriculum VI. Teacher and Student Versions.* (Available from EDRS; ED 015 917.)

A teacher's guide for twelfth grade that includes discussions of Hamlet's character, problems in the characterization of Claudius, the ghost, and Hamlet. The play's three part structure is examined as is its resolution.

Maloney, Henry B. **"Half a Hamlet Better Than None."** *English Journal* 48 (February 1959): 94–96.

Provides ten questions for students to answer (after seeing a 1-1/2 hour TV *Hamlet*) in preparation for reading the play.

Mizener, Arthur. *"Hamlet."* In his *Teaching Shakespeare,* pp. 103–28. New York: New American Library, 1969.

Includes an analysis of the play by act and scene, short-answer and discussion questions, and a sample test.

Mooney, Alfred Leland. **"Students Write a New Ending."** *English Journal* 43 (December 1954): 522.

Teaching *Hamlet* includes discussion and student compositions of a variant ending to the play.

Page, M. Myriam. **"Reexamining Certain Methods in the Teaching of Literature."** *English Journal* 34 (June 1945): 326–29.

Includes reference to the study of *Hamlet*.

Parker, Richard K. **"Polonius' Indirections: A Controlling Idea in *Hamlet*."** *English Journal* 57 (March 1968): 339–44.

The paradox that often the most direct path to knowledge is the indirect path suggests the method for getting students to come to grips with *Hamlet*; offers good ideas for a college prep oratory class.

Poethen, Wilhelm Von. **Hamlet im Deutschunterricht."** *Wirkendes Wort* (Düsseldorf) 9 (1959): 99–109.

Quinn, James E. **"Rosencrantz and Guildenstern Are Alive in the Class- room."** *Missouri English Bulletin* 26 (October 1969): 16–19.

Stoppard's play leads to lively class discussion and provides insights into *Hamlet*.

Rogover, E. S. **Studying *Hamlet* at School. Methodological Aid to Teaching.** Leningrad: A. I. Gerzen Pedagogical Institute, 1971.

Stauffer, Ruth M. **"Experiencing *Hamlet*."** In *Conducting Experiences in English,* edited by Angela M. Broening, pp. 25–27. New York: Appleton- Century-Crofts, 1939.

Presents a lesson plan "to read *Hamlet* for its revelation of character" together with teacher and pupil activities and an evaluation of results.

Thomas, Cleveland A. **"Focus for Teaching *Hamlet*."** *English Journal* 47 (January 1958): 8–14, 40.

Gives "plan" for one focus: what weakness in Hamlet's nature con- tributes to his downfall?

Traci, Philip. **"Joseph Papp's Happening and the Teaching of *Hamlet*."** *English Journal* 58 (January 1969): 75–77.

Any Shakespearean production "can work as a kind of profitable source study in reverse. That is, by analyzing the differences between text and production, we can arrive at more meaningful interpretations of the Shakespearean text."

Wilson, Theodore H. **"A Real Prince of Denmark."** *English Leaflet* 26 (May 1927): 63–69.

Advocates looking at Hamlet as a seventeenth century theater goer would and see "a prince of untainted mind, of unsullied conscience . . . [who] held to his highest ideals."

Young, Francis B. *"Hamlet:* **Shakespeare's Play Told as a Short Story."** *Scholastic* 28 (April 1936): 4–6, 12, 30.

Version is from *Six Stories from Shakespeare* (Appleton-Century Co., 1935).

Zink, Priscilla M. **"Hamlet-Caviare to the Generals."** *English Journal* 44 (January 1955): 37–38.

Lower IQ pupils enjoyed *Hamlet* because play was originally intended for the same kind of audience found at the movies today. Reading of play is enhanced by constant review of the plot and a careful introduction to drama.

See also, in General section, Bailey, Bolenius, Brichto, Klein, McLean, Marsh, G., Mary Barbara, Peters, Rosinger, Sherman, Stephenson.

1 Henry IV

Chapman, Frank. *"1 Henry IV."* *Use of English* (London) 5 (Autumn 1953): 12–15.

Summarizes, for teaching purposes, L. C. Knights' approach to the play.

Evans, Bertrand. *"1 Henry IV* **and** *Henry V* **(Grade 11 or 12)."** In his *Teaching Shakespeare in the High School,* pp. 243–54. New York: Macmillan, 1966.

Horton, Stephen. **"Horseplay at the Boar's Head."** *English Leaflet* 47 (June 1948): 87–88.

Discusses *1 Henry IV* II.4.

Howes, Alan B. *"1 Henry IV."* In his *Teaching Literature to Adolescents: Plays,* pp. 57–61. Glenview, Ill.: Scott, Foresman, 1968.

Discusses how discovery and reversal are used to develop the main plot and how the testing and maturation of Hal "transcends and includes both main plot and subplot, and action is complete within the play."

Sale, William. *"1 Henry IV."* In *Teaching Shakespeare,* edited by Arthur Mizener, pp. 297–326. New York: New American Library, 1969.

Includes an analysis of the play by act and scene, short-answer and discussion questions, and a sample test.

Smith, Hallett D. **"Teaching Shakespeare's *1 Henry IV*."** *English Leaflet* 62 (Spring 1963): 7–17.

1 Henry IV can be taught "to high school students as readily as to college freshmen." Gives detailed discussion of the problems encountered and dramatic effects that students should understand. Considers different kinds of language and their uses, structure (narrative and dramatic), and the great themes of the play "presented in powerful poetic and comic language, heightened and reinforced by dramatic situations and actions."

See also, in General section, Marsh, P., Palmer.

2 Henry IV

Atthill, Robin. **"Set Books: 13. *Henry IV, Part 2*."** *Use of English* (London) 9 (Summer 1958): 253–58.

The difficulty of teaching the play is in presenting it as a whole in correct perspective which requires some knowledge of *1H4* and *H5*.

See also, in General section, Bridge, Felsher, Hudson, Illsley, Marsh, G., Simons, Stephenson, Taylor, Tisdel, Trent.

Henry V

Jenks, Tilli. **"A Unit in Shakespeare."** *North Carolina Education* 4 (December 1944): 122.

Tenth grade pupils rewrite and take part in all phases of staging *Henry V* and other plays.

Rowe, D. F. **"Set Books: 10. *Henry V*."** *Use of English* (London) 7 (Winter 1956): 106–10.

Provides a list of twenty-seven questions for pupils to answer. Provides sketching commentary to help guide students' answers. Read play silently first; then aloud after pupils are given a chance to prepare parts beforehand.

Julius Caesar

Barnes, T. R. **"Set Books: 11. *Julius Caesar*."** *Use of English* (London) 8 (Summer 1957): 233–36.

The first question for the teacher is not so much "What is this play about?" as "How much of this play can this particular class be expected to understand, and what aspect of it will, for a start, appeal to them?"

Barnet, Sylvan. **"The Tragedy of** *Julius Caesar.*" In *Teaching Shakespeare,* edited by Arthur Mizener, pp. 49–75. New York: New American Library, 1969.

Analysis of play, short-answer and discussion questions, and a sample test.

Baumann, Edith L. *"Julius Caesar:* **Is It True?"** *Clearing House* 30 (December 1955): 208–10.

High school sophomores are given outlines questions about human nature and find appropriate passages in *Julius Caesar* to illustrate principle of answer.

Beckoff, Samuel. **"A Reevaluation of Shakespeare's** *Julius Caesar.*" *High Points* 20 (October 1938): 56–60.

Urges that the play be taught at a higher level than junior high.

Bramfitt, G. N. **"The Tragedy of Cassius."** *School* (Toronto) 24 (February 1936): 504–06.

Chase, Rosemary. **"Play** *Is* **the Thing."** *Independent School Bulletin* 31 (February 1972): 55–56.

Oral reading of *Julius Caesar* has pupils acquire many language skills.

Clark, Earl John. **"The Final Irony of Cassius."** *Wisconsin English Journal* 12 (January 1970): 29–30.

Argues that Cassius is the victim of Pindarus's faulty interpretation of events.

Cohen, Hilda C. **"A** *Julius Caesar* **Project."** *High Points* 38 (October 1956): 73–76.

Following study of *Julius Caesar* class committees work on various aspects of Roman history and mythology.

Dean, Leonard F. *"Julius Caesar* **and Modern Criticism."** *English Journal* 50 (October 1961): 451–56. Reprinted in *Scholarly Appraisals of Literary Works Taught in High Schools,* edited by Stephen Dunning and Henry W. Sams, pp. 29–34. Champaign, Ill.: National Council of Teachers of English, 1965.

Discusses how *Julius Caesar* "is now almost unanimously read as a problem play marked by political, ethical, and psychological ironies of a decidedly modern and painfully human kind."

Dias, Earl J. **"Shakespeare or Hemingway—Or Both?"** *English Journal* 34 (May 1945): 278–80.

Views Shakespeare as representative of the "classical" approach to literature.

Evans, Bertrand. ***"Julius Caesar* (Grade 9 or 11)."** In his *Teaching Shakespeare in the High School,* pp. 165–77. New York: Macmillan, 1966.

Farmer, Paul. **"On Reading Literature."** In *Perspectives on English,* edited by Robert C. Pooley, pp. 187–96. New York: Appleton-Century-Crofts, 1960.

Uses three passages from *Julius Caesar* to illustrate the importance of close and careful reading in order to have reader come to terms with various structural devices.

Foster, Guy L. **"Teaching *Julius Caesar* to Slow Learners."** *English Journal* 49 (December 1960): 632–34.

A five week unit emphasizes "plot, characters, and the play as good literature."

Gadlin, Barry. **"Two Tragedies: *Julius Caesar* and *Jesus Christ Superstar.*"** *Illinois English Bulletin* 61 (January 1974): 10–14.

Identifies similarities between character, theme, plot structure, and dramatic devices.

Gray, Cecelia E. **"Listening to *Julius Caesar.*"** *English Journal* 36 (March 1947): 152–53.

Discusses Welles's recording of the play.

Handwerker, Bernard. **"When Should Shakespeare First Be Taught in the Schools?"** *High Points* 43 (March 1961): 69–71.

Suggests *Julius Caesar* as an introductory play for bright eighth or ninth graders.

Hawley, Hattie L. **Teaching English in Junior High Schools: A Study of Methods and Devices.** Boston: Houghton Mifflin, 1924.

Questions on *Julius Caesar* for ninth year work (pp. 127–29).

Hoetker, James, and Engleman, Alan. **Shakespeare's *Julius Caesar:* The Initial Classroom Presentation. An Introduction to Theatre.** Vol. 2, rev. ed. St. Ann, Miss.: Central Midwestern Regional Educational Library, 1969. (Available from EDRS; ED 035 657.)

Contains detailed lesson plans for the English teacher inexperienced in drama.

Holland, Norman N. *"Julius Caesar:* A Close Reading." In *Steps to Reading Literature 1,* edited by B. Spacks and P. Spacks, et al., pp. 101–50. New York: Harcourt, Brace & World, 1964.

Presents four units for programmed instruction for grades 10–12, "a summing up," suggestions for discussion and composition.

Howes, Alan B. *"Julius Caesar."* In his *Teaching Literature to Adolescents: Plays,* pp. 35–39. Glenview, Ill.: Scott, Foresman, 1968.

"To fully appreciate the play, students must keep their eyes on both (the public and private) worlds within the play at once, keeping a proper distance from each so that the complex relationships between the two can be perceived." Discusses public (political) world and private (personal) one in play; urges students be made aware of and appreciate tension "between personal ideal and public expediency."

Hübner, Paul. "Lehrstück und Leichenschan: Shakespeare *Julius Caesar* als Auftakt des Shakespeare—Jahres bei Stroux," *Christ und Welt* (Stuttgart) 17 (1964): 3, 18.

"Julius Caesar." Senior Scholastic, 7 April 1947, p. 20.

Six stills from British Information Service film.

Katterjohn, Elsie. "Shakespeare for the Retarded." *Shakespeare Newsletter* 7 (December 1957): 45.

Explains how her text *Julius Caesar in Modern English* is not a substitute for Shakespeare but was prepared for "classes reading below grade level."

Kitzhaber, Albert R. *"Julius Caesar. Plutarch's Lives. Autobiography." Literature Curriculum IV. Student Version.* (Available from EDRS; ED 010 817. Teacher Version, ED 010 818.)

Tenth grade student guide.

Kitzhaber, Albert R. "Literature Curriculum IV . . . Tests for *Julius Caesar* and *Autobiography.*" (Available from EDRS; ED 015 940.)

Examination questions for tenth graders.

Lane, Mary. "Extra! Extra!" *English Journal* 27 (February 1938): 137–39.

Students put out newspaper covering first three acts of *Julius Caesar* and learn a lot in the process.

Larrick, N. **"Mob Scene in *Julius Caesar.*"** *Virginia Teacher* 17 (February 1936): 33–34.

Lederer, Richard H. **"*Julius Caesar:* An Approach to the Teaching of Drama."** *English Leaflet* 64 no. 1 (1965): 13–18.

Demonstrates selective process of dramatist's creative process by comparing *Julius Caesar* with source in Plutarch.

Leeb, David. **Permanent Key—Indexed Study Guide to Shakespeare's *Julius Caesar.*** New York: Research Associates Inc. of America and Bantam Books, 1966.

Lillard, Kathryn B., and Fox, Doris. **"Another Stab at *Julius Caesar.*"** *Texas Outlook* 52 (February 1968): 36–37, 53.

Three teachers team-teach sophomores, two classes meeting together for four periods each day, and three classes meeting for two periods. A six-week period provided a twenty-seven-day unit.

Lisman, Helen. **"Teaching Plan for *Julius Caesar.*"** *English Journal* 30 (April 1941): 316.

Class had "Roman Party."

Malone, Thomas J. **"It worked for me . . . a tape recorder for Mark Anthony."** *Wisconsin English Journal* 5 (February 1963): 27.

Tape recorder allows students to imitate actors' performance and perform scenes for comparison.

Mary Julia Anne, Sister. **"*Caesar* is a Modern Play."** *Catholic School Journal* 65 (May 1965): 41–42.

Introduces sophomore study of *Julius Caesar* by discussing pupils' favorite movies, the qualities of a good play or movie, and how to visualize Shakespearean scenes and characters.

Miller, Joy. **"Methods That Work with *Julius Caesar.*"** *FOCUS: Teaching English in Southeastern Ohio* 2 (May 1976): 13–18.

Ninth grade teacher explains how she exposes pupils to *Julius Caesar* through audio-visual materials, including recording of the full play.

Murphy, Geraldine. **"Advanced Play Reading: Shakespeare."** In her *The Study of Literature in High School,* pp. 285–99. Waltham, Mass.: Blaisdell, 1968.

An excellent examination of "the structure, the language, and the world of *Julius Caesar* to show on what grounds this play recommends itself as a 'right' introduction to Shakespeare."

Nelson, Drucella. **"Scenes from the Classroom:** *Julius Caesar***—Junior Grade."** *Wisconsin English Journal* 2 (April 1960): 11, 14.

Reports on class dramatization of assassination scene.

Riley, Roberta. **"Five or Six Plays Are Better Than One;** *Julius Caesar* **Yields to Tenth Grade Drama Workshop."** *California English Journal* 9 (1973): 27–30.

Rodgers, Bertha. **"Introducing** *Julius Caesar.***"** *English Leaflet* 31 (February 1932): 169–71.

A teacher learns: "place active responsibility upon students and they will not fail you."

Ryerson, Edward. **"***Julius Caesar* **Once Again."** *English Journal* 47 (January 1958): 1–7.

Argues that teachers must decide if their ninth grade classes will be able to relate to the play, and offers analysis of the play's "teachable characteristics."

Sargeant, Seymour H. **"***Julius Caesar* **and the Historical Film."** *English Journal* 61 (February 1972): 230–33, 245.

Compares Shakespearean dramatic techniques with those of the historical film.

Spiegler, Charles G. **"***Julius Caesar***—A Liberal Education: A Modern Approach to the Teaching of a Classic."** *High Points* 18 (May 1936): 25–34.

The teacher should relate play to current events and to awareness of social phenomena.

Schultz, P. **"Shakespeare's** *Julius Caesar* **im englischen Unterricht.** Berlin: Mathiesen, 1941.

Stuart, Milo. **"***Julius Caesar* **Again."** *English Journal* 32 (April 1943): 216–18.

Students imagine they have been carried back to ancient Rome by a time machine and write letters to twentieth century friends.

See also, in General section, Blakely, Bolenius, Brichto, Chubb, Crawford, DeBoer, Harrison, Hudson, Illsley, Jones, M., Leonard, S., McLean, Marsh, G., Martin, McGraw, MacIsaac, Palmer, Poethen, Rodes, Royster, Simons, Stephenson, Taylor, Tisdel, Townsend, Trent, Wood.

King Lear

Evans, Bertrand. **"Lear."** In his *Teaching Shakespeare in the High School,* pp. 271–74. New York: Macmillan, 1966.

Guyol, Hazel Sample. **"A Temperance of Language: Goneril's Grammar and Rhetoric."** *English Journal* 55 (March 1966): 316–19.

"Goneril's controlled language reflects her controlled and limited universe."

Siegel, Paul N. **"Willy Loman and King Lear."** *College English* 17 (March 1956): 341–45.

Death of a Salesman is a successful tragedy that is focused, like *King Lear,* on the theme "Know Thyself."

See also, in General section, Poethen, Stephenson.

Macbeth

Baker, Franklin T. **"Literature in the Secondary School."** In *Teaching English in the Elementary and Secondary School,* edited by G. R. Carpenter, et al., pp. 250–82. New York: Longmans, Green, 1903.

Provides list (pp. 277–78) of fifteen topics to consider when teaching *Macbeth.*

Bartling, Charles E. **"On Teaching *Macbeth* and Shakespeare."** *English Journal* 49 (January 1960): 38–39.

Advocates committee method by which students spend two weeks on "background" in preparation for reading the play in one week. See also, in this section, Turner.

Bates, Arlo. **"The Study of *Macbeth."*** In his *Talks on Teaching Literature,* pp. 165–92. Boston: Houghton Mifflin, 1906.

First reading of the play should be by teacher to give the students the plot. Then the class may attend to details. Oral readings by pupils should focus on selection of central motive (ambition) and the study of difficult passages. Avoid pedantry during the second reading. Tests should allow the students "to feel and to reason in terms of [their] own experience."

Briggs, Martyn. **"It's Mad This, Sir."** *Creative Drama* (Birmingham) 4 no. 8 (1976): 23–26.

In an attempt to "translate" Shakespeare, students stage bits and pieces of *Macbeth* in a modern "production."

Calitri, Charles. *"Macbeth* **and the Reluctant Reader."** *English Journal* 48 (May 1959): 254–61.

Shakespeare must be presented to the reluctant reader in familiar terms. The teacher must find bridges between medieval Scotland and present day America, between Shakespeare's characters and people in the everyday life of the student.

Conlin, Matthew T. **"Teaching** *Macbeth* **as Tragedy."** *Connecticut English Journal* 2 (Spring 1970): 10–17.

Five elements of the tragic are considered: view, plot, hero, language, and effect.

Cunningham, J. V. *"Macbeth* **in Three Days."** *High Points* 43 (October 1961): 71.

Argues for the use of records or tapes by different performers.

Dean, Leonard F. *"Macbeth* **and Modern Criticism."** *English Journal* 47 (February 1958): 57–67.

Short synthesis of recent criticism with selected reading list.

Dettmers, H. A. **"Teaching** *Macbeth* **Visually."** *Michigan Education Journal* 25 (April 1948): 412.

Describes blackboard techniques for depicting plot problems.

Edgerly, Lydia. **"Shakespeare in 1951."** *English Journal* 40 (December 1951): 573–74.

Describes junior girls' response to film and recordings of *Macbeth.*

Evans, Bertrand. *"Macbeth* **(Grade 11 or 12)."** In his *Teaching Shakespeare in the High School,* pp. 177–91. New York: Macmillan, 1966.

Flatter, Richard. *Macbeth.* Frankfurt am Main: M. Diesterweg, 1958.

Commentary on the play with a survey of the principal theories underlying the main ideas.

Fleege, Urban. **"Streamlining Shakespeare."** *English Journal* 30 (May 1941): 408–11.

Having students write their own version of *Macbeth* in "the streamlined English of today" led students to another unit on the play. Only two limitations were imposed: (1) fidelity to plot in all but minor details, and (2) "the action reflecting the traits of the various characters had to be true to the characters in Shakespeare's play."

Gallman, Mary N. *"Macbeth Lives Again."* *English Journal* 41 (September 1952): 370–71.

The students tell the story from the viewpoint of different characters.

Hall, Evelyn W. **"Color Him Red."** *English Journal* 56 (April 1967): 564–65.

The students follow the central image of blood act by act, which leads to a discussion of related elements such as diction, images, and nature.

Hart, Evalee. **"A Comparative Study: *Macbeth* and *Richard III."*** *English Journal* 61 (September 1972): 824–30.

A comparison of the two plays reveals maturing of Shakespeare's artistry, clarifies the nature of tragedy, provides a better understanding of character, and reflects contemporary thought.

Henry, George H. **"The Growth of a Unity."** *English Journal* 37 (September 1948): 341–47.

Offers approaches to the meaning of *Macbeth* designed to meet contemporary student interest.

Herman, G. **"Macduff's Boy: A Reply to Professor Syrkin."** *Use of English* (London) 9 (Autumn 1957): 40–42.

"How Well Do You Know *Macbeth?"* *English Journal* 46 (September 1957): 354.

High school pupils design a "special test" for teachers.

Holmes, E. M. **"Shakespeare without Pain."** *English Journal* 42 (May 1953): 270–71.

When teacher "dares" students to read Shakespeare, class accepts and selects *Macbeth.* Gives an account of how the play was studied.

Howes, Alan B. *"Macbeth."* In his *Teaching Literature to Adolescents: Plays,* pp. 68–73. Glenview, Ill.: Scott, Foresman, 1968.

The teacher should help students achieve insights into the interplay of internal and external forces working on Macbeth, and the changes in his character. Seven principles for the teacher to follow are: (1) present the play selectively, (2) juxtapose significant passages, (3) stick to the major points, (4) concentrate on character in action rather than the mechanics of plot, (5) avoid stereotypes in the discussion of character, (6) involve students in the play through questions which move from what to why, and (7) make students aware of their feelings as members of an audience.

Hughes, Daniel E. **"The 'Worm of Conscience' in *Richard III* and *Macbeth.*"** *English Journal* 55 (October 1966): 845–52.

The role of conscience is general in *Richard III*, but polarized in *Macbeth*.

Kitzhaber, Albert R. **"Drama: Tragedy (*Oedipus, Macbeth, Ghosts*), Comedy (*The Rivals, Major Barbara*).**" *Literature Curriculum V. Teacher and Student Versions.* (Available from EDRS; ED 015 909.)

An eleventh grade unit comparing comedy and tragedy.

Ladd, William. **"*Macbeth*—As a Reading Production."** *English Journal* 33 (September 1944): 374–77.

Macbeth used in oral interpretation, with twenty speaking parts prepared for by using recordings.

"*Macbeth* in the Socialized Recitation." *High Points* 7 (May 1925): 48.

Each pupil is assigned an act and conducts a lesson.

Makey, Hermann O. **"In the Literature Class."** *English Journal* 39 (September 1950): 360–66.

Offers various ways of presenting the opening scene of *Macbeth* that allow students to see how different the play would be if Shakespeare were writing it today.

Morris, F. J. A. **"*Macbeth.*"** *School* (Toronto) 25 (1936): 25–31.

O'Malley, R. **"Set Books: 8. *Macbeth.*"** *Use of English* (London) 6 (Summer 1955): 230–34.

"With almost any class an intelligent interest in the play can soon be created." Includes list of fifteen points to discuss in *Macbeth* III.2.

Parry, Martin. **"The Tragedy of *Macbeth.*"** In *Teaching Shakespeare,* edited by Arthur Mizener, pp. 13–47. New York: New American Library, 1969.

Includes an analysis of the play by act and scene, short-answer and discussion questions, and a sample test.

Reynolds, William J. **"When Thou Doest *Macbeth,* Do It Quickly."** *English Journal* 47 (February 1958): 90–91.

Suggests extensive preparation for class study of *Macbeth* through essays such as Shaw's "Better than Shakespeare," and "Valedictory," Thurber's "The Macbeth Murder Mystery," and De Quincey's "On the

Knocking at the Gate in *Macbeth,*" followed by rapid reading and discussion in class.

Robinson, Miles A. **"How We Studied** *Macbeth.*" *English Journal* 20 (May 1931): 419–20.

Students learn to dramatize select scenes with attention to stagecraft: i.e., where the actors move on stage, their gestures, delivery, etc.

Ruth, Mary A. **"Two Devices Applied to** *Macbeth.*" *English Journal* 37 (January 1948): 46.

Describes student responses to writing the story of *Macbeth* as a modern newspaper might carry it.

Saalbach, Raymond C. **"*Macbeth* in Review."** *English Journal* 39 (December 1950): 574–77.

Describes successful review unit used in an eleventh grade class.

Sonntag, Wolfgang. **"*Macbeth* in Englischunterricht, Forschung-Methodik-Praxis."** *Die Neueren Sprachen* (Marburg) (August 1965): 353–68.

Proposes method of teaching *Macbeth* through appropriate questions to elicit students' response.

Syrkin, Marie. **"Youth and Lady Macduff."** *Use of English* (London) 8 (Summer 1957): 257–61.

Considers the relevance for today's youth of the murder of Lady Macduff and her children.

Taggert, L., and Haefner, George E. **"Two Methods of Teaching** *Macbeth.*" *English Journal* 23 (September 1934): 543–53.

Concludes that student-guided class was more aggressive and discussion tended to be more heated and emotional than in the teacher-guided group. Objective tests given both groups, however, proved the student-guided group less effective.

"Teaching Shakespeare." *High Points* 7 (March 1925): 39–40.

Reports on high school pupils acting out *Macbeth* in class.

Turner, Rosemary. **"*Macbeth.*"** In *Teaching Secondary English: Alternative Approaches,* edited by Thomas Brown, Mary Gallagher, and R. Turner, pp. 85–88. Columbus, Ohio: Merrill, 1975.

Students should read the play prior to class reading or discussion. Gives questions by which to motivate students.

Watson, Mary H. *"Macbeth* **Outgrows the Classroom."** *English Journal* 39 (January 1950): 33–34.

> Reports on several projects used to interest students, e.g., posters and handbills, dress dolls in Elizabethan costume, Shakespeare's songs, music, model of Globe, group recordings, and play production.

See also, in General section, Arnold, Blakely, Bolenius, Bridge, Chubb, DeBoer, Gribble, Hudson, Illsley, Klein, Marsh, G., Martin, McGraw, Morgan, Peters, Poethen, Rodes, Sherman, Simons, Stephenson, Tisdel, Trent, Vogel, Walker.

Midsummer Night's Dream

Eidenier, Elizabeth. **"Bottom's Song: Shakespeare in Junior High."** *English Journal* 60 (February 1971): 208–11.

> Shows how editing *Midsummer Night's Dream* to fit eighth graders' needs and abilities can help students to identify with the various roles.

Elledge, Scott. *"Midsummer Night's Dream."* In *Teaching Shakespeare,* edited by Arthur Mizener, pp. 159–81. New York: New American Library, 1969.

> Includes an analysis of the play by act and scene, short-answer and discussion questions, and a sample test.

Emery, John P. **"The Theme of** *Midsummer Night's Dream."* *English Leaflet* 59 (February–March 1960): 1–3.

> "The theme is the importance of both realism and antithetical romance in the life of every individual."

Evans, Bertrand. *"Midsummer Night's Dream* **(Grade 9 or 11)."** In his *Teaching Shakespeare in the High School,* pp. 191–207. New York: Macmillan, 1966.

Holleran, James V. **"The Pyramus—This be Theme in** *Midsummer Night's Dream."* *California English Journal* 3 (1967): 20–26.

Kadushin, Charles. **"Shakespeare and Sociology."** *Columbia University Forum* 9 (Spring 1966): 25–31.

> Reports on the reactions to New York Shakespeare Festival interracial production of *Midsummer Night's Dream* in 1964.

Kahdy, N. **"Eighth Grade Shakespeare."** *High School Journal* 38 (October 1954): 7–8.

The class project is to produce *Midsummer Night's Dream* with puppets, and includes building a stage, designing scenery, and learning the voice parts.

Lee, Agnes Patricia. *"Midsummer Night's Dream:* A Project." *High School Teacher* 5 (September 1929): 216-17.

Leonard, Pauline W. *"Midsummer Night's Dream* in Junior High Schools." *English Journal* 12 (March 1933): 227-29.

Midsummer Night's Dream deserves to be first play studied because of its relative simplicity of language, rhythm, beautiful poetry, and famous characters, and because, "it is peculiarly an English play."

Mendelson, Florence G. "Shakespeare in the Winchell Era." *High Points* 17 (March 1935): 54.

Sophomore pupils paraphrase *Midsummer Night's Dream* in modern idiom.

Meszaros, Patricia K. "Prolegomena for a Student's Dramatic Edition of Shakespeare with an Edition of *Midsummer Night's Dream.*" Ph.D. dissertation, University of Maryland, 1971. *Dissertation Abstracts* 32 (1971): 3261A.

The introduction surveys modern criticism and Shakespeare's plays in the classroom. The text of *Midsummer Night's Dream* abandons "un-Shakespearean act and scene divisions and locality designations, but left-hand pages facing the text . . . offer expanded stage directions and stage diagrams consistent with Elizabethan stage practice, designed to heighten the reader's awareness of visual and aural elements of the play. . . ."

See also, in General section, Hudson, Lease, Lloyd, Marsh, G., McGraw, Royster, Simons, Taylor, Tisdel, Townsend, Trent, Wood.

Merchant of Venice

Aubert, William. "Hvorfor velger lektorene *Merchant of Venice?* (Why Do Secondary School Teachers Choose *Merchant of Venice?*)" *Samtiden* (Oslo) 80 (1971): 552-56.

An answer to G. Meyer partly in support of *Merchant of Venice.* See also, in this section, Meyer.

Carlin, Jerome. "The Case against *The Merchant of Venice.*" *English Journal* 42 (October 1953): 388-90.

"Shylock is not a noble figure," nor can the play be used to dispel any feelings of anti-Semitism.

DeHaven, Ethel M. **"The Sheik of Venice."** *English Journal* 19 (September 1930): 565–67.

Tenth graders become enthused when *Merchant of Venice* is read selectively by the teacher in the simplified language of the pupils. Bassanio, for example, was identified as a "sheik" who needed cash in a hurry.

Downer, Alan. *"Merchant of Venice."* In *Teaching Shakespeare,* edited by Arthur Mizener, pp. 77–101. New York: New American Library, 1969.

Includes an analysis of the play by act and scene, short-answer and discussion questions, and a sample test.

Johansson, Ernest H. **"Getting Straight with Shakespeare's *Merchant of Venice."* FOCUS: Teaching English in Southeastern Ohio* 2 (May 1976): 34–45.

Outlines an approach to the play for juniors and seniors in high school that includes an examination of the play's narrative and the nature of a comic plot.

Kitzhaber, Albert R. *"The Merchant of Venice."* Literature Curriculum III. Student Version.* (Available from EDRS; ED 010 815. Teacher Version, ED 010 816.)

Ninth grade student guide to the play presents alternate approaches.

LaBrant, Lou L. **"How to Read a Play."** In her *The Teaching of Literature in the Secondary School,* pp. 68–83. New York: Harcourt, Brace, 1931.

How to teaching the reading of *Merchant of Venice* in the ninth grade.

"Leah, Miss Grenshaw, and Shylock." *English Journal* 38 (December 1949): 580–83.

An imaginative account of a Jewish girl's experience in class studying Shakespeare.

Leonard, Albert. **"Should *Merchant of Venice* Offend Jewish Students?"** *English Journal* 41 (October 1952): 432–33.

The teacher should provide Elizabethan background and show how Shylock was vengeful because of his mistreatment by the Christians. Note also how Shakespeare allows his audience sympathy with Shylock.

Leshem, Hayim. **"Ha-soher mi-Venezia mi-behinah hinukhit (Didactic**

Aspects of *Merchant of Venice*)." In *Mehkarim ve-iyunim (Researches and Studies),* pp. 261–64. Tel Aviv: Leshem, 1976.

On teaching and studying *Merchant of Venice* in Israel today.

McGraw, H. Ward. **"Shylock: A Lesson in Character Interpretation for the Ninth and Tenth Years."** *English Journal* 19 (March 1930): 227–30.

A lesson plan which assumes that the play already has been read for the study and for first impressions.

Malm, M. H. **"Interpreting Shakespeare to Youth."** *English Journal* 26 (December 1937): 317–19.

Merchant of Venice comes alive for pupils after the teacher provides background on theater and Shakespeare. The class reads the play and acts it out.

Marder, L. **"Shakespeare No Anti-Semite."** *American Judaism* 12 (Fall 1962): 18.

Outlines evidence to prove that Shakespeare is not anti-Semitic and urges teachers to stress these points when they teach *Merchant of Venice.*

"*Merchant of Venice* Not Studied in the New York Public Schools." *New York Evening Sun.* 2 April 1936.

Meyer, G. **"Kjpmannen: Venedig som artium spensum (*MV* as a Set Book for the Secondary School Examination)."** *Samtiden* (Oslo) 80 (1971): 548–51.

Finds *Merchant of Venice* interesting because of its anti-semitism. See also, in this section, Aubert.

Palmer, Dora E. **"A Good Deed in a Naughty World."** *English Journal* 35 (September 1946): 370–75.

Merchant of Venice contributes to a better understanding of religion and intercultural education. Describes the use of recordings and gives samples of student papers.

Perrin, Porter G. **"*The Merchant of Venice,* Etc."** *English Journal* 40 (October 1951): 446.

Suggests that the play "isn't very interesting to young people."

Phillips, Addison L. **"Shutting Out Shylock."** *Journal of Education* (London) 120 (December 1937): 399–400.

Neither Italians nor Jews should be offended by the play because it is "a lesson in sympathy and tolerance" for youth. He would, however, cut the scurrilous abuse of the Jew from the play.

Rust, Dorothy Ann. **"Give Shakespeare a Break."** *Journal of Education* (London) 122 (February 1939): 48–50.

Offers suggestions for teaching. Advises the teacher not to minimize the sense of drama; and gives questions for study of *Merchant of Venice.*

Shapiro, Alan. **"Should the *Merchant of Venice* Offend Jewish Students?"** *English Journal* 41 (October 1952): 432–33.

Suggests that "only through frank discussion of prejudice . . . can the student learn about it."

Summers, Vivian. *"The Merchant of Venice."* *Use of English* (London) 12 (Spring 1961): 161–66.

Merchant of Venice is a good choice for a class tackling Shakespeare for the first time because of its obvious merits (a gripping plot, court-room drama, comic relief, fine poetry, good acting parts, and a compelling central figure). Follows G. W. Knight's *Principles of Shakespearean Production* (1936) in her interpretation of the play.

Taubman, Nora S. **"When the New Generation Reads *Merchant of Venice.*"** *High Points* 17 (January 1935): 39–40.

The cynicism of third term pupils is overcome when the teacher reads the play in class, omitting difficult passages.

Treichler, M. **"Free-acting Shakespeare."** *Independent School Bulletin* 31 (May 1972): 64–65.

Ninth graders enact the play in their own words, become involved with the play, and improve their verbal skills.

Webster, Edward H., and Smith, D. V. **Teaching English in the Junior High School.** Yonkers-on-the-Hudson, N.Y.: World Book, 1927.

Pp. 193–94 suggest an illustrated booklet of *Merchant of Venice* as a teaching device.

Wyatt, E. V. *"Merchant of Venice."* *Catholic World* 181 (May 1955): 149.

See also, in General section, Bailey, Blakely, Bolenius, Hudson, Marsh, G., McGraw, Royster, Stephenson, Taylor, Trent.

Othello

Adler, Doris. **"The Rhetoric of *Black* and *White* in *Othello.*"** *Shakespeare Quarterly* 25 (Spring 1974): 248–57.

Costello, Patrick. **"Salinger and Honest Iago."** *Renascence* 16 (1964): 171–74.

Iago sees love only as lust and J. D. Salinger tells us that this is happening in our own society.

Fogel, Ephim. *"Othello."* In *Teaching Shakespeare,* edited by Arthur Mizener, pp. 183–214. New York: New American Library, 1969.

Includes an analysis of the play by act and scene, short-answer and discussion questions, and a sample test.

Goldstein, R. M. *"Othello."* *High Points* 37 (October 1955): 46–50.

Immaculate Clare, Sister. **"The Problem of Suffering in Shakespeare's** *Othello."* *Catholic Educator* 27 (1957): 178–80.

Mary Philip, Sister. **"The Tragedy** *Othello."* *High School Teacher* 7 (December 1931): 373.

Though he ensnares the naive Othello, Iago ends as wretchedly as he has lived.

Schlegelmilch, Wolfgang. **"Shakespeare** *'Othello'* **in Oberprima."** *Praxis des neusprachlichen Unterrichts* (Dortmund) 7 (1960): 148–50.

See also, in General section, Brichto, Schevill, Sherman.

Richard II

Hommrich, Sister Rita Catherine. *"Richard II."* In *Teaching Shakespeare,* edited by Arthur Mizener, pp. 269–96. New York: New American Library, 1969.

Includes an analysis of the play by act and scene, short-answer and discussion questions, and a sample test.

See also, in General section, Illsley, Stephenson, Taylor.

Richard III

Felsher, Roy L. **"Two Shakespearean History Plays:** *Richard III, Henry V."* In *Teaching Literature in Grades Seven through Nine,* edited by Edward B. Jenkinson and Jane Stouder Hawley, pp. 117–43. Bloomington: Indiana University Press, 1967.

An excellent, succinct discussion.

Hart, Evalee. **"A Comparative Study:** *Macbeth* **and** *Richard III."* *English Journal* 61 (September 1972): 824–30.

A comparison of the two plays reveals the maturing of Shakespeare's artistry, clarifies the nature of tragedy, provides a better understanding of character, and reflects contemporary thought.

Hodgins, Frank, and Hodgins, Audrey. **"Teaching Guide for *Richard III.*"** *English Journal* 45 (March 1956): 138–40, 144.

Richard as an arch-dissembler can provide education and moral insights; for use in conjunction with NBC-TV production.

Hughes, Daniel E. **"The 'Worm of Conscience' in *Richard III* and *Machbeth.*"** *English Journal* 55 (October 1966): 845–52.

The role of conscience is general in *Richard III* but polarized in *Macbeth.*

Leas, Susan E. ***"Richard III,* Shakespeare and History."** *English Journal* 60 (December 1971): 1214–16, 1296.

Suggestions for exploring the nature of history and the writing of history as a way of preparing to read *Richard III.*

See also, in General section, Felsher, Poethen, Stephenson.

Romeo and Juliet

Andrews, Tom, and Austell, Jan. **"Who Are These People?"** *Media and Methods* 5 (1968): 27–29, 35.

Students viewed Zeffirelli's film *Romeo and Juliet* before reading the text, which enabled them "to see" the words of the play more clearly and to become more involved in the action of the play.

Arnold, Lois V. ***Romeo and Juliet* Individualized Literature Unit.** Cincinnati, Ohio: American Book Co., 1971.

Benedict, Stewart H., comp. ***"Romeo and Juliet* and *West Side Story* by A. Laurents, L. Bernstein and S. Sondheim."** In his *A Teacher's Guide to Modern Drama,* pp. 215–21. New York: Dell, 1967.

Provides topics and questions for discussion, composition, and special projects, and two short tests to check reading.

Cohen, Lauren W. ***"Romeo and Juliet*: Living Is Being Relevant."** *English Journal* 59 (December 1970): 1263–65, 1269.

Tenth graders in an all black inner-city school began with a study of family trees; then proceeded to enactment of the play, with student directors and student actors assigned in advance. For evaluation, students could either write a newspaper account of the action or update a major scene.

Elliot, Marian. *"Romeo and Juliet."* In *Teaching Shakespeare,* edited by Arthur Mizener, pp. 129–57. New York: New American Library, 1969.

Includes an analysis of the play by act and scene, short-answer and discussion questions and a sample test.

Evans, Bertrand. *"Romeo and Juliet* (Grade 10 or 11)."* In his *Teaching Shakespeare in the High School,* pp. 223–38. New York: Macmillan, 1966.

Goldberg, Sam. *"Romeo and Juliet* and 'Vocational' Boys."* *English Journal* 39 (March 1950): 159–60.

Success with having boys enact III.i. in class before a week of discussions when student panels were assigned the different acts.

Hanke, Jeanette J. *"Romeo and Juliet* and the Disadvantaged."* *English Journal* 59 (February 1970): 273–76.

Relates working with small groups that discussed and enacted scenes. Students became very involved.

Herzberg, Max J. "Sources and Stage History of *Romeo and Juliet.*" *Educational Screen* 21 (December 1955): 21–27.

Sketches the literary background of the story and indicates the changes made by Shakespeare, as well as by later dramatic imitators of Shakespeare.

Lewis, Anthony J. "Responses to Prejudice in *Romeo and Juliet, Merchant of Venice* and *Lear.*" *English Journal* 61 (April 1972): 488–94.

"Juliet, Morocco, and Shylock, as the victims of prejudiced environments, are quick to assert in very physical terms that they are people, not labels." Lear comes to an understanding of the unity of men, "precisely what Juliet knew intuitively and what Morocco and Shylock fall back on when faced with the specter of prejudice."

Perrine, Laurence. "When Form and Content Kiss/Intention Made the Bliss: The Sonnet in *Romeo and Juliet.*" *English Journal* 55 (October 1966): 872–74.

A sonnet pattern in *Romeo and Juliet* I.v. suggests a good exercise for students: ask if this is accident or design.

Pettet, E. C. **"The Imagery of *Romeo and Juliet*."** *English* (London) 8 (Autumn 1950): 121–26.

"Fate and premonition" revealed in play's imagery (of "images of strife, contrast, contradiction, and paradox").

Robinson, Katherine, ed. *"Romeo and Juliet."* *Scholastic Scope,* 13 September 1968, pp. 4–11.

Taylor, Gary J. *"Romeo and Juliet* and *West Side Story*: **An Experimental Unit."** *English Journal* 51 (October 1962): 484–85.

Comparison of *Romeo and Juliet* with modern stage and movie production.

See also, in General section, Crawford, Lasser, Marsh, G., Palmer, Stephenson.

Taming of the Shrew

Evans, Bertrand. *"Shrew."* In his *Teaching Shakespeare in the High School,* pp. 262–64. New York: Macmillan, 1966.

See also, in General section, Stephenson.

The Tempest

Caputi, Anthony. *"Tempest."* In *Teaching Shakespeare,* edited by Arthur Mizener, pp. 327–52. New York: New American Library, 1969.

Includes an analysis of the play by act and scene, short-answer and discussion questions, and a sample test.

Evans, Bertrand. *"Tempest."* In his *Teaching Shakespeare in the High School,* pp. 274–77. New York: Macmillan, 1966.

Gillie, Christopher. *"The Tempest."* *Use of English* (London) 7 (Autumn 1955): 37–41.

Should not approach play only as allegory or fairy story with good poetry: recognize the "unreality" of play found in the place (magical island) and in the magicianship of Prospero and Ariel.

Syna, Seymour. *"The Tempest:* **A Production with College Actors Designed to Tour Grade Schools."** Ed.D. dissertation, Columbia University, 1969. *Dissertation Abstracts* 31 (1970): 506A.

A one-hour performance was well received by pupils prepared in advance by use of a study guide. Teachers were unable to integrate production into their classwork.

"*The Tempest* at Washington Irving." *High Points* 8 (December 1926): 30.

Pupils design marionette costumes.

Two Gentlemen of Verona

Stephenson, William E. **"The Adolescent Dream-world of the *Two Gentlemen of Verona.*"** *Shakespeare Quarterly* 17 (1966): 165–68.

Twelfth Night

Adams, Barry. *"Twelfth Night."* In *Teaching Shakespeare,* edited by Arthur Mizener, pp. 243–68. New York: New American Library, 1969.

Includes an analysis of the play by act and scene, short-answer and discussion questions, and a sample test.

Evans, Bertrand. *"Twelfth Night."* In his *Teaching Shakespeare in the High School,* pp. 264–68. New York: Macmillan, 1966.

Gillie, Christopher. *"Twelfth Night."* *Use of English* (London) 4 (Spring 1953): 136–40.

Though commonly regarded as a safe introduction to Shakespeare, *Twelfth Night* is more complex and interesting than is usually recognized.

Perkins, Derek C. **Model Answers on Shakespeare's *Twelfth Night.*** Swansea: Celtic Educational Series, 1967.

Winter's Tale

Evans, Bertrand. *"Winter's Tale."* In his *Teaching Shakespeare in the High School,* pp. 268–71. New York: Macmillan, 1966.

Teaching Shakespeare in College

General

Alexander, Peter. **"The Schoolmaster from the Country."** *Times Literary Supplement* (London), 23 April 1964, p. 327.

Major changes in the view of Shakespeare's education and art since 1916.

Ashland Studies in Shakespeare. (A book of articles, prints, and suggestions for projects: designed to accompany classwork in the Field Course established by the English Department at Stanford University in collaboration with the Oregon Shakespeare Festival of 1955.) Ashland, Oregon, 1955.

Brief review in *Shakespeare Quarterly* 8 (1957): 243.

Bache, William B. **"A Procedure for Teaching a Shakespeare Play."** *Shakespeare Newsletter* 28 (April 1978): 17.

Students are "given a seminal scene" and a handout designed to alert them to its various tensions, emphasis, basic strategy, etc.

Barber, C. L. **"On the Use of Talking Passages."** *Shakespeare Newsletter* 25 (April 1975): 11.

Considers "how quotation, reading from the text, can best counter tendencies toward empty abstraction."

Beckerman, Bernard. **"Some Problems in Teaching Shakespeare's Plays as Works of Drama."** In *Teaching Shakespeare,* edited by W. Edens, et al., pp. 305–16. Princeton: Princeton University Press, 1977.

Discusses four interdependent impediments to teaching or studying the distinctive dramaturgic features of Shakespeare's work: (1) the difficulty in isolating exclusively dramatic elements of a play, (2) the inability to perceive movement behind language, (3) the lack of adequate examples of performance for the classroom, and (4) the absence of a satisfactory vocabulary with which to talk about the drama. These impediments must be overcome in order to develop the perception needed to articulate the dramatic movement in Shakespeare.

Bender, Robert M. **"Shakespeare Illustrated: A Report on Some Recent Experiments in Teaching."** *Shakespeare Newsletter* 25 (April 1975): 20.

Describes extensive use of media, especially of slides (including over 800 of an entire production of *Twelfth Night*), synchronized with a professional recording of the play.

Bergeron, David M. **"Plays Within Plays in Shakespeare's Early Comedies."** In *Teaching Shakespeare,* edited by W. Edens, et al., pp. 153–73. Princeton: Princeton University Press, 1977.

Argues that as a dramatic device, "the play-within-the-play represents a possibility for a happy combination of concern for theatrical practice as well as the more literary aspect of drama." Explores *Shr, LLL, MND,* and *TN.*

Bergman, Fredrick. **"Shakespeare in Indiana: A Report on the 'Shakespeare Meeting' of the Indiana College English Association."** *Shakespeare Quarterly* 4 (1953): 337–41.

The discussion groups on "Problems in Teaching Shakespeare" agreed on "the necessity of developing appreciation as the first goal of teaching the plays. Recorded and filmed teaching aids were generally approved. And the greatest aim, stemming from the developed appreciation, is to produce enthusiasm for the plays."

Berkeley, David S. **A Guide to Shakespeare's Comedies and Histories.** Stillwater: Oklahoma State University Bookstore Press, 1964.

Lists questions on plays for students to answer. A separately published key provides answers.

Berkeley, David S. **A Guide to Shakespearean Tragedy.** Stillwater: Oklahoma State University Bookstore Press, 1960.

Contains study questions on *Rom, JC, Hamlet, Macbeth, Lear, Othello,* and *Ant* in addition to general information on tragedy. A separately published key provides answers.

Blanshard, Rufus A. **"Shakespeare's Funny Comedy."** *College English* 21 (October 1959): 4–8.

A short essay that points to humorous elements not explained by function.

Blinderman, Abraham. **"I Actually Know Not Too Much on Shakespeare."** *College English* 37 (December 1975): 353–57.

An analysis of student responses to questions about what they know of

Shakespeare, what he has written, what they have read, and what they think of Shakespeare's writing.

Bowden, William R. **"Here Comes One with a Paper."** *Teaching Shakespeare: Ideas for the Classroom* 1 (Fall 1976): 4–5.

Suggests four helpful devices: (1) short assignment in *primary* research (e.g., analysis of a scene or a take home examination), (2) the use of an appendix as a compendium of evidence, (3) use of 3 × 5 cards to collect quotations for questions, and (4) writing a composite exam answer for students.

Bowden, William R. **"Teaching Structure in Shakespeare:** *1 Henry IV, Twelfth Night, Hamlet."* *College English* 23 (April 1962): 525–31.

Suggests that the teacher convey a sense of structure with an analysis by means of parallel columns that give students a perspective of the whole play and a sense of the skill by which the dramatist manipulates multiple plots. Outlines given for the three plays.

Brooks, Cleanth, and Heilman, R. B., eds. **Understanding Drama: Twelve Plays.** New York: Holt, Rinehart & Winston, 1945.

Includes text, discussion, study questions, and analysis of *1H4* (pp. 317–88) and *Lear* (pp. 586–661), with notes and questions on *Othello* (pp. 661–68), *Macbeth* (pp. 668–73), and *Ant* (pp. 673–74).

Carroll, D. Allen. **"The Presentation of Shakespeare."** In *Teaching Shakespeare,* edited by W. Edens, et al., pp. 48–63. Princeton: Princeton University Press, 1977.

Maintains that like the presentation of a play each day's classroom presentation should have a visible, effective structure. Urges focus on the text.

Chan, Mimim, and Kwok, Helen. **"Figuratively Speaking: A Study of the Cantonese-Speaking Undergraduate's Response to Figures of Speech in Shakespeare."** *Shakespeare Quarterly* 25 (1974): 209–27.

Discusses similarities and differences between Chinese and English figurative language.

Clayton, Thomas. **"How Many Beds Did Shakespeare Share?: Lexis, Praxis, Opsis, and the Teaching of Shakespearean Drama."** *Shakespeare Newsletter* 23 (April 1973): 12.

Abstract of paper concerned with different teaching-emphases: Presenting the play through words (lexis), through the action (praxis), or through the spectacle (opsis) implied by the words and the action of play.

Crow, John. **"Deadly Sins of Criticism, or, Seven Ways to Get Shakespeare Wrong."** *Shakespeare Quarterly* 9 (1958): 301–06.

Wittily exposes most of the follies of contemporary criticism.

Devine, Mary E., and Clark, Constance M. **"The Two Faces of Gertrude."** *Teaching Shakespeare: Ideas for the Classroom* 1 (Fall 1977): 1–2.

Suggests students make an equally valid case for a sympathetic and an unsympathetic interpretation of the same character by approaching a role from the point of view of an actor creating that character on stage. Provides two views of Gertrude in *Hamlet.*

Duncan, Charles F. **"A Blackboard Model of Shakespearean Irony."** *College English* 34 (March 1973): 791–95.

Blackboard demonstration can draw student "away from preoccupations with mono-thematic messages" and lead to other appreciations. Provides diagrams for *Macbeth, Ant, Lear,* and *JC,* and for comedy and tragedy in general.

Emslie, McDonald. **"Burning Bradley."** *Shakespeare Newsletter* 4 (September 1954): 30.

Suggests a pattern-recognition approach which eschews Bradley and emphasizes an ability to read poetry.

Enright, D. J. **Shakespeare and the Students.** London: Chatto & Windus, 1970.

This book "has arisen directly out of teaching . . . [*Lear, Ant, Macbeth, WT*]: that is to say, out of a fairly intimate acquaintance not only with students' difficulties but also . . . with the things they find all too easy."

Enstrom, Frederic A. **"Humanism as the Key to Shakespeare's Relevance."** *FOCUS: Teaching English in Southeastern Ohio* 2 (May 1976): 46–52.

Uses *Hamlet* and *MND* to illustrate the thesis that "Shakespearean drama requires us to pierce the surface to search for the essence of the human experience."

Fagin, N. Bryllion. **"Segregated Shakespeare."** *Commonweal,* 26 February 1960, pp. 591–92.

Touches on the problems of teaching Shakespeare to black college students in the segregated South.

Falk, Robert. **Shakespeare in America: A Survey to 1900."** *Shakespeare Survey* 18 (1965): 102–18.

Discusses the reception and influence of actors, editors, and critics; and the use of the themes and language of Shakespeare in America.

French, William W. **"Tapping the Energy of Shakespeare: One Way to Teach the Plays."** *Shakespeare Newsletter* 27 (April 1977): 10.

Suggests that students write plays in response to some part of a Shakespeare play that moves them.

Frey, Charles. **"Teaching Shakespeare's Romances."** *College Literature* 4 (Fall 1977): 252–56.

Outlines approach for undergraduate study of *WT, Temp, Cym,* and *Per.*

Grace, William J. **"Discussion Questions."** In his *Approaching Shakespeare,* pp. 205–28. New York: Basic Books, 1964.

Discussion questions on Shakespeare as a dramatic artist, as poet, and in terms of the beautiful.

Granville-Barker, Harley, and Harrison, G. B., eds. **A Companion to Shakespeare Studies.** New York: Macmillan, 1934; Doubleday Anchor paperback.

Collection of fifteen essays which serve as guide to various areas of Shakespearean scholarship. Of particular interest is T. S. Eliot's survey of Shakespearean criticism from Dryden to Coleridge. Paper edition replaces original reading lists with an updated annotated bibliography.

Gutmann, Ethel Feurlicht. **"Teacher Extraordinary of Shakespeare."** *Hunter Alumni Quarterly* (Spring 1964): 11–12.

Tribute to Helen Gray Cone (d. 1934).

Haas, Rudolf. **"Shakespeare als pädagogische Herausforderung."** *Shakespeare Jahrbuch* (Weimar) 112 (1976): 128–53.

The teaching challenges presented by Shakespeare.

Harrison. G. B. **"Shakespeare in the Classroom."** In his *Profession of English,* pp. 150–63. New York: Harcourt, Brace & World, 1962. Reprinted Garden City, N.Y.: Doubleday-Anchor, 1967.

Shakespeare for college sophomores can best be studied as drama, and we can learn to be the "director and the full cast of our unseen performance," if we keep in mind the full dramatic context of the action on the stage.

Heilman, Robert B. **"Shakespeare in the Classroom: Scientific Object vs. Immediate Experience."** In *Teaching Shakespeare,* edited by W. Edens, et al., pp. 3–26. Princeton: Princeton University Press, 1977.

Advocates "a balanced style" which implies a middle ground with regard to both the objective and subjective positions by which "one may check scientific and sensibilitarian excesses that equally diminish the literary object."

Hellenga, Robert R. **"Shakespeare: Our Contemporary?"** *Teaching Shakespeare: Ideas for the Classroom* 1 (Fall 1976): 7.

"The reality of the modern role is almost invariably denied, whereas the reality of the Elizabethan role is almost invariably affirmed."

Hortmann, Wilhelm. **Shakespeare-Unterricht zwischen Text und Theater.** Duisburg, W. Germany: W. Braun Verlag, 1976.

Hulme, Hilda M. **"Shakespeare's Language."** *Shakespeare Newsletter* 14 (April–May 1964): 43.

Hyder, Clyde Kenneth. **George Lyman Kittredge: Teacher and Scholar.** Lawrence: Kansas University Press, 1963.

Portions detail Kittredge's contributions to Shakespeare study.

Jackson, Elizabeth. **"The Kittredge Way."** *College English* 4 (May 1943): 483–87.

Summarizes teaching method of G. L. Kittredge.

Jamison, William A. **"The Case for a Complete Shakespeare."** *Shakespeare Quarterly* 25 (1974): 258–59.

Reports on teaching all the plays over a two term period, allowing sophomore students exposure to the context of the Shakespeare canon.

Jones, Edward T. **"Though It Be Not Written Down: Assigning an Annotated Bibliography."** *Teaching Shakespeare: Ideas for the Classroom* 1 (Fall 1977): 6.

Suggests assigning an annotated bibliography as alternative to formal paper in Shakespeare course.

Jones, Eldred. **"Shakespeare's Presence in Africa."** *Shakespeare Newsletter* 26 (December 1976): 49.

A glance at Shakespeare in Africa where his works have long been part of the school curriculum with *Hamlet, Macbeth, Lear,* and *Othello* most favored after *JC.* Comparisons between major tragedies and African scapegoat rituals have provided new insights.

Joseph, Bertram. **"The Problem of Bradley."** *Use of English* (London) 5 (Winter 1953): 87–91.

Points out that at least the "character" approach was eminently teachable and satisfying.

Kernodle, George R. **"Basic Problems in Reading Shakespeare."** *Quarterly Journal of Speech* 35 (1949): 36–43.

Concerns three problems in giving a poetic reading of Shakespeare's lines: (1) poetic form where "rhythm and line patterns are as powerful as the imagery in creating the lyric effect"; (2) grammatical and rhetorical form with attention to complex phrasing and emphasis; (3) emotional coloring.

Keyishian, Harry. **"Examining Shakespeare's Plays Through Focus on Secondary Characters."** *Shakespeare Newsletter* 27 (April 1977): 10.

Suggests students look at the play through eyes of secondary characters.

Knight, G. Wilson. **"The Teacher as Poetic Actor."** In *Teaching Shakespeare,* edited by W. Edens, et al., pp. 290–304. Princeton: Princeton University Press, 1977.

"The primary need for actor or for literary student alike is to listen to his own vocal dramatization . . . and see how it works."

Knights, L. C. **"Imaginative Energy: or Why Read Shakespeare?"** *New Theatre Magazine* 5 no. 2 (1964): 26–28.

Shakespeare "calls out the latent energies of our minds, and extends the boundaries of our consciousness."

Krieger, Elliot. **"Shakespearean Crossroads: Teaching Shakespeare Through Induction."** *College English* 39 (November 1977): 286–89.

The inductive method—allowing students to discover evidentary material to support one interpretation over another—accomplishes several goals: (1) "to demonstrate . . . that the text is not a fixed, given phenomenon. . . ."; (2) "it shows that non-active and discriminating reading of the text is the method by which we construct or . . . arrive at an interpretation. . . ." Examples of "Instances" from *1H4* and *Macbeth* illustrate moments in a play to be taught.

Lecky, Eleazer. **"The Enduring Shakespeare."** *Teachers College Record* 65 (April 1964): 563–71.

Examines ways in which Shakespeare can be considered genuinely alive today and ways "the number of readers for whom Shakespeare endures" can be increased.

Lodge, Evan. **"Education Shakespeare Digest."** *Shakespeare Newsletter* 13 (September 1963): 33; 14 (September 1964): 66.

Lyttle, Charles F. **"Teaching Shakespearean Drama."** *Shakespeare Association Bulletin* 18 (1943): 62–65.

Argues for classroom dramatization and the use of films and recordings.

McDonald, Daniel. **"Anyone Can Teach Shakespeare."** *Journal of General Education* 22 (October 1970): 187–92.

"A good generalist teacher . . . can indeed teach Shakespeare" if he avoids concentrating on textual and historical matters and sticks to discussion of plot, characters, and themes.

MacEachen, Dougald B. **"Analyzing a Play."** *College English* 25 (April 1964): 549–50.

Some questions to direct students in reading any play.

MacFadden, Fred R. **"Report on Opportunities for Teaching and Researching the Literature of Shakespeare Using the Computer."** *Computer Studies in the Humanities and Verbal Behavior* (The Hague) 4 (June 1973): 3–8.

Lists sixty-eight research projects in Shakespeare stylistics and pedagogy adaptable to some kind of computer processing.

McLean, Andrew. **"Annotated Bibliography."** In *Teaching Shakespeare,* edited by W. Edens, et al., pp. 317–33. Princeton: Princeton University Press, 1977.

A selected bibliography on teaching Shakespeare in schools and colleges.

McLean, Andrew, ed. **Shakespeare in the Classroom: Resources and Media Aids.** Kenosha: UW-Parkside's Center for Teaching Excellence, 1977.

Includes articles on teaching Shakespeare, a film glossary, and bibliographies on teaching Shakespeare, Shakespeare on film, film and other media, and audio-visual resources. Reviewed in *Shakespeare Newsletter* 28 (April 1974): 14; and by R. V. Graybill in *Ralph, for Medieval-Renaissance Teaching* 6 (January 1979): 3.

MacLean, Hugh. **"Shakespeare in the Classroom: Titles and the Text."** *English Record* 23 (1972): 27–33.

Stresses the importance of first teaching students the significance of the full titles of Shakespeare's plays.

McManaway, James G. "**Shakespeare in the United States.**" *PMLA* 79 (1964): 513–18.

Mentions Shakespeare as taught in the schools.

McNamee, Lawrence F. "**New Horizons in the Teaching of Shakespeare.**" *College English* 23 (April 1962): 583–85.

Advocates an auditory approach.

Marder, Louis. "**Steps Toward a Methodology of Teaching Shakespeare.**" *Shakespeare Newsletter* 28 (May 1978): 21–22.

Summary of Virgil Whitaker's lecture at the 1978 Shakespeare Association of America calling for teachers to present a methodology that will enable students to come to grips with the play.

Marder, Louis. "**On Teaching, Criticizing, and Presenting Shakespeare: The Ripeness and Readiness is All.**" *Shakespeare Newsletter* 28 (April 1978): 12.

Argues that "eclecticism is the only valid approach to Shakespeare in good criticism and good teaching."

Marder, Louis. "**Teaching Shakespeare: 'New' Area of Interest.**" *Shakespeare Newsletter* 28 (February 1978): 1, 6.

Comments on how pedagogical concerns are no longer discussed only by secondary school teachers. Provides report on model teaching symposium held at the University of Wisconsin-Parkside.

Marder, Louis. "**Reflections on Teaching Shakespeare.**" *Shakespeare Newsletter* 27 (April 1977): 10.

"No teacher is an island unto himself. . . . Knowledge plus proper pedagogy can make Shakespeare a pleasant and richly rewarding experience."

Marder, Louis. "**A Working Method for Teaching Shakespeare.**" *Shakespeare Newsletter* 25 (April 1975): 10. Reprinted in *Shakespeare in the Classroom,* edited by A. McLean, pp. 3–4. Kenosha: UW-Parkside's Center for Teaching Excellence, 1977.

Suggests students read play after some background materials are presented; use themes, images, plot, etc. "to get into the plays via the analysis, and illustrate how all the elements illuminate and enhance the play, making it relevant to our lives, more comprehensible, and therefore more pleasurable and edifying."

Marder, Louis. "**Teaching Shakespeare: Is There Method?**" *College English*

25 (April 1964): 479-87. Reprinted in *Shakespeare in School and College.* Champaign, Ill.: National Council of Teachers of English, 1964.

A structural approach is "an interesting and effective way of entering the heart of the play and working through it."

Marder, Louis. **"A Shakespeare Philosophy for the Twentieth Century."** *Teachers College Record* 65 (April 1964): 572-82.

The concept of man and of order pervading Shakespeare is meaningful today.

Marder, Louis. **"Teaching Shakespeare—Past and Present."** *Shakespeare Newsletter* 10 (December 1960): 45.

Acknowledges that many feel Shakespeare is now being overtaught, so that students don't get the appreciation they should from the plays. Emphasizes that notes must be used for "discovering and eliciting meaning and stimulating curiosity."

Marder, Louis. **"What to Teach Who."** *Shakespeare Newsletter* 4 (December 1954): 46.

Suggests a Shakespeare course for English majors, and another designed for general appreciation.

Marder, Louis. **"Teaching Shakespeare—'Methods' Past and Present."** *Shakespeare Newsletter* 4 (May 1954): 22.

An appreciation of Shakespeare, drama, the particular play, literature, and life in general should be given to students according to age and intelligence. Shakespeare's syntax should not be overly analyzed.

Marder, Louis. **"Teaching Shakespeare—The Methods."** *Shakespeare Newsletter* 4 (April 1954): 14.

"Know how much to give, what to give, when to stop" in a class. Teachers must stimulate and satisfy the students in order for them to enjoy Shakespeare. Describes a "project" method (recreating plays, scenes, characters, etc.) and "Fairchild's procedure" (one play each semester, every line analyzed).

Marder, Louis. **"Teaching Shakespeare Effectively."** *Shakespeare Newsletter* 4 (April 1954): 15.

Summarizes past methods and emphasizes need to keep the attention and interest of the students.

Marder, Louis. **"Teaching Shakespeare—The Problems."** *Shakespeare Newsletter* 4 (February 1954): 2.

"Teacher's colleges are turning out teachers who are proficient in method and deficient in subject matter." Advises that prospective teachers should be given a "broad survey-analysis of successful approaches to Shakespeare."

Menezes, A. **"Has Shakespeare Fallen on Evil Tongues?"** *Literary Criterion* (Mysore) 6 (1963): 79-85.

Describes teaching Shakespeare to college students in India.

Milward, Peter. **"Teaching Shakespeare in Japan."** *Shakespeare Quarterly* 25 (1974): 228-33.

Comments on reactions and problems of Japanese students' studying Shakespeare. Students who prefer character analysis find *Midsummer Night's Dream* their favorite comedy, and enjoy doing their own productions.

Milward, Peter. **An Introduction for Shakespeare's Plays.** Tokyo: Kenkyusha, 1964.

"Modern Approaches to Shakespeare." *Times Educational Supplement* (London), 28 August 1937, p. 304.

Reports on a conference that divided modern approaches to Shakespeare into three groups: (1) scholarly, those who study the 'world' of Shakespeare, (2) critical, those concerned with poetic imagery, and (3) dramatic, those dealing with producing and performing the plays.

Moulton, Richard Green. **The Modern Study of Literature: An Introduction to Literary Theory and Interpretation.** Chicago: University of Chicago Press, 1915.

Discusses Shakespeare's plots in the evolution of Romantic drama with illustrations from *MV, Lear* and *WT* (pp. 184-93); also comments on "motive force" personages in the tragedies, and the complex plot of *TN* (pp. 393-402) and on the literary significance of metrical changes in *Temp* (pp. 484-86).

Muliyil, G. **"Why Shakespeare for Us?"** *Literary Criterion* (Mysore) 6 (1963): 86-93.

Argues the need for Shakespeare in our technological world.

Muller-Schwefe, Gerhard. **"Shakespeare in der Universität."** *Praxis des neusprachlichen Unterrichts* (Dortmund) 12 (1965): 1-7.

"NEH Aids Teaching Projects." *Shakespeare Newsletter* 25 (April 1975): 16.

Describes various ways NEH supports the teaching of Shakespeare.

Ornstein, Robert. **Shakespeare in the Classroom.** Urbana, Ill.: Educational Illustrators, 1960.

An important discussion for teaching Shakespeare at all levels.

Partridge, Edward. **"Re-presenting Shakespeare."** *Shakespeare Quarterly* 25 (1974): 201–08.

Students need to be made aware of the thorough interrelationship of auditory, semantic, architectonic, choreographic, and scenic elements of a play. Teachers must try to re-create the play by explication, analysis, and interpretation.

Perret, Marion. **"Shakespeare for Sophomores and 'Rude Mechanicals'."** *Shakespeare Newsletter* 28 (April 1978): 17.

Finds *1H4, Rom,* and *Hamlet* "especially useful with sophomore and tech students."

Peterson, Bertil. **"Skolteatern i Umea."** *Tidning för Sveriges läroverk* (Stockholm) 60 (1960): 17, 544.

Chiefly about Shakespeare in Umea.

Petronella, Vincent F. **"Teaching Shakespeare's Development as Poetic Dramatist."** *Indirections* (Ontario Council of Teachers of English) 1 (1976): 37–41.

Uses passages from *Rom,* IV.i.90–106, and *Hamlet,* I.v.58–73, to discuss Shakespeare's development in detail.

Quattrocki, Edward. **"Classroom Presentations of Shakespeare."** *FOCUS: Teaching English in Southeastern Ohio* 2 (May 1976): 26–33.

Explains two college classroom projects, a classroom production of an edited version of a Shakespeare play and a method for stimulating class discussion.

Rabkin, Norman. **"Shakespeare and the Graduate English Curriculum."** In *Teaching Shakespeare,* edited by W. Edens, et al., pp. 67–78. Princeton: Princeton University Press, 1977.

Suggests more and better of what we have been doing for those who intend to specialize in Renaissance literature and theater and to teach Shakespeare, but argues against graduate courses in Shakespeare for the non-specialist, who needs the kind of course normally offered to under-graduates, the aim of which is "to provide a model of the intelligent reader of Shakespeare, trusting of his emotional responses, ready to use secondary knowledge when he feels it necessary but not to let it seem more important than the text . . . above all ready to make himself an active audience."

Rao, V. Srinivasa. **"Shakespeare and the Indian Graduate."** *Literary Half-Yearly* (Bangalore) 1 (1960): 69–70.

Pleas for a comparative study of the experiences of Shakespeare students throughout India and wherever English is not the mother tongue.

Reaske, Christopher R. **"Drama."** In his *The College Writer's Guide to the Study of Literature,* pp. 79–113. New York: Random House, 1970.

Answers questions (What is drama? What does drama do? What makes drama art?) by drawing freely from Shakespeare's plays to illustrate structure, characters, gesture, and language, etc.

Richmond, Hugh M. **"The Berkeley Shakespeare Program."** *Teaching Shakespeare: Ideas for the Classroom* 1 (Fall 1977): 4–5.

Reports on the development of an interdisciplinary program which supplements a large lecture course.

Richmond, Hugh M. **"Shakespeare College at Berkeley."** *Shakespeare Newsletter* 25 (April 1975): 19.

Reports on an innovative undergraduate interdisciplinary experiment.

Rogers, William Hudson. **Shakespeare and English History.** Totowa, N.J.: Littlefield, Adams, 1966.

Gives the historical background of ten historical plays, followed by a resume of the play and the manner in which Shakespeare used historical fact for his dramatic purposes. Discusses main characters of each play and gives series of genealogical tables showing the relationship of various characters to each other.

Rose, Mark. **"Theatrical Approaches in the Classroom and Post-New Critical Assumptions."** *Shakespeare Newsletter* 26 (May 1976): 31, 39.

Explains that largely as a result of the social upheavals of the 1960s, performance-oriented teaching that rejects the work of art as an artifact represents "a fundamental challenge to the old New Critical orthodoxy."

Rosenblatt, Louise M. **Literature as Exploration.** New York: Appleton-Century-Crofts, 1938.

Antony and Cleopatra is used to illustrate how students learn to understand the portrayal of a character in fiction while in "real" life they would probably make a harsh moral judgment.

Schevill, James. **"Bright Enigma, All Thy Puzzles Glitter."** *Teachers College Record* 65 (April 1964): 591–602.

Discusses the "mysterious clarity" of Shakespeare's plays.

Schoenbaum, Samuel. **"The Teaching of Shakespeare."** *University of Kansas Bulletin of Education* 17 (1963): 108–14.

The experience of teaching British university students, who were prepared to handle complex textual studies, suggests that American students may enjoy and profit from "the close rigorous reading of texts." English majors in America should "come to grips with the complexities and obscurities of diction, syntax, and allusion."

Schott, Penelope Scambly. **"The Student Director Auditions of the Mind, or One More Shakespeare Assignment."** *Teaching Shakespeare: Ideas for the Classroom* 1 (Fall 1976): 2–4.

Emphasizes "the role of the reader as director and producer in the theater of the mind." Abstracted in *Shakespeare Newsletter* 27 (April 1977): 10.

Schott, Penelope Scambly. **"The Chronicle of Wasted Time: Some Observations on Shakespeare in High Schools and How to Recover."** *CEA Forum* 6 (December 1975): 2–3, 10–11.

Objects to teaching Shakespeare as a "social grace" and as a monument to be overcome.

Scott, Elledge. **"What Literature Do College-Bound Students Read?"** *English Journal* 46 (March 1958): 147–50.

Based on study of 300 entering freshmen at Carleton College, author asks "Why should 2/3 and more of the most literate 18 year olds in America know *Macbeth* and *Julius Caesar* when fewer than 1/3 know *Romeo and Juliet, As You Like It, Henry IV,* or *Midsummer Night's Dream!*"

Shakespeare in School and College. Champaign, Ill.: National Council of Teachers of English, 1964.

Collects nine essays from the April (1964) issues of *College English* and *English Journal* by Wright, Barber, Hosley, Dye, Shapiro, Ornstein, Veidemanis, Mardis, and Taylor.

Shakespeare Quarterly 25 (Spring 1974).

Special issue on methods and approaches to teaching Shakespeare.

Shakespeare Survey (Cambridge) 17 (1964).

Special issue on "Shakespeare in His Own Age." Seventeen essays on "The Daily Life," "Philosophy and Fancy," and "Art and Entertainment."

"Shakespearean Switch." *Newsweek,* 29 August 1955, p. 52.

Yale Professors Mack and Prouty inaugurate a new summer-session Shakespeare course, designed especially for teachers. The course is also described in *New York Times Magazine,* 28 August 1955, p. 47.

Shaw, William P. **"Teaching Shakespeare's Plays with Student Workbooks."** *Shakespeare Newsletter* 27 (April 1977): 10.

Workbook stimulates quality and quantity of class preparation and discussion.

Siegel, Paul N. **"Shakespeare and Our Time's Malaise."** *Teacher's College Record* 64 (April 1964): 583–90.

"Shakespeare can help to renew our spirits so that we can seek . . . salvation out, and he can give us some idea of what it consists. . . ."

Siegel, Paul N. **"In Defense of Bradley."** *College English* 19 (February 1948): 250–56.

Sprague, Arthur C. **"Kittredge on Shakespeare: A Long Time After."** *Shakespeare Newsletter* 28 (May 1978): 24.

A personal reminiscence of Kittredge as teacher and scholar.

Stone, W. B., and Eastman, R. M. **"Criticism Liberal and Left: An Exchange."** *College English* 33 (May 1972): 891–907.

Svendsen, Kester. **"Formalist Criticism and the Teaching of Shakespeare."** *College English* 27 (October 1965): 23–27.

Argues for "the primacy of formalist literary theory in teaching Shakespeare to beginners." Formalist criticism is concerned "with sensitivity to structures, with that interaction of elements which is form and which generate force."

Thompson, Karl F. **"Facing the Fact of Fiction."** *Shakespeare Newsletter* 4 (May 1954): 22.

"Let the student retain his own individuality and do not force him to surrender it by demanding that he too feel the emotions exhibited by the characters in the play . . . Let him rather observe the behavior of Shakespeare's characters as that of other individuals and then comment on *their* experiences."

Thorpe, R. **"Ridding confession finds but ridding shrift."** *Improving College and University Teaching* 15 (Summer 1967): 188.

First year instructor finds freshmen ill prepared to read Shakespeare and decides to 'translate' text as a way of making students enthusiastic.

Vancura, Zdenek. **"Shakespeare—Whose Contemporary?"** *Charles University on Shakespeare,* edited by Zdenek Stříbrný and Jarmila Emmerova, pp. 39–53. Praha: Universita Karlova, 1966.

A discussion of Shakespeare's historical and artistic background. Shakespeare can be our contemporary only to the extent that we are able to share his humanism.

Velz, John W. **"Shakespeare Inferred."** In *Teaching Shakespeare,* edited by W. Edens, et al., pp. 27–47. Princeton: Princeton University Press, 1977.

Because there is more to Shakespeare than can be taught in a semester, author devises methods (e.g., arrangement of syllabus) of encouraging students to infer a part of what he has neither the time nor the talent to teach.

Woodbridge, Elizabeth (Mrs. E. Morris). **The Drama: Its Law and Its Technique.** Boston and Chicago: Allyn and Bacon, 1898.

An adaptation and modification of Freytag's *Die Technik des Dramas* (1863) to make it suitable for college students with generous examples taken from Shakespearean plays.

Wooden, Warren W. **"Shakespeare's Globe Theatre in Appalachia."** *Shakespeare Newsletter* 28 (April 1978): 15.

Reports on scale model of Globe at Marshall University "displayed as a teaching tool for students."

Yoshio, Nakano. **"English Literature in Japan."** *Japan Quarterly* 6 (1959): 165–74.

Includes notes on the teaching of Shakespeare's plays and Shakespeare in the Japanese theatre.

Zahorski, Kenneth J. **"The Next Best Thing . . . Shakespeare in Stereo."** *College English* 39 (November 1977): 290–93.

At evening record listening sessions, students are asked to imagine themselves viewing a stage performance. Questionnaire at end allows space for reactions and questions that identify areas of concern for classroom discussion.

Individual Plays and Non-dramatic Poetry

Antony and Cleopatra

Bowling, Lawrence E. **"Duality in the Minor Characters in *Antony and Cleopatra.*"** *College English* 18 (February 1957): 251–55.

Explores the dual interests of Pompeius, Lepidus, Octavia and Enobarbus that lead them to failure.

Mills, Laurens J. **The Tragedies of Shakespeare's *Antony and Cleopatra.*** Bloomington: Indiana University Press, 1965.

Schwartz, Elias. **"The Shackling of Accidents: *Antony and Cleopatra.*"** *College English* 23 (April 1962): 550–58.

Lovers play a "taudry game" to known rules and pleasant ends.

See also, in General section, Brooks, Duncan, Berkeley, Enright, Rosenblatt.

Coriolanus

Neumeyer, Peter F. **"Ingratitude Is Monstrous: An Approach to *Coriolanus.*"** *College English* 26 (December 1964): 192–98.

Discusses theme: ingratitude is the violation of order.

Proser, Matthew. **"*Coriolanus*: The Constant Warrior and the State."** *College English* 24 (April 1963): 507–12.

Explores Coriolanus's relationship to war, to the community, and to his mother to explain single image we have of him.

Vickers, Brian. **"Teaching *Coriolanus*: The Importance of Perspective."** In *Teaching Shakespeare,* edited by W. Edens, et al., pp. 228–70. Princeton: Princeton University Press, 1977.

Believes that *Coriolanus* has been the most misjudged of the major tragedies because critics have ignored the existence of a structure of perspectives in the play. Argues that the image Coriolanus and Virgilia have of each other is the only true perspective in the play.

Comedy of Errors

Barber, C. L. **"Shakespearean Comedy in *Errors.*"** *College English* 25 (April 1964): 493–97.

"Shakespeare's sense of comedy as a moment in a larger circle leads him . . . to frame farce with action which presents the weight of age and the threat of death, and to make the comic resolution a renewal of life . . . a rebirth."

Hamlet

Alling, Eliza. **"Dear Will."** *Shakespeare Quarterly* 25 (1974): 264–71.

Hamlet sends Shakespeare letters telling his story.

Bonjour, Adrien. **"On Artistic Unity in *Hamlet.*"** *English Studies* 21 (1939): 193–202.

A "symphonic conception of death pervading the whole play contributes . . . to the unity of *Hamlet.*"

Cooperman, S. **"Shakespeare's Anti-Hero: Hamlet and the Underground Man."** *Shakespeare Studies* 1 (1965): 37–63.

Contrasts *Hamlet* and *Notes from the Underground* concluding that in both "affirmation—that faith itself—is based upon consciousness and suffering."

Dachslager, E. L. **"On Teaching *Hamlet.*"** *CEA Critic* 33 (1971): 8–11.

Argues that since *Hamlet* "deals with a state of affairs which is itself indefinable and evasive," the teacher should give students "awareness of the quality of the play which makes it difficult—if not impossible—to teach."

Emslie, MacDonald. **"*Hamlet* and Hamilton."** *English Language Teaching* 23 (1969): 289–98.

How to bring *Hamlet* alive for first-year university students.

Friedman, Neil, and Jones, Richard M. **"On the Mutuality of the Odeipus Complex. Notes on the Hamlet Case."** *American Imago* 20 (1963): 107–31.

"Far from 'resisting' the standard oedipal interpretation of Prince Hamlet, Shakespeare can be instrumental in broadening the psycho-analytic theory of the oedipus complex itself." In the light of Erik H. Erikson's psychosocial development scheme, Hamlet illustrates "the child as victim."

Gray, Henry David. **"Some Methods of Approach to the Study of *Hamlet.*"** *Studies in Philology* 45 (April 1948): 203–15.

Discusses (1) aesthetic or intuitive, (2) historical, and (3) 'dramaturgic' approaches, arguing the latter should "take its rightful place among the other necessary methods of approach to the study of *Hamlet.*"

Hellenga, Robert R. *"Hamlet* **in the Classroom."** *College English* 35 (October 1973): 32–39.

Offers certain questions that allow student and teacher to explore play together. See also, in this section, Hill.

Hentz, Ann Louise. *"Hamlet*: **The Anatomy of a Task."** *College English* 27 (April 1966): 523-28.

Describes how Hamlet's task of revenge leads him to discern between human frailty and corruption.

Hill, Alma Blinn. **"Hamlet as an Undergraduate."** *College English* 36 (September 1974): 122–25.

A reply. See also, in this section, Hellenga.

Kemp, Lysander. **"Understanding Hamlet."** *College English* 13 (October 1951): 9–13.

A tongue-in-cheek suggestion that because Hamlet Sr. was asleep when poisoned, he only assumes Claudius was the murderer; at the play-within-a-play, Claudius bolts because he visualizes his murder contemplated by Hamlet Jr.

Knapp, Peggy Ann. **"'Stay illusion,' or How to Teach** *Hamlet."* *College English* 36 (September 1974): 75–85.

Suggests presenting students with contrary scholarship in order to enrich their understanding of the play; discusses three opposed readings of the play.

Levine, Richard A. **"The Tragedy of Hamlet's World View."** *College English* 23 (April 1962): 539–46.

"Hamlet is a tragic hero, but his purgation is negative. . . . his tragic flaw, his vacillating and faulty world view, is reconciled by the last act of the play by means of the negative purgation which he experiences."

Lewis, Roger. **"An Approach to** *Hamlet* **with College Students."** *Use of English* (London) 25 (Autumn 1973): 21–26.

Students edit experimental production aimed at involving the audience in a discussion of the play after its showing.

McElroy, Davis D. **"'To Be, Or Not To Be'—Is That the Question?"** *College English* 25 (April 1964): 543-45.

Hamlet has three alternatives evidenced by use of *chiasmus:* to do nothing, to kill the king, or to kill himself. His suicide is considered late. See also, in this section, Soule.

Mary Cleophas, R. S. M., Sister. **"Absent Thee from Felicity."** *CEA Critic* 26 (October 1964): 1, 4–5, 8.

Suggests three approaches: (1) to show film version, (2) to study the "music" of the play, and (3) to study the artistic developments in Acts I, III, V to see if the play is a failure as Eliot suggests.

Mack, Maynard. **"The World of *Hamlet*."** *Yale Review* 41 (Summer 1952): 502–23.

Emphasizes Hamlet's world's "interrogative mood"; its riddlesome language and action, and its built-in mysteriousness "where uncertainties are of the essence."

Ornstein, Robert. **"Teaching *Hamlet*."** *College English* 25 (April 1964): 502–08.

"Like Hamlet, we might conclude that our task is not to analyze or dissect but to comprehend—to gain that sense of the whole of the dramatic action, and of the meaning of the whole, which makes so many of the speculations and hypotheses of the past seem irrelevant."

Ornstein, Robert. **"The Mystery of *Hamlet*: Notes toward an Archetypal Solution."** *College English* 21 (October 1959): 30–36.

Contends that as a scapegoat, Hamlet's archetypal role is that he is "Dying God as Juvenile Delinquent."

Poethen, Wilhelm Von. **"*Hamlet* im Deutschunterricht."** *Wirkendes Wort* (Düsseldorf) 9 (1959): 99–109.

Argues teacher must have a methodological groundwork before teaching the play. Suggests an exact interpretation of Act I on which the tragedy builds, focusing on three important aspects: (1) the metaphysical element (the ghost), (2) the corrupt world surrounding Hamlet, and (3) Hamlet's internal dilemma. Following a summary of *Hamlet* criticism, concludes that the teacher must maintain an "Elizabethan reading" of the text.

Sacks, Claire, and Whan, Edgar, eds., *Hamlet*: **Enter Critic.** New York: Appleton-Century-Crofts, 1960.

An anthology of thirty-eight selections of *Hamlet* criticism from 1736 to 1959 with suggested study questions.

Seiler, Robert M. **"Prufrock and Hamlet."** *English* 21 (Summer 1972): 41–43.

Shoemaker, Francis. **"Extensions and Exemplification of a Modern Aesthetic Approach to World Literature:** *Hamlet* **as Example."** In his *Aesthetic Experience and the Humanities,* pp. 192–227. New York: Columbia University Press, 1943.

Surveys recent trends in *Hamlet* scholarship (especially by G. W. Knight, J. D. Wilson, J. W. Draper), Elizabethan culture and attitudes, and a scene-by-scene analysis of the play.

Soule, George. **"Hamlet's Quietus."** *College English* 26 (December 1964): 231.

Takes issue with McElroy's definition of *quietus* as death and suggests Hamlet is thinking of discharging his debt to the Ghost to whom he had promised revenge. See also, in this section, McElroy.

Sternlicht, Sanford. *"Hamlet*: **Six Characters in Search of a Play."** *College English* 27 (April 1966): 528–31.

Sees Hamlet as "actor-personality" whose role playing allows him direct contact with reality. Notes that Hamlet plays six parts: student prince, mourner, melancholy philosopher, mad hero of a revenge play, disappointed lover and soldier.

Utter, Robert P. **"In Defense of Hamlet."** *College English* 12 (December 1950): 138–44.

Supplements articles by Wagenknect (January 1949) and McCanse (May 1949) with the suggestion that Hamlet should be thought of as "a hero full of many desirable qualities."

Williams, Clyde V. **"Buffalo Bill Might Be Defunct, But the Bard Isn't: An Essay On Relevance."** *Cimarron Review* no. 21 (October 1972): 30–36.

The relevance of *Hamlet* is explored by reference to *Rosencrantz and Guildenstern are Dead* and *Hair,* "both of which illustrate to us that the modern artist finds in Shakespeare a continuing source of creative inspiration."

Williamson, Claude C. H., ed. **Readings on the Character of Hamlet.** New York: Macmillan, 1950.

A useful miscellany of Hamlet criticism to 1947.

Wilson, Robert F. **"Lovesickness and Hamlet's Tragedy."** *The Leaflet* 70 (November 1971): 34–38.

Examines Hamlet's four love relationships (with his dead father, Gertrude, Ophelia, and Horatio) and concludes male friendship "provides soil for Hamlet's revived faith in human and divine love."

See also, in General section, Berkeley, Bowden, Devine, Enstrom, Klein, Perret, Petronella.

1 Henry IV

Bass, Eben. **"Falstaff and the Succession."** *College English* 24 (April 1963): 502–06.

Wise king is one who can banish vanity—Falstaff—and avoid follies of Richard II.

Eastman, Richard M. **"Political Values in *1 Henry IV*: A Demonstration of Liberal Humanism."** *College English* 33 (May 1972): 901–07.

Part II of "Criticism, Liberal and Left: An Exchange" argues that the liberal-humanist is flexible "in appreciating *1 Henry IV* as a theater piece of heroic comedy; in assessing the historical context . . . ; in marshalling the play . . . in a criticism of our ongoing life."

Hinman, Myra. **"Teaching *1 Henry IV* to Beginning College Students."** *Shakespeare Quarterly* 25 (1974): 153–60.

Discusses problems of reading drama imaginatively.

Knoepelmacher, V. C. **"The Humors As Symbolic Nucleus in *1 Henry IV*."** *College English* 24 (April 1963): 497–501.

"Shakespeare's subtle metaphoric use of the Elizabethan theory of humors provides the basis for a symbolic nucleus which binds the play's abundant references to blood, sickness and the four elements to those related to heavenly bodies and to time, and stresses the Christian import of Prince Hal's transcendence."

Stone, William B. **"Literature and Class Ideology: *1 Henry IV*."** *College English* 33 (May 1972): 891–900.

Part I of "Criticism, Liberal and Left: An Exchange" provides a prolegomenon to a Marxist critique of the play.

Templeton, Robert G. **"The Problems of Teaching Shakespeare."** *English Leaflet* 48 (October–November 1949): 83–109.

Reports on teaching *1 Henry IV* at the Massachusetts Institute of Technology, using various techniques and devices.

See also, in General section, Brooks, Bowden, Krieger, Perret.

Henry V

Berkelman, Robert. **"Teaching *Henry V.*"** *College English* 13 (November 1951): 94–99.

The teacher will not rest with calling this Shakespeare's most patriotic play and Henry his ideal king but "will seize this rich opportunity to cultivate his students' powers of discrimination." Points out difference between jingoism of portions of *H5* and the muted power of Gaunt's tribute to England in *R2*.

Berman, Ronald S. **"Shakespeare's Alexander: Henry V."** *College English* 23 (April 1962): 532–39.

Notices that Henry V belongs in "the enigmatic tradition of Alexander" and in certain ways he is "a reconstruction of Plutarch's Alexander."

1, 2, 3 Henry VI

Gerould, D. C. **"Principles of Dramatic Structure in *Henry VI.*"** *Educational Theatre Journal* 20 (October 1968): 376–88.

Explains that the unity of the trilogy is thematic with the action unfolding according to a pattern of repetition and variation on a theme.

Julius Caesar

Bonjour, Adrien. **The Structure of *Julius Caesar.*** Liverpool: Liverpool University Press, 1958.

Shows how carefully balanced the whole structure is in broad outline, how subtly secondary themes are fitted into the general scheme to enhance its significance, and how essentially structural the very imagery of the drama is.

French, William W. **"Homage to *Julius Caesar*: or Why Teach the Hoary Old Thing?"** *Shakespeare Newsletter* 26 (May 1976): 24.

Lists reasons that the play was taught in the nineteenth century (to aid in the study of Latin, to espouse morality and patriotism), and is still taught today (parallels contemporary world, explores the self, and provides examples of political rhetoric).

Mack, Maynard. **"Teaching Drama: *Julius Caesar.*"** In *Essays on the Teaching of English,* edited by J. Gordon and Edward S. Noyes, pp. 320–36. New York: Appleton-Century-Crofts, 1960.

A good teacher begins to ask "Why?" in the first scene of the first act because the first episode "dramatizes instantaneously the oncoming theme of the play: that a man's will is not enough."

Manning, John. **"Shakespearean Tragedy in General Education."** *Improving College and University Teaching* 6 (Winter 1958): 12–17.

Presents a method for teaching *Julius Caesar* which provides for historical background, detailed reading of the play (with questions for each act and scene), and a final synthesis.

Schwartz, Elias. **"On the Quarrel in *Julius Caesar*."** *College English* 19 (January 1958): 168–70.

Infers that Brutus's anger (IV.iii.) is caused by the unconscious haunting thought of having killed his friend Caesar to no purpose.

See also, in General section, Duncan, Berkeley.

King Lear

Baker, James V. **"An Existential Examination of *King Lear*."** *College English* 23 (April 1962): 546–50.

Existential categories—instruments for inquiring into a problem—applied to *King Lear*.

Cubeta, Paul M. **"*Lear*'s Comic Spirit: 'Come, Let's Away to Prison."** In *Teaching Shakespeare,* edited by W. Edens, et al., pp. 138–52. Princeton: Princeton University Press, 1977.

Suggests that "to follow the teaching of *AYL* with *Lear* is one way to reveal how Shakespeare constantly returns to comic subjects and strategies for transmutation into tragedy."

Dye, Harriet. **"The Appearance-Reality Theme in *King Lear*."** *College English* 25 (April 1964): 514–17.

Fitts, Dudley. **"Poetry of *Lear*."** In *Lear,* edited by F. Fergusson and C. J. Sisson, pp. 21–29. New York: Dell, 1960.

Holland, Norman N. **"Transactive Teaching: Cordelia's Death."** *College English* 39 (November 1977): 276–85.

The aim of transactive teaching is "To make the role of self in literary experience explicit" and is achieved by a three-step process: "Articulate your response to the work. Ask what you are bringing to it. Ask what in and around it interacts with what you are bringing." Student responses open up new perspective on *King Lear* as the tragedy of the impotence of old age.

Mack, Maynard. *King Lear* **in Our Time.** Berkeley: University of California Press, 1965.

Studies structure and psychology and what this critic has learned from his students.

Mroczkowski, P. J. **"Comparative Reception of** *King Lear*: **An Experiment in International Education."** *Shakespeare Quarterly* 25 (1974): 234–47.

Polls responses by Polish, French, and English university students to *King Lear*.

Pearson, P. H. **"How the Action Starts in** *King Lear***."** In his *The Study of Literature,* pp. 195–210. Chicago: A. C. McClurg and Co., 1913.

An "exercise in appreciation" analyzes "the inciting force in the action" which begins, unlike other tragedies, without any crime in the background antedating the action. Lear's fatal division was not made without some public deliberation and only after those immediately concerned in it had been advised. Cordelia's response is unsuited to such a "stale occasion if solemn formality" and contrasts with the statesmanship of the court; she had been "keyed up" by "the jealous glances and evil forces playing about her."

Rosenberg, Marvin. **The Masks of King Lear.** Berkeley: University of California Press, 1972.

A detailed scene-by-scene analysis that juxtaposes the major interpretations of literary critics with those of actors.

Savvas, Minas. **"***King Lear* **as a Play of Divine Justice."** *College English* 27 (April 1966): 560–62.

"Ultimately, the play must be viewed as pessimistic, amoral, even nihilistic."

Taylor, Warren. **"Lear and the Lost Self."** *College English* 25 (April 1964): 509–13.

"Meaning in a play by Shakespeare . . . centers . . . in experiences common to all men." "In the fullness of his own vision of Lear . . . Shakespeare counters what Lear is with what he might have been."

Wentersdorf, Karl P. **"Structure and Characterization in** *Othello* **and** *King Lear***."** *College English* 26 (May 1965): 645–48.

An application of Freytag's *Technic des Dramas* method—three parts of tragedy are exposition, conflict and catastrophe—to *Othello* and *Lear*.

See also, in General section, Brooks, Duncan, Berkeley, Enright, Moulton.

Macbeth

Elliott, G. R. **Dramatic Providence in** *Macbeth*: **A Study of Shakespeare's Tragic Theme of Humanity and Grace.** Princeton: Princeton University Press, 1958.

A scene-by-scene analysis that is designed to show how dramatic tension is achieved by the constant possibility that Macbeth may be converted from self-centered remorse to Christian repentance.

Hill, Knox C. **"Drama and Fiction."** In his *Interpreting Literature,* pp. 51–98. Chicago: University of Chicago Press, 1966.

Suggests procedures reader may profitably follow in studying *Macbeth.*

Rosenberg, Marvin. **The Masks of Macbeth.** Berkeley: University of California Press, 1978.

Examines major interpretations together with observations on rehearsals and performances to explore the mysteries of the play.

Stanley, J. Lyndon. *"Macbeth:* **The Tragedy of Evil."** *College English* 22 (February 1961): 305–11.

"Shakespeare's vision here is of a world in which men can hardly do better amid the forces of circumstance; and in which, if men do no better, they must suffer and lose not only the world but themselves as well."

Wertheim, Albert. **"'Things Climb Upward to What They Were Before': The Reteaching and Regreening of** *Macbeth."* In *Teaching Shakespeare,* edited by W. Edens, et al., pp. 114–37. Princeton: Princeton University Press, 1977.

The challenge for the teacher is to enable students to encounter Shakespeare as the poetic dramatist; *Macbeth* "can be a stimulating illustration of Shakespeare's probing mind, for it brings the darkness and bloodiness of tragedy to the brighter and green confines of romance."

See also, in General section, Berkeley, Brooks, Duncan, Enright, Klein, Krieger.

Measure for Measure

Hamilton, A. C. **"On Teaching the Shakespeare Canon: The Case of** *Measure for Measure."* In *Teaching Shakespeare,* edited by W. Edens, et al., pp. 95–113. Princeton: Princeton University Press, 1977.

"The meaning of any part of a play is given by its context in the play, and the meaning of the play is given by its context in the Shakespeare canon."

Lascelles, Mary. **Shakespeare's** *Measure for Measure.* London: Athlone Press, 1953.

Provides a scene-by-scene analysis with discussion of sources and analogues.

Midsummer Night's Dream

Huntley, John F. **"An Objective Test for Literary Comprehension."** *College English* 39 (November 1977): 361–67.

Provides a sample fifteen minute test on *Midsummer Night's Dream* which asks students to place passages in chronological order.

See also, in General section, Bergeron, Enstrom.

Merchant of Venice

Dachslager, E. L. **"Teaching Literary Antisemitism."** *College English* 39 (November 1977): 315–25.

Includes a discussion of *Merchant of Venice,* admonishing the teacher "to distinguish the reality (real Jews) from the imitation (Shylock) . . . [and] to explain *where* the imitation came from."

Maccoby, Hyam. **"The Figure of Shylock."** *Midstream* 16 (1970).

Merchant of Venice is "a piece of profound anti-Semitism."

Marder, Louis. **"In Defense of Shakespeare and Shylock."** *Shakespeare Newsletter* 13 (May 1963): 28.

A reply. See also, in this section, Siegel.

Rosenberg, Edgar. **From Shylock to Svengali.** Palo Alto: Stanford University Press, 1960.

Recognizes that with Shylock, Shakespeare "gave classic expression to the myth of the Jew-villain."

Schappes, Morris U. **"Shylock and Anti-Semitism: Evidence That the Backbone of the Play Is Anti-Semitic."** *Jewish Currents* 16 (June 1962): 7–13, 37–39.

Argues that the play as a whole is "unalterably anti-semitic."

Siegel, Paul N. **"Shylock the Puritan."** *Columbia University Forum* 5 (Fall 1962): 14–20.

Shylock is a puritan caricature and Shakespeare was "depending on his audience to associate Judaism, Puritanism and usury." See also, in this section, Marder.

Walden, Daniel. **"Three Cases of Literary Antisemitism."** *Sh'ma,* 24 December 1976, pp. 26–28.

Argues that *Merchant of Venice* not be staged but "reserved for serious study by students of Shakespeare."

See also, in General section, Moulton.

Much Ado About Nothing

Hartley, Lodurck. **"Claudio and the Unmerry War."** *College English* 26 (May 1965): 609–14.

Claudio's actions are consistent within the framework of the play.

Heffner, Ray L., Jr. **"Hunting for Clues in *Much Ado About Nothing."*** In *Teaching Shakespeare,* edited by W. Edens, et al., pp. 177–227. Princeton: Princeton University Press, 1977.

The teacher of Shakespeare should possess some of the attributes of the fictional detective; he "must be content with proximate truth, with an endless series of tentative and exploratory readings, knowing that his view of the case will again be modified and extended the next time he teaches the course." Treats play as a case for detection, "running through a few solutions proposed by editors, critics, and directors" and posing his own solution at end.

Othello

Matthews, G. M. **"Othello and the Dignity of Man."** In *Shakespeare in a Changing World,* edited by Arnold Kettle, pp. 123–45. London: Lawrence and Wishart, 1964.

Argues that *Othello* is not a vaguely timeless story of jealousy but a modern instance of a black man's love for a white woman.

Miller, Helen Rand. **"*Othello* in a Community College."** *English Journal* 39 (April 1950): 218–19.

Gives a composite of student papers and describes her experience in teaching *Othello* to college sophomores.

Mudford, Peter G. *"Othello* **and the 'Tragedy of Situation'."** *English* 20 (Spring 1971): 1–6.

An approach to overcome the impasse reached by verbal and psychological criticism.

Mueller, William R. **"The Class of '50 Reads** *Othello."* *College English* 10 (1948): 92–97.

Suggests that *Othello* should be read as a work of art; not read as a vignette from life nor as a detailed report of an actual event but as a portrayal of strong passions in action.

Rosenberg, Marvin. **The Masks of Othello.** Berkeley: University of California Press, 1961.

Uses the insights of literary critics and famous actors for scene-by-scene analysis.

Wentersdorf, Karl P. **"Structure and Characterization in** *Othello* **and** *King Lear."* *College English* 26 (May 1965): 645–48.

An application of Freytag's *Technik des Dramas* (1863) method—three parts of tragedy are exposition, conflict and catastrophe—to *Othello* and *Lear.*

See also, in General section, Frey.

Richard II

Weingarten, Samuel. **"The Name of King in** *Richard II."* *College English* 27 (April 1966): 536–41.

Explains that verbal symbols are more important than the things for which they stand, and "King" is a word from which Richard cannot disassociate himself.

Richard III

Clemen, Wolfgang. **A Commentary on Shakespeare's** *Richard III.* Translated by Jean Bonheim. London: Methuen, 1968.

An excellent scene-by-scene commentary.

Pennel, Charles A. **"On Introducing Shakespeare:** *Richard III."* *College English* 26 (May 1965): 643–45.

Most obvious advantage of beginning with *Richard III* is that it is melodrama.

Romeo and Juliet

Auden, W. H. **"Commentary on the Poetry and Tragedy of *Romeo and Juliet.*"** In *Romeo and Juliet,* edited by F. Fergusson and C. J. Sisson. New York: Dell, 1958.

Evans, Robert O. **The Osier Cage: Rhetorical Devices in *Romeo and Juliet.*** Lexington: University of Kentucky Press, 1966.

"An exegesis of Shakespeare's rhetoric, particularly his use of certain of the tropes and figures of speech so familiar to writers in the Renaissance."

Rosenheim, Edward W., Jr. **What Happens in Literature: A Guide to Poetry, Drama, and Fiction.** Chicago: University of Chicago Press, 1960.

"Reading Dramatic Literature" (pp. 93–124) is principally concerned with *Romeo and Juliet.*

Shapiro, Stephen A. **"*Romeo and Juliet*: Reversals, Contraries, Transformations, and Ambivalences."** *College English* 25 (April 1964): 498–501.

Concentrates on reversals in II.vi. and III.i.

Taylor, Gary J. **"*Romeo and Juliet* and *West Side Story*: An Experimental Unit."** *English Journal* 51 (October 1962): 484–85.

See also, in General section, Bergeron, Perret, Petronella.

Taming of the Shrew

Schleiner, Winfried. **"Deromanticizing the *Shrew*: Notes on the Teaching of Shakespeare in a Women in Literature Course."** In *Teaching Shakespeare,* edited by W. Edens, et al., pp. 79–92. Princeton: Princeton University Press, 1977.

Uses *Taming of the Shrew* to exemplify the theme of "wives willfully tested" in a general course on the image of women in literature.

See also, in General section, Bergeron, Lease.

The Tempest

Bowling, Laurence E. **"The Theme of Natural Order in *The Tempest.*"** *College English* 12 (January 1951): 203–09.

The Tempest is "one of the most intellectual and ideological of all Shakespeare's works." Practically every character is guilty of trying to break the great chain of being, to invert the natural order. All ends well when the characters are restored to their proper status.

Hilberry, C. *"The Tempest*: Act IV."* College English* 23 (April 1962): 586–88.

Relates Prospero's "Our revels now are ended" speech to action in Act IV.

Lodge, David. **"Conrad's *Victory* and *Tempest*: An Amplification."** *Modern Language Review* 59 (1964): 195–99.

Supplements previous evidence of *The Tempest*'s influence.

See also, in General section, Frey, Moulton.

Twelfth Night

Downer, Alan S. **"1952: Feste's Night."** *College English* 22 (November 1960): 117–23.

Discusses the importance of Feste to resolution of play.

Downer, Alan S. **"1952: Feste's Night."** *College English* 22 (November 1960): 117–23.

Discusses the place of disguise and the role of the fool in *Twelfth Night*.

See also, in General section, Bergeron, Bowden, Moulton.

Troilus and Cressida

Richards, I. A. **"*Troilus and Cressida* and Plato."** *Hudson Review* 1 (1948): 362–76.

Argues that the play deserves a place in general education because many of the lines are great statements like Plato's.

Thompson, Karl F. **"*Troilus and Cressida*: The Incomplete Achilles."** *College English* 27 (April 1966): 532–36.

Seen live, the play's turning point is Ulysses' address to Achilles; yet, the play is more interesting as drama for the classroom than for the stage.

See also, in General section, Enright, Frey, Moulton.

Winter's Tale

Ellis, John. **"Rooted Affection: The Genesis of Jealousy in *A Winter's**

Tale." *College English* 25 (April 1964): 545–47.

Speculates that Leonte's suppressed love for Polixenes is the ground for his anger.

Non-dramatic Poetry

Alverez, A. **"How to Read a Poem (III): Shakespeare's 'The Phoenix and the Turtle'."** *Mandrake* 2 (Autumn/Winter 1955–56): 395–408.

A close reading employing four approaches to the poem.

Barber, C. L. **"An Essay on the Sonnets."** In *Sonnets,* edited by F. Fergusson and C. J. Sisson, pp. 7–23. New York: Dell, 1960.

Berkelman, Robert. **"The Drama in Shakespeare's Sonnets."** *College English* 10 (December 1948): 138–41.

Suggests that the sonnets are "marvelously condensed dramas," especially Sonnets 129, 144, 30, 73, and 146.

Clark. W. R. **"Poems for Study: Winter."** *Clearing House* 36 (November 1961): 187–88.

Considers "When icicles . . ."(*Love's Labour's Lost* V.ii.)simply as poetry.

Clark, W. R. **"Poems for Study: Sonnet 116."** *Clearing House* 34 (January 1960): 316.

Crompton, Louis. **"Literature and Our Gay Minority."** *Iowa English Bulletin Yearbook* (Fall 1973): 11–13.

Uses Shakespeare's sonnets as an illustration of classroom attitudes toward literature.

Daiches, David. **"Shakespeare's Poetry."** In *The Living Shakespeare,* edited by Robert Gittings, pp. 44–53. London: Heinemann, 1960.

Davis, Jack M., and Grant, J. E. **"A Critical Dialogue on Shakespeare's Sonnet 71."** *Texas Studies in Literature and Language* 1 (1959): 214–32.

Sonnet 71 is used to illustrate a variety of critical approaches—Neo-Aristotelian, Archetypal, and Eclectic. Discusses "the way words modify one another in poetry," and the inadequacy of paraphrastic criticism.

Dunning, Stephen. **Teaching Literature to Adolescents: Poetry.** Glenview, Ill.: Scott, Foresman, 1966.

Suggests that "skeleton statements" may be a way of starting toward a meaning in the sonnets. Sonnet 73 examined, pp. 66–69.

Evans, Bertram. **"A Note on Teaching the Sonnets."** In his *Teaching Shakespeare in High School,* pp. 278–93. New York: Macmillan, 1966.

Suggests an "irreducible minimum" of thirty-six sonnets that should be "distributed among all grades from nine through twelve." Suggests that sonnets 18, 29, 73, and 116 are appropriate for grades nine or ten, while sonnets 105, 107, 119, 129, and 130 are appropriate for grades eleven or twelve.

Frederick, E. C. **"I Taught Shakespeare to the Buzzards."** *Instructor* 80 (January 1971): 116.

Teaches Sonnet 130 to slow reading pupils by selecting certain words, having pupils define them and build a sentence around them, and then having them write a poem to a pretended girl or boy friend. This is done without showing the poem or telling it is Shakespeare. Later, poems are compared and discussed.

Gleeson, James F. **"Introducing Shakespeare."** *English Journal* 56 (December 1967): 1293–94.

As an introduction to Shakespeare for ninth and tenth graders, suggests that students summarize sonnets in their own words while hearing them read aloud. Students must listen carefully, recognize ideas involved, select details, and recast ideas. Recommends beginning with sonnets 18, 29, 30, 91, 106, 116, 130 and 138.

Gordon, Edward J. **"Sonnet 73."** In his *Writing About Imaginative Literature,* pp. 87–89. New York: Harcourt Brace Jovanovich, 1973.

Explains aspects of the sonnet that are necessary for explication.

Hedberg, Johannes. **"Enjoying a Shakespeare Sonnet in Class."** *Moderna Sprak* (Saltsjo-Duvnas) 59 (1965): 5–10.

Explains how the Shakespearean poem can be vitalized by cutting away the "boils and abscesses."

Helton, Tinsley. **"Contemporary Trends in Shakespeare Sonnet Scholarship."** *Wisconsin English Journal* 8 (1965): 13–16.

Discusses theories on biography, dating, themes and word play in sonnets.

Jorgensen, Virginia. **"Poetry in the Classroom: Of Love and Hate: Shakespeare's Sonnet 90."** *English Journal* 53 (September 1964): 459–61.

Sees that Sonnet 90 "has been a recreation of a state of mind comprehensible to the high school student."

Koch, Kenneth. **"William Shakespeare: Songs."** In his *Rose, Where Did You Get That Red? Teaching Great Poetry to Children,* pp. 90–101, 226–32. New York: Vintage Books, 1974.

Suggests that many of Shakespeare's songs appeal to children's sense of fantasy and sensuous feeling for nature. Exercises are suggested for using several songs.

MacLeish, Archibald. **"The Proper Pose of Poetry."** *Saturday Review* 5 (March 1955): 11–12, 47–49.

An analysis of Sonnet 116 answers question "What is the language of poetry?"

Matthews, Charles, and Blum, Margaret M. **"To the Student of Poetry: An Essay on Essays."** *CEA Critic* 35 (January 1973): 24–27.

An analysis of Sonnet 116 illustrates suggestions for students writing essays on poetry.

McLean, Andrew. **"Teaching Shakespeare's Poetry: A Checklist."** *Teaching Shakespeare: Ideas for the Classroom* 1 (Fall 1977): 7.

Annotates twenty-four items.

Prince, Frank T. **William Shakespeare: The Poems.** London: Longmans, Green for the British Council and National Book League, 1963.

An overview.

Radley, Virginia L., and Redding, David C. **"Shakespeare: Sonnet 110, a New Look."** *Shakespeare Quarterly* 12 (1961): 462–63.

Sonnet 110 has nothing to do with theater. It involves "the Poet's recognition of his own transgressions against ideal love" and thus against his friend of old. Offers a line-by-line paraphrase.

Russ, Jon R.. **"Time's Attributes in Shakespeare's Sonnet 126."** *English Studies* 52 (1971): 318–23.

Illustrates the importance of punctuation to provide a coherent reading of the sonnet.

Schroeter, James. **"Shakespeare's Not 'To-Be-Pitied Lover'."** *College English* 23 (January 1962): 250–55.

Takes issue with the New Critics' approach to Sonnet 73.

Stocking, Fred. **"Shakespeare's Temperance."** In *The Hues of English, NCTE Distinguished Lectures,* pp. 11–32. Champaign, Ill.: National Council of Teachers of English, 1969.

Shows how Shakespeare's universality may be recognized through an analysis of 'temperance' in Sonnet 18, which is "clear, precise, perfectly controlled, harmonious."

Sylvester, Bikford. **"Natural Mutability and Human Responsibility: Form in Shakespeare's** *Lucrece.***"** *College English* 26 (April 1965): 505–11.

Points out patterns in the imagery and structure that coalesce in a coherent scheme.

Taaffe, James, and Lincks, John. **"Reading the Poetry of William Shakespeare."** In their *Reading English Poetry,* pp. 1–15. New York: The Free Press, 1971.

Good commentary and questions on sonnets 1, 2, 15, 17, 60, 65, 33, 129, plus two songs from *Love's Labour's Lost.*

Waddington, Raymond B. **"Shakespeare's Sonnet 15 and the Art of Memory."** In *The Rhetoric of Renaissance Poetry,* edited by T. O. Sloane and R. B. Waddington, pp. 96–122. Berkeley: University of California Press, 1974.

An analysis within relevant historical contexts that uses Sonnet 15 to illustrate how certain kinds of reflective lyrics should be read.

Warner, John M. **"Shakespeare's 'Winter' and 'Spring' and the Radical Teaching of Poetry."** *CEA Critic* 34 (March 1972): 16–19.

Argues that clarity of perception is a requisite for radical awareness. These two songs offer a simple exercise that reveals the acuteness and complexity of poetic seeing.

Teaching Shakespeare as Performance

Adland, David. **The Group Approach to Shakespeare.** New York: Longman, 1976.

A series of practical drama books provides group plays, play scripts, improvisations and stage design projects for pairs and groups. The play text is not included.

Adland, David. **Group Drama. Teacher's Book . . . A Companion to the Group Drama Approach to Shakespeare, pupils books 1-4.** London: Longman, 1964.

Alington, A. F. **Drama and Education.** Oxford: Basil Blackwell, 1961.

Shows that British students instructed by a "stage-centered" approach were acquiring solid understanding of the nature of drama and were well prepared to answer Shakespeare questions on national examinations.

Armstrong, William A. **"The Art of Shakespearean Production in the Twentieth Century."** *Essays and Studies* 15 (1962): 74–87.

Survey of English theatre's shift to spectacular production (Beerbohm Tree) through Elizabethan staging (Granville-Barker) to personal interpretations (Peter Brook, T. Guthrie).

Arnold, Elizabeth M. **"No More Hurly-Burly."** *English Journal* 41 (January 1952): 37–38.

Emphasizes performance in class discussion—as if the play were to be staged.

Arnold, Ruth K. **"Shakespeare in the Garden."** *English Journal* 40 (June 1951): 325–29.

Emphasizes reading aloud as a "revelation in itself," as a socializing force, and as a preparation of students for public readings.

Bacon, Wallace A. **"Teaching Shakespeare Through Performance: A Tried, Effective Way of Learning."** *Chronicle of Higher Education,* 6 December 1976, p. 16.

A reply to M. G. Scully notes that Northwestern University has been teaching Shakespeare through performance for about 100 years.

Bacon, Wallace A. **"Problems in the Interpretation of Shakespeare."** *Speech Teacher* 22 (November 1973): 273–81.

Makes a plea "for the primacy of the language in performance . . . to make most useful what Shakespeare has done at his finest."

Bacon, Wallace A. **"On the Teaching of Interpretation."** *College English* 11 (February 1950): 397–400.

A useful general discussion to explain "what modern work in interpretation is." See also, in this section, Scully, Swander.

Bailey, Margery. **"Shakespeare in Action."** *College English* 15 (March 1954): 307–15.

"Too often we forget [Shakespeare] as a dramatist and poet fused"—sees need to study Shakespeare's plays in action.

Ballet, Arthur H. **"Oral Interpretation in the English Class."** *English Journal* 39 (December 1950): 360–67.

"All the effort that should be expended in a good job of oral interpretation seems obviously better used in an attempt to read a passage from Shakespeare than a verse from Edgar Guest."

Barnes, T. R. **"Cutting Shakespeare."** *Journal of Education* (London) 39 (1957): 395–96.

Suggestions for staging and acting.

Barnes, T. R. **"Producing Shakespeare in School."** *Use of English* 3 (March 1952): 151–56.

Notes stage problems and enumerates principles of production. "To think of the words, is to think of the verse."

Barry, Jackson G. **"Shakespeare with Words: The Script and the Medium of Drama."** *Shakespeare Quarterly* 25 (Spring 1974): 161–71.

In teaching Shakespeare, emphasis should be placed on how "the scenes and its speeches are created out of the possibilities provided by a stage and actors."

Beckerman, Bernard. **"The Flowers of Fancy, the Jerks of Invention, or, Directional Approaches to Shakespeare."** In *Shakespeare 1971,* edited by C. Leech and J. M. R. Margeson, pp. 200–14. Toronto: University of Toronto Press, 1972.

Argues that from the director's comprehensive insight "new frames emerge that will electrify Shakespeare's words anew."

Bentley, Gerald E. **Shakespeare and His Theatre.** Lincoln: University of Nebraska Press, 1964.

Includes argument that "all teachers and critics ought to cling painfully to the central concept that William Shakespeare was essentially a man of the theatre and not a poet writing for readers."

Berry, Ralph, ed. **On Directing Shakespeare: Interviews with Contemporary Directors.** New York: Harper & Row, 1977.

Boas, Guy. **Shakespeare and the Young Actor: A Guide to Production.** 2d. ed. London: Barrie & Rockliff, 1961.

Discusses boy actors as Shakespeare's men and women, and the plays produced at Sloane School (staging, rehearsal, and speech). Gives special attention to twelve plays.

Brien, Alan. **"Back to School."** *Spectator,* 19 August 1961, p. 283.

Michael Croft's Youth Theatre production of *Julius Caesar.*

Brown, John R., ed. **Shakespeare in Performance: An Introduction Through Six Major Plays.** New York: Harcourt Brace Jovanovich, 1976.

Presents texts of *Rom, 1H4, TN, Othello, Lear,* and *Temp* in center column of three columns, with gloss on right and a running theatrical commentary on left.

Brown, John R. **"The Theatrical Element of Shakespeare Criticism."** In *Reinterpretations of Elizabethan Drama,* edited by Norman Rabkin, pp. 177–95. New York: Columbia University Press, 1969.

Examines the effect that renewed theatrical consciousness has had on criticism.

Brown, John R. **Shakespeare's Plays in Performance.** London: Arnold; New York: St. Martin's, 1966.

Brubaker, E. S. **Shakespeare Aloud: A Guide to His Verse on Stage.** Lancaster, Pa.: By the Author, 1976.

Useful discussion on verse dialogue for those who like to read Shakespeare aloud.

Burkman, Katherine H. **Literature Through Performance.** Athens: Ohio University Press, 1977.

Includes "Shakespeare's Mirror," a selection of scenes from Shakespeare's plays, connected by narrative and interspersed with songs first conceived as a teaching script.

Clark, John Lewis. **"Shakespeare in American Colleges: From Declamation to Drama."** In his "Dramatic Activity in the Colleges and Universities of the United States Prior to 1905," pp. 111–53. Ph.D. dissertation, Stanford University, 1956. *Dissertation Abstracts* 16 (1956): 178.

Clay, James, and Krempel, Daniel. **The Theatrical Image.** New York: McGraw-Hill, 1967.

Includes discussion of *Hamlet* (1922), *Tro* (1938, 1956), and *Lear* (1962) and film versions: *MND* (1936), *Macbeth* (1948), *Hamlet* (1948).

Cole, Toby, and Chinoy, Helen K., eds. **Directors on Directing: A Source Book of the Modern Theater.** Rev. ed. Indianapolis, Ind.: Bobbs-Merrill, 1963.

"Staging Shakespeare: A Survey of Current Problems and Opinions," pp. 403–40, presents statements from Gielgud, Guthrie, Olivier, Houseman, Webster, Brook, Hall, Langham, Ball, Papp, Vaughan and Zeffirelli.

Cook, H. Caldwell. **"Acting Shakespeare in the Classroom."** In his *The Play Way: An Essay in Educational Method,* 2d. ed., pp. 183–221. New York: Stokes, 1919.

The "play way"—having students act out as much of a Shakespeare play as their abilities and imaginations permit—gives students opportunities to study characterization, staging, narration, poetry, history and language.

Crawford, Mary M., and Phillips, Leroy. **"Shakespeare as We Like Him."** *English Journal* 26 (December 1937): 811–16.

Suggestions for staging in a classroom.

Crump, Michael. **"Principles of Shakespearean Production in a Secondary Modern School."** *Use of English* (London) 15 (Winter 1963): 99–102.

Davies, Derek J. **"Getting Shakespeare Taped."** *Use of English* (London) 7 (Spring 1956): 184–88.

Suggests the teacher tape his or her own recording of the play under study and tailor it to class needs.

De Reyes, C. M. **"Appendix on Dramatic Production."** Included in many volumes of the series *Junior School Shakespeare*. London and Glasgow: Blackie & Son.

E., Sh. **"Students Stage *King Lear* for Their Diploma."** *Teatr* (Moscow) 6 (1960): 185–86.

Describes occasion in Sarakov People's theatre, Sofia, Bulgaria.

Eaves, Morris. **"The Real Thing: A Plan for Producing Shakespeare in the Classroom."** *College English* 31 (February 1970): 463–72.

Project involves dividing class into four groups to work on "texts, sets, costumes, acting and directing, and reviewing." Includes bibliography.

Evans, C. R. **"Plays in Production: *Twelfth Night* in the Open Air."** *Use of English* (London) 20 (Autumn 1968): 37–40.

Describes a fifth form production.

Faust, Richard, and Kadushin, Charles. **Shakespeare in the Neighborhood: Audience Reaction to *Midsummer Night's Dream*, As Produced by Joseph Papp for the Delacorte Mobile Theater.** New York: Twentieth Century Fund, for the Bureau of Applied Social Research of Columbia University, 1965.

Finds that middle class neighborhood audiences recall play in generalities while lower class audiences remember particular scenes or episodes.

Fell, Kenneth. **"Producing the School Play."** *Use of English* (London) 6 (Autumn 1954): 32–37.

Discusses the producer's job with illustrations from *Antony and Cleopatra*.

Fidone, William. **"Three Tiers for the Bard."** *Scholastic Teacher,* 29 November 1956, p. 4T.

Shakespeare is brought to life for senior high students as they prepare for viewing live production at Hofstra College on three level stage.

Foakes, R. A. **"The Player's Passion: Some Notes on Elizabethan Psychology and Acting."** *Essays and Studies* 7 (1954): 62–77.

Warns those critics who make excessive use of Elizabethan psychology in their approach to Shakespeare: Elizabethan acting was thought at the time to be lifelike.

"Free Will—Adult Western Version." *Time,* 8 June 1959, p. 48.

Review of a London performance of a Western adaptation of *Midsummer Night's Dream* produced by the students of Howard Payne College.

Gilbert, Miriam. **"Teaching Dramatic Literature."** *Educational Theatre Journal* 25 (March 1973): 86–94.

Describes a provocative approach to making students aware of the stage production by having them stage a scene. Examples from various Shakespearean plays are included.

Glover, William. **"Some Notes on Shakespearean Acting and Sundry Ramblings on the State of the American Theatre."** *FOCUS: Teaching English in Southeastern Ohio* 2 (May 1976): 53–56.

Calls for "vision" and new directions in the American theatre.

Golden, Joseph. **"Three Deadly Sins in Staging Shakespeare."** *English Record* 15 (December 1964): 2–5.

Warns against piety, novelty, pedantry.

Goldman, Michael. **"Acting Values and Shakespearean Meaning: Some Suggestions."** *Mosaic* 10 (Spring 1977): 51–58.

"We should pay attention to Shakespeare as a writer for actors. . . . to what he gives his actors and requires of them, and to the ways he uses actors to shape an audience's response."

Gould, Gerald. **"Producing Shakespeare with Amateurs."** *Amateur Stage* 19 (1964): 30–31.

Granville-Barker, Harley. **More Prefaces to Shakespeare.** Princeton: Princeton University Press, 1974.

Discusses *MND, WT, Macbeth, H5,* and *Hamlet* and continues classic discussion of Shakespeare in performance found in *Prefaces to Shakespeare,* 4 vols. (1968).

Hagen, John. **"*Hamlet* Produced."** *Use of English* (London) 19 (Autumn 1967): 26–29.

Activities surrounding a school production.

Halio, Jay L. **"'This Wide and Universal Stage': Shakespeare's Plays as Plays."** In *Teaching Shakespeare,* edited by W. Edens, et al., pp. 273–89. Princeton: Princeton University Press, 1977.

Advocates the use of performance as a teaching technique through the critical use of Shakespeare in performance (e.g., coming to grips with the text) and the students' own performances of scenes from Shakespeare's plays.

Hallet, Charles A. **"A Shakespeare Workshop."** *College English* 32 (April 1971): 790–96.

Offers a modest workshop technique that is adaptable to almost any level: assigns same limited section of a scene to two casts, each with its own director. Shows that more than one reading of the play is possible. Provides list of opposing views for various scenes to try with students.

Hamil, Louise Knudsen. **"Try Shakespeare—It's Fun."** *Alabama School Journal* 56 (October 1938): 9.

A dramatics teacher has pupils revise and rework scenes and speeches for dramatic exercises.

Hammack, J. Alan. **"Settings for Shakespearean Productions."** *Players Magazine* 41 (January 1965): 96–98.

Contains brief bibliography of additional sources for usable pictures of settings.

Hanratty, Jerome. **"School Plays in Production:** *Arden of Feversham.***"** *Use of English* (London) 11 (Spring 1960): 176–80.

Harbage, Alfred. **"Shakespearean Staging."** *Shakespeare Newsletter* 14 (April–May 1964): 31.

Heniger, Mrs. Alice M. (Herts). **The Children's Educational Theatre.** New York: Harper, 1911.

Includes a discussion of productions of *Temp* and *AYL.*

Henneman, Dennis. **"The Class Play: Shakespeare or Trivia?"** *English Journal* 53 (November 1964): 595–96.

Advises even small high schools to stage the classics.

"I Henry IV." *Studies in the Mass Media* (April 1962): 1–20.

The entire issue is "a guide that will help the 68,000 students" who will see *I Henry IV* at Stratford, Connecticut. Introduction by Joseph Verner Reed. Also includes Paula Silberstein, "Audio-Visual Aids in the Teaching of Shakespearean Plays" (a bibliography), pp. 18–20.

Hirsch, Samuel. **"Drama as Theatre."** *Journal of Education* 148 (1965): 14–21.

Offers practical suggestions to the teacher for implementing "performance" in the mind of the student.

Holmes, Martin. **Shakespeare and His Players.** London: John Murray, 1972.

The importance of the text as a vehicle for performance is central concern; offers practical and sensible discussion.

Horn, Robert D. **"Shakespearean Performances as Criticism, Ashland, 1962."** *Shakespeare Quarterly* 13 (1962): 547–52.

Concerns performances of *Err, AYL, 1H4,* and *Cor.*

Horn, Robert D. **"Our Friend Shakespeare."** *School Activities* 32 (September 1960): 15–17.

Notes on staging and acting in school productions.

Hughes, R. E. **"Conveyors Are You All."** *Education* 80 (1960): 279-82.

Discusses staging and acting Shakespeare in schools.

Hughes, W. R. **"*Macbeth* Goes African."** *Scholastic Teacher,* 22 September 1954, p. 43.

An account of a Liberian performance.

Johnson, Albert. **Shakespeare Vignettes: Adaptations for Acting.** South Brunswick and New York: A. S. Barnes, 1970.

Designed for classroom performance by a director with experience in television. Thirty-minute adaptations of *MV, Shrew, Rom, Macbeth, Hamlet,* and *Othello.*

Kapteyn, James. **"Producing Shakespeare in [Secondary] School."** *Scholastic Teacher,* 22 November 1957, p. 111.

Kildahl, Erling E. **"Directing Shakespeare's Plays."** *Communication Education* 5 (November 1956): 296–304.

Practical advice on director's attitude and on selecting, cutting, directing, and acting the play. Primarily for college and high school groups.

Kiley, Frederick S. **"A Barrage of Slings and Arrows."** *Clearing House* 32 (January 1958): 284–86.

Recounts a series of mishaps plaguing school productions.

Kirstein, Lincoln. **"On Producing *Midsummer Night's Dream*."** In *Midsummer Night's Dream,* edited by F. Fergusson and C. J. Sisson, pp. 16–27. New York: Dell, 1960.

Knight, G. Wilson. **Shakespearean Productions.** 3d ed. London: Routledge and Kegan Paul, 1968.

Deals especially with the tragedies.

Krentz, Irving. **"Ideas and Ideals in Producing Shakespeare."** *Shakespeare Newsletter* 11 (December 1961): 50.

Discusses tension between ideal paradigm of production and an actual production.

Lasser, Michael, and Dalton, William. **"Theater in the Classroom."** *Clearing House* 49 (January 1976): 221–23.

Class studies *Macbeth,* views Welles' film and enacts scenes, all of which allows tenth graders alternatives to passive learning.

Leary, William G. **Shakespeare Plain: The Making and Performing of Shakespeare's Plays.** New York: McGraw-Hill, 1976.

Lee, Marion H. **"Playing *a Midsummer Night's Dream*: An Introduction to Period Acting for American College Students."** Ph.D. dissertation, Columbia University, 1968. *Dissertation Abstracts* 28 (1968): 4304A.

Legatt, Alexander. **"The Extra Dimension: Shakespeare in Performance."** *Mosaic* 10 (Spring 1977): 37–49.

Explores how scholars "have been using theatrical performances as evidence for their own interpretations," noting that a performance is unstoppable, presents moments of tension between the verbal and the visual, and is inevitably selective.

Loney, R., and Mackay, P. **The Shakespeare Complex: A Guide to Summer Festivals and Year Round Repertory in North America.** New York: Drama Book Specialists, 1975.

Low, J. T. **"*Love's Labour's Lost.*"** *Use of English* (London) 12 (Summer 1961): 242–44.

An appropriate choice for college production because it concerns young men who give up women for their studies only to learn "that true education comes from a careful study of women."

Ludwig, J. F. **"Shakespeare with Few Males."** *Players Magazine* 37 (February 1961): 103–04.

Experiments at Russell Sage College "demonstrate that with some compromise Shakespeare can be produced in the high school or small college."

McDowell, John H. **"Analyzing *Julius Caesar* for Modern Production."**

Quarterly Journal of Speech 31 (October 1945): 303–14.

Illustrates a director's preparation for a performance using an Elizabethan styled stage.

McGuire, Philip C., and Samuelson, David A., eds. **Shakespeare: The Theatrical Dimension.** New York: AMS Press, 1978.

Fourteen essays exemplify "non-literary" criticism, i.e., examines the plays as they are experienced in the theatre.

McMahon, Charlene. **"Notes on the Production of 'Pyramus and Thisbe'."** In *The Dynamics of English Instruction, Grades 7–12,* edited by George Hillocks, Bernard J. McCabe, and James F. Campbell, pp. 343–48.

Student teachers report on 150 ninth graders' production of *Pyramus and Thisbe* play.

Mattingly, Alethea S. **"The Playing Time and Manner of Delivery of Shakespeare's Plays in the Elizabethan Theatre."** *Communication Monographs* 21 (March 1954): 29–38.

Meszaros, Patricia K. **"Notes on a Workshop Approach to Shakespeare."** *Shakespeare Quarterly* 25 (1974): 188–97.

Suggests having the students meet in a theater rehearsal room; the unit of measure is always the scene that the students block out while listening to a recording.

Monroe, Elizabeth A. **"The Group Reading of Drama: Its Essence and Aesthetic Principles."** Ph.D. dissertation, University of Wisconsin, 1963. *Dissertation Abstracts* 24 (1963): 2620.

Motter, Charlotte Kay. **"Shakespeare on the High School Stage."** In her *Theatre in High School: Planning, Teaching, Directing,* pp. 123–28. Englewood Cliffs, N.J.: Prentice-Hall, 1970.

Briefly discusses cutting Shakespearean plays, staging, and evaluating.

Nardin, James T. **"Modern Criticism and the Closet Drama Approach."** *College English* 26 (May 1965): 591–97.

Comments on widespread influence of Brooks and Heilman's *Understanding Drama* (1945) and advocates that students "be taught to construct a performance of the play in their minds."

Nathan, Norman. **"Shakespeare: 'The Play's the Thing'."** *English Journal* 56 (October 1967): 964–69.

Good survey of how "attitudes, philosophical views, and the relationship of characters to each other [can] be indicated by the way the lines are spoken," and how knowledge of the play prior to viewing it can lead us to ignore basic concepts and details in the play.

Neilson, Francis. **A Study of *Macbeth* for the Stage.** Mineola, N.Y.: Davenport Press, 1952.

Scene-by-scene discussion in terms of the stage action.

Olfson, Lewy. **Radio Plays from Shakespeare: Ten Plays Adapted for Royalty-Free Performance.** Boston: Plays, 1958.

Phillips, A. L. **"Shakespeare Not Closet Drama."** *School and Society* 46 (1937): 689–91.

Students will benefit from seeing the plays but even better results occur when they act the play themselves.

Pollack, Daniel B. **"Peter Brook: A Study of a Modern Elizabethan and His Search for New Theatrical Forms."** Ph.D. dissertation, New York University, 1972. *Dissertation Abstracts* 34 (1973): 447A.

Includes a discussion of Brook's stage productions of *Lear* (1962) and *MND* (1970) as well as other Shakespearean productions.

Purdom, Charles B. **Producing Shakespeare.** London: Sir Isaac Pitman, 1950.

Summarizes production principles of William Poel and H. Granville-Barker, and the final chapter describes the author's production of *Winter's Tale.*

Purdom, Charles B. **What Happens in Shakespeare: A New Interpretation.** London: John Baker, 1963.

Deals with the plays' quality as drama: "It is as drama that Shakespeare is an education in the imagination and the feelings."

Reeves, James. **"The Shakespearean Score."** *Use of English* (London) 11 (Summer 1960): 230–32.

Criticizes modern Shakespearean production. Pleads that in order "to make Shakespeare come alive again theatrically" it is necessary to restore the text to its central importance, as distinct from the production and interpretation of individual roles.

Rehner, Herbert A. **"Choral Speaking in the Theatre."** *Players Magazine* 31 (April 1955): 160–61.

Discussion of this technique for the use of amateur groups with *JC* and *Rom.*

Riffle, Nancy. "**Shakespeare's Stage: A Bibliography.**" *Shakespeare Newsletter* 12 (November 1962): 90.

Scully, Malcolm. "**Teachers of Shakespeare Using New Techniques.**" *Chronicle of Higher Education,* 11 October 1976, p. 5.

Reports on new emphasis on performance, focusing on work by Gilbert and Shand. See also, in this section, Bacon, Swander.

"**Shakespeare at School.**" *New York Times Magazine,* 31 March 1957, p. 63.

Concerns the Theatre in Education Shakespeare productions in sixteen Connecticut high schools.

Shand, G. B. "**Theatrical Techniques in Shakespeare Teaching.**" *English Quarterly* (Waterloo) 10 (Winter 1977/78): 25–36.

Outlines various theatrical techniques for the classroom such as (1) scene preparation, (2) four group tasks (see also, in this section, Eaves, Morris), (3) a workshop (see also, in this section, Hallet, Charles), and (4) stage related exercises (see also, in this section, Gilbert).

Shand, G. B. "**Classroom as Theatre: A Technique for Shakespeare Teachers.**" *English Quarterly* (Waterloo) 8 (Spring/Summer 1975): 13–19.

Suggests that informal classroom-theater "often clarifies what might be seen as aspects of the fiction of the play" and that preparing scenes "teaches students to see the play on stage with the mind's eye while reading." Furthermore, there is "a sense of group identification and creativity achieved" when students come together to choose a scene, learn lines, and perform for their classmates.

Sharp, William L. "**Subtexts in Shakespeare.**" In his *Language in Drama: Meanings for the Director and the Actor,* pp. 45–70. Scranton, Pa.: Chandler, 1970.

"Subtext" is the unspoken or underlying intention in the character that must be realized by the actor. Develops suggestions in J. R. Brown's "Shakespeare Subtexts," *Tulane Drama Review* 8 (Fall 1963): 72–94; 8 (Winter 1963): 85–102.

Soderwall, Margreta. "*Macbeth* **pa skolscen—sedd genom elevogon ('*Macbeth* acted at school for pupils' eyes').**" *Modersmalslararnas forenings arsskrift,* pp. 13–20. Lund, 1961.

Speaight, Robert. "**Shakespeare in American Colleges.**" *Shakespeare Newsletter* 9 (April 1959): 15.

Discusses the dichotomy between the scholar and the director, and the role of the university theater.

"Staging Shakespeare: Symposium." *Theatre Arts* 45 (August 1961): 60–65, 79–80.

Summarized in "On Directing and Producing Shakespeare." *Shakespeare Newsletter* 11 (December 1961): 49–50.

Styan, J. L. **"Direct Method Shakespeare."** *Shakespeare Quarterly* 25 (1974): 198–200.

The direct method of teaching Shakespeare is to discover him by playing him.

Styan, J. L. **The Shakespeare Revolution: Criticism and Performance in the Twentieth Century.** New York: Cambridge University Press, 1977.

Traces historical changes in various approaches to staging Shakespeare and the impact of major critics on Shakespeare production.

Styan, J. L. **"Shakespeare Show and Tell."** *Teaching Shakespeare: Ideas for the Classroom* 1 (Fall 1976): 1–2.

Argues that "Shakespeare emerges most richly when returned to his own medium . . . [i.e.] to Shakespeare's essential drama of non-illusion on the floor of the naked classroom."

Styan, J. L. **"Shakespeare Teaches Shakespeare."** *Shakespeare Newsletter* 35 (April 1975): 16.

"Students can learn much from performing bits of the play in class in teams."

Styan, J. L. **Shakespeare's Stagecraft.** Cambridge: University Press, 1967.

Swander, Homer. **Letter.** *Chronicle of Higher Education,* 7 February 1977, p. 15.

Responds to Scully by saying that the battle for accepting new approaches to teaching Shakespeare's plays has just begun.

Swander, Homer. **"Teaching Shakespeare as Performance."** *Shakespeare Newsletter* 25 (April 1975): 19.

"There is no legitimate way to teach his plays—*as plays*—that does not prepare everyone involved for those meetings of actors and audiences for which play scripts are written." See also, in this section, Bacon, Scully.

Theatre's Different Demands: An Approach to the Classroom Teaching of Plays. Connecticut State Department of Education, 1970.

A sequential plan to introduce high school students to acting and to provide an understanding of dramatic literature, especially Shakespearean drama.

Thespis. **"School Shakespeare Productions."** *English* (London) 11 (Summer 1957): 187–88.

Trewin. J. C. **Shakespeare on the English Stage, 1900–1964.** London: Barrie and Rockliff, 1964.

A selective survey of productions which "seeks to outline theories and experiments, changes and chances." Well illustrated.

Turner, Mary M. **"Why Not Produce Shakespeare?"** *Clearing House* 12 (January 1938): 302–05.

Argues that Shakespeare plays are inexpensive to produce, employ simple settings, and that students enjoy acting in them.

Versteeg, Robert. **"A Multi-Media Production of *Romeo and Juliet.*"** *Educational Theatre Journal* 21 (October 1969): 259–74.

Reports on "a serious experiment in using electronic devices and filmic principles as fully integrated elements in a re-creation of Shakespeare's play."

Vilhauer, William. **"Why Not Do a Classic?"** *Players Magazine* 34 (February 1958): 103–04.

Suggestions for producing Shakespeare and Greek drama in secondary schools. Recommends *Shr, AYL,* and *MND.*

Watkins, Ronald. **On Producing Shakespeare.** 2d. ed. New York: Blom, 1964.

Watkins, Ronald. **"The Actor's Task in Interpreting Shakespeare."** *Use of English* (London) 9 (Winter 1957): 104–09.

Emphasizes the power of spoken word.

Watkins, Ronald. **"Producing Shakespeare in an Elizabethan Setting."** *College English* 11 (December 1949): 159–60.

Until all the conditions in which Shakespeare worked are accepted "we cannot see the art of the greatest of poetic dramatists in its truest light; . . . to recapture Shakespeare's stagecraft, we must reproduce the essentials of his theater."

Webster, Margaret. **"On Directing Shakespeare."** In *Producing the Play,* edited by John Gassner, pp. 436–43, rev. ed. New York: Holt, Rinehart & Winston, 1953.

Shakespeare's plays give the director room for interpretation of the text and for flexibility in staging.

Weninger, Lloyd F. **"Time Spent on *Julius Caesar.*"** *Carnegie Magazine* 13 (April 1939): 86–90.

Discusses the laborious and exacting work by the staff and the 1600 student hours spent in this production.

Whiting, William E. **"The Bard on the High School Stage."** *English Record* 15 (December 1964): 6–8.

Advocates classroom study, frequent performance, and recurrent practice to build up a student-community audience for an annual Shakespeare play.

Willy, Margaret. **" School Shakespeare."** *Drama: The Quarterly Theatre Review* n.s. 42 (Autumn 1956): 58.

Mentions several all boys' school productions.

Teaching Shakespeare
with Other Authors

Adler, Jacob H. **"Shakespeare and Christopher Fry."** *Educational Theatre Journal* 11 (1959): 85–98.

Delineates some parallels between Fry's comedies and Shakespeare's; shows that the comedies of both playwrights are ambiguous and complex.

Baum, Bernard. **"*Tempest* and *Hairy Ape*: The Literary Incarnation of Mythos."** *Modern Language Quarterly* 14 (1953): 258–73.

Argues that Shakespeare's world is one with a rational principle of order, and may be contrasted with the dynamic world of O'Neill's "naturalistic mythos."

Beyle, Henri [Stendhal]. **Racine and Shakespeare.** Translated by Guy Daniels. Foreword by Andre Maurois. New York: Collier, 1962.

Bhattacherje, M. M. **"Spenser and Shakespeare."** *Visvabharati Quarterly* (West Bengal) 27 (1961): 106–21.

Discusses major similarities and differences.

Browne, Ray B. **"Shakespeare in American Vaudeville and Negro Minstrelsy."** *American Quarterly* 12 (1960): 374–91.

Recalls ways in which Shakespeare permeated American popular entertainment in the nineteenth century.

Christ, Henry I. **"*Macbeth* and the Faust Legend."** *English Journal* 46 (1957): 212–13.

Sees six parallels and notes especially the possible influence of Marlowe.

Chute, Marchette. **"Chaucer and Shakespeare."** *College English* 12 (October 1950): 15–19.

Discusses general similarities between them.

Doyle, Thomas L., and Hoffman, M. D., eds. **Romeo and Juliet and Cyrano de Bergerac.** Noble's Comparative Classics. New York: Noble & Noble, 1959.

Drew, Arnold P. **"Emily Brontë and** *Hamlet.*" *Notes and Queries* 199 (February 1954): 81–82.

Finds a pattern in *Hamlet* IV.i. for a scene in Chapter 12 of *Wuthering Heights.* Cathy's mad speech shows resemblances to Ophelia's.

Duncan, Edward. **"Unsubstantial Father: A Study of the** *Hamlet* **Symbolism in Joyce's** *Ulysses.*" *University of Toronto Quarterly* 19 (1950): 126–40.

Ellis-Fermor, Una. **"Ibsen and Shakespeare as Dramatic Artists."** *Edda A.* (Oslo) 43 Bd. 56 (1956): 364–79.

Estarellas, Juan. **"*Don Quixote* and *Hamlet* as Symbols of Contrasting Cultural and Educational Patterns."** *Topic* 2 (Spring 1962): 15–23.

Frenz, Horst, and Mueller, Martin. **"More Shakespeare and Less Aeschylus in Eugene O'Neill's** *Mourning Becomes Electra.*" *American Literature* 38 (1966): 85–100.

Finds closer similarities between Shakespere and O'Neill than between Aeschylus and O'Neill.

Gates, W. B. **"Bret Harte and Shakespeare."** *South-Central Bulletin* (Winter 1960): 29–33.

Gates, W. B. **"Shakespearean Elements in Irving's** *Sketch Book.*" *American Literature* 30 (1959): 450–58.

Germer, Rudolf. **"Die Bedeutung Shakespeares für T. S. Eliot."** *Shakespeare Jahrbuch* (Weimar) 95 (1959): 112–32.

Discusses Shakespearean elements in Eliot's poems, especially "Prufrock" and "The Waste Land."

Gibian, George. **Tolstoj and Shakespeare.** The Hague: Mouton, 1957.

"Tolstoj enjoyed disliking Shakespeare and disagreeing with other critics." That disagreement "was based in part on Tolstoj's adherence to the literary criteria and tastes of the French eighteenth century neoclassicists and in part on Tolstoj's personal religious and puritanical fanaticism."

Girdler, Lew. **"*Wuthering Heights* and Shakespeare."** *Huntington Library Quarterly* 19 (1956): 385–92.

Finds "striking parallels in theme, characterization, structure, and literary devices, as well as some similarities in situation and in phraseology."

Gleckner, Robert F. **"Eliot's 'The Hollow Men' and Shakespeare's** *Julius Caesar.***"** *Modern Language Notes* 75 (1960): 26–28.

Shows how Caesar is a "pervasive force" in Eliot's poem.

Goldstone, Richard H. **"Experiments with A-V Aids: I. In Teaching Shakespeare."** *College English* 13 (March 1952): 319–22.

Concerns comparison of *Othello* with Verdi's opera.

Grushow, Ira. **"*Brave New World* and *Tempest.***"** *College English* 24 (1962): 42–45.

Finds *Tempest* themes and allusions in Huxley's similarly "open-ended" novel.

Gwynn, Frederick L. **"*Hamlet* and Hardy."** *Shakespeare Quarterly* 4 (1953): 207–08.

Finds the Closet Scene of *Hamlet* to be a partial source of a scene in *The Return of the Native.*

Hernberger, Charles Fredrick, Jr. **"Tragic Perspective in Tudor Biography and Shakespeare."** Ph.D. dissertation, Boston University, 1960. *Dissertation Abstracts* 21 (1960): 895.

Analyzes the historical background of Shakespeare's tragedies in terms of structure and significance. Takes up More's *Richard III,* Roper's *More,* and Cavendish's *Wolsey.*

Heydrick, Benjamin A., and Mag, A. A., eds. *Macbeth* and *The Emperor Jones.* Noble's Comparative Classics. New York: Noble & Noble, 1958.

Hodgart, M. J. C. **"Shakespeare and Finnegan's Wake."** *The Cambridge Journal* 6 (1953): 735–52.

Hugo, Howard E. **"The Madman of the Heath and the Madwoman of Chaillot."** *Chrysalis* 3–4 (1952): 3–11.

Compares *King Lear* with the Giradoux play.

James, D. G. **"Keats and *Lear.***"** *Shakespeare Survey* (London) 13 (1960): 58–68.

Claims that the impact of *King Lear* on Keats can scarcely be exaggerated. Shakespeare and Keats "reached the limits of the imagination's power in their beholdment of sorrow as heightening beauty and of serenity as containing suffering." Both recognized that the end of poetry is to excite "speculations" not give answers.

Jones, William M. **"The Iago of *Brave New World.*"** *Western Humanities Review* 15 (1961): 275–78.

Notes the influence of *Othello* on Aldous Huxley's novel.

Julius Caesar in Shakespeare, Shaw and the Ancients, edited by G. B. Harrison. New York: Harcourt, Brace, 1960.

Provides texts of *Julius Caesar* and Shaw's *Caesar and Cleopatra* plus classical selections.

Kirwan, Katherine; Parker, G.; and Barratta, M. **"A Guide Through *Rosencrantz and Guildenstern Are Dead.*"** *Kentucky English Bulletin* 20 (Winter 1970–71): 35–39.

Knight, G. Wilson. **"Byron and *Hamlet.*"** *Bulletin of the John Rylands Library* 45 (1962): 115–47.

Notes similarities between Byron's life and *Hamlet.*

Knight, G. Wilson. **Shakespeare and Tolstoy.** (English Association Pamphlet, 88). London: Oxford University Press, 1934.

Lennam, T. **"The Happy Hunting Ground."** *University of Toronto Quarterly* 29 (1960): 386–97.

Focuses largely on the Shakespearean elements in the "Scylla and Charybdis" episode of Joyce's *Ulysses.*

Lerner, Laurence. **"Racine and the Elizabethans."** *Essays in Criticism* 12 (1962): 353–69.

Uses *Lear, Macbeth,* and *Othello* for contrast with Racine.

Mendel, Sydney. **"The Revolt against the Father: The Adolescent Hero in *Hamlet* and *The Wild Duck.*"** *Essays in Criticism* 14 (1964): 171–78.

Points out that Gregers and Hamlet are much alike, but while Shakespeare "shares the misanthropic vision" of his "adolescent" hero, Ibsen is less than sympathetic.

Muir, Kenneth. **Last Periods of Shakespeare, Racine, and Ibsen.** Detroit: Wayne State University Press, 1961.

MacNalty, Arthur Salusbury. **"Shakespeare and Sir Thomas More."** In *Essays and Studies 1959,* edited for the English Association by D. M. Stuart, n.s. 12 (1959): 36–57.

More's life and work influenced Shakespeare. The two men were kindred spirits.

Major, John M. *"Comus* and *The Tempest."* Shakespeare Quarterly 10 (1959): 177–83.

"The many resemblances in form, theme, dramatic situation, characterization, atmosphere, and language" indicate "that *The Tempest* provided *Comus* with a good deal more than an occasional verbal echo, or some hints for a character or two—that, in fact, it served as an actual model for Milton's poem."

Peery, William. **"Shakhisbeard at** *Finnegan's Wake."* University of Texas Studies in English 30 (1951): 243–57.

A study of the Shakespearean allusions and quotations in the Joyce work.

Potts, Abbie F. **Shakespeare and the** *Faerie Queene.* Ithaca: Cornell University Press, 1958.

Polak, A. Laurence. *"The Tempest* and *The Magic Flute."* English 9 (1952): 2–7.

Notes resemblances between the two works.

Pujals, Esterban. **"Shakespeare y Lope de Vega."** Revista de Literatura (Madrid) 1 (1952): 25–45.

Rider, Maurice L. **"'In Glorious Titles He Excels'."** English Journal 54 (January 1965): 52–55.

Examines the many authors who owe their titles to Shakespeare.

Romeo and Juliet. West Side Story. New York: Dell, 1965.

Schultheiss, Thomas. **"Lord Hamlet and Lord Jim."** Polish Review 11 no. 4 (1966): 101–33.

Discusses the influence of *Hamlet* on composition, meaning, and structure of Conrad's story.

Schutte, William M. **Joyce and Shakespeare: A Study in the Meaning of** *Ulysses.* New Haven: Yale University Press, 1957.

Sherbo, Arthur. **"Conrad's** *Victory* and *Hamlet."* Notes and Queries 198 (November 1953): 492–93.

Notes verbal echoes of *Hamlet* in the Conrad novel.

Spivack, Charlotte. *"Macbeth* and **Dante's** *Inferno."* North Dakota Quarterly 28 (1960): 50–52.

Reflecting its "medieval Christian heritage," *Macbeth* contains "the dual

Dantesque theme of the equivocal nature of evil and its double-dealing consequence."

Steene, Birgitta. **"Shakespearean Elements in the Historical Plays of Strindberg."** *Comparative Literature* 11 (1959): 209–20.

Shakespeare's influence on Strindberg as evidenced in *Folkungasagan, Gustav Vasa,* and *Erik IV.*

Stroud, T. A. *"Hamlet* **and** *The Seagull."* *Shakespeare Quarterly* 9 (1958): 746–47.

Examines extent of Chekhov's indebtedness—in mood, characters, and plot, with speculations about the dramatic genre intended by Chekhov in relation to *Hamlet.*

Thaler, Alwin. **"Shakespeare and Milton Once More."** In *SAMLA Studies in Milton: (Essays in John Milton and His Works),* edited by J. Max Patrick. Gainesville: University of Florida Press, 1953, pp. 80–99.

Adds new evidence of Milton's close knowledge of Shakespeare and dependence on him for imagery and phrase.

Thaler, Alwin. **Shakespeare and Sir Philip Sidney. The Influence of** *The Defense of Poesy.* Cambridge: Harvard University Press, 1947.

Torrens, James. **"Eliot's Poetry and the Incubus of Shakespeare."** *Thought* 52 (1977): 407–21.

Trowbridge, Clinton W. **"Hamlet and Holden."** *English Journal* 57 (January 1968): 26–29.

Shows how A. C. Bradley's analysis of Hamlet's character may be applied to Holden Caulfield in *The Catcher in the Rye.*

Uhler, John E. **"Goethe and Shakespeare."** In his *Goethe After Two Centuries,* pp. 97–102.

Goethe's life and work parallels Shakespeare's.

Vandiver, Edward P., Jr. *"The Return of the Native* **and Shakespeare."** *Furman Studies* 47 (November 1964): 11–15.

Evidence of Shakespeare's influence on Hardy.

Vandiver, Edward P., Jr. **"Cooper's** *The Prairie* **and Shakespeare."** *PMLA* 69 (1954): 1302–04.

The pedantic language of Dr. Battius patterned after that of Holofernes.

Vandiver, Edward P., Jr. **"Thackeray and Shakespeare."** *Furman Studies* 34 (1951): 30–45.

Vogelback, A. L. **"Shakespeare and Melville's** *Benito Cereno.*" *Modern Language Notes* 67 (1952): 113–16.

Compares Melville's Babo with Iago.

Walker, Roy. **"Shakespeare v. Shaw."** *The Shavian* (London) (February 1959): 7–9.

A comparison of the moral structures of Shaw's *Caesar and Cleopatra* and Shakespeare's *Antony and Cleopatra.*

Winner, T. G. **"Chekhov's** *Seagull* **and Shakespeare's** *Hamlet:* **A Study of a Dramatic Device."** *American Slavic Review* 15 (1956): 103–11.

Yaggy, Elinor. **"Shakespeare and Melville's** *Pierre.*" *Boston Public Library Quarterly* 6 (1954): 43–51.

Traces Shakespearean influences in *Pierre.*

Part Two

Title Abbreviations

Ado: *Much Ado About Nothing*	**MM:** *Measure for Measure*
Ant: *Antony and Cleopatra*	**MND:** *Midsummer Night's Dream*
AWW: *All's Well That Ends Well*	**MV:** *Merchant of Venice*
AYL: *As You Like It*	**Othello:** *Othello*
Cor: *Coriolanus*	**Per:** *Pericles*
Cym: *Cymbeline*	**R2:** *Richard II*
Err: *Comedy of Errors*	**R3:** *Richard III*
Hamlet: *Hamlet*	**Rom:** *Romeo and Juliet*
1H4: *1 Henry IV*	**Shr:** *Taming of the Shrew*
2H4: *2 Henry IV*	**Temp:** *The Tempest*
H5: *Henry V*	**TGV:** *Two Gentlemen of Verona*
1-3H6: *1-3 Henry VI*	**Tim:** *Timon of Athens*
H8: *Henry VIII*	**Tit:** *Titus Andronicus*
JC: *Julius Caesar*	**TN:** *Twelfth Night*
John: *King John*	**TNK:** *Two Noble Kinsmen*
LLL: *Love's Labor's Lost*	**Tro:** *Troilus and Cressida*
Lear: *King Lear*	**Wiv:** *Merry Wives of Windsor*
Macbeth: *Macbeth*	**WT:** *Winter's Tale*

Shakespeare in Feature Films and on Television

General

Agate, James E. **"Shakespeare and the Masses."** In his *Around Cinemas.* 2d series, pp. 277–80. London: Home & Van Thal, 1948.

"Reasonable understanding of Shakespeare and a comprehensive understanding of the masses" are needed for anyone about to film Shakespeare.

Aicken, Frederick. **"Shakespeare on the Screen."** *Screen Education* (London) no. 21 (September–October 1963): 33–36.

Because a full text does not blend with the naturalism of the setting and a mobile camera, it is impossible to screen Shakespeare faithfully, and at the same time do justice to the visual medium.

Albert, R. N. **"Annotated Guide to Audio-Visual Materials for Teaching Shakespeare."** *English Journal* 54 (November 1965): 704–15.

Alpert, Hollis. **"Film and Theater."** In his *The Dreams and Dreamers,* pp. 233–51. New York: Macmillan, 1962.

General observations about Shakespeare on film and brief comments on Mankiewicz's *JC.* Suggests that the screen could be a better medium for presenting Shakespeare than the stage, but observes that newer and better film techniques are needed.

Alpert, Hollis. **"Movies are Better than the Stage."** *Saturday Review* 23 July 1955, pp. 5–6, 31.

Film-versions contribute more to the popular appreciation of Shakespeare than stage productions.

Anderegg, M. A. **"Shakespeare on Film in the Classroom."** *Literature/Film Quarterly* 4 (Spring 1976): 165–75.

Explores the gains and losses of a Shakespeare-on-Film course.

Anstey, Edgar. **"Scenes from Shakespeare."** *Spectator,* 13 July 1945, p. 35.

Describes how British Film Council stages films and short excerpts from

Shakespeare for screening overseas and for classroom study.

Atkinson, E. J. Rupert. **Key to the Adaptations of the Best of Shakespeare's Plays to the Stage-Cinema-Interaction for the Production of Drama.** New York: The Knickerbocker Press, 1920.

Ball, Robert H. **"On Shakespeare Filmography."** *Literature/Film Quarterly* 1 (Fall 1973): 299–306.

Comments on recent studies and updates his work on silent film.

Ball, Robert H. **Shakespeare on Silent Film.** New York: Theatre Arts Books, 1968.

The most thorough treatment of this subject. Includes stills, a useful bibliography, a series of indices, and a glossary of terms.

Ball, Robert H. **"Pioneers and All: The Beginnings of Shakespeare Film."** *Theatre Survey* 1 (1960): 18–42.

Ball, Robert H. **"Shakespeare in One Reel."** *Quarterly of Film, Radio, and Television* 8 (Winter 1953): 139–49.

Surveys the early period of Shakespeare films.

Ball, Robert H. **"If We Shadows Have Offended."** *Pacific Spectator* 1 (1947): 97–104.

Discusses film productions of Shakespeare's plays.

Barasch, Frances K. **"S[hakespeare] F[ilm] at MLA, Chicago, 1977."** *Shakespeare on Film Newsletter* 2 (April 1978): 8.

Reports on discussion of problems in the criticism and teaching of Shakespeare on film.

Barbetti, Emilio. **"Shakespeare Teatro e Cinema."** *Teatro Scenario* (Milan), 1 May 1952, pp. 42–43.

Barnes, T. R. **"Random Thoughts on Shakespeare in the Cinema."** *Use of English* (London) 8 (Autumn 1956): 7–11.

Advises that it is better to see Shakespeare on film than not at all, even though films present distorted view of the play.

Barnet, Sylvan. **"The Film Versions of Shakespeare."** In his *A Short Guide to Shakespeare,* pp. 188–200. New York: Harcourt Brace Jovanovich, 1974.

A brief survey of films.

Bazin, André, and Bitsch, Charles. **"Entretien avec Orson Welles."** Cahiers du Cinema (Paris) no. 84 (June 1958): 1–13.

Interview touches on Shakespeare passim.

Bourgeois, J. **"La sujet et l'expression au cinéma à propos d'***Hamlet*** et de** *Macbeth.*" *La Revue du Cinema* (Paris) 3 (October 1948): 57–62.

Discusses relationship between theater and cinema. "Whereas Olivier simply tried and succeeded in renewing a theatrical staging by the cinema, Welles tried to rethink each dramatic method employed by Shakespeare in function of a new mode of expression."

Brace, Keith. **"76 Shakespeare Films . . . But So Few at 'Oscar' Level."** *Birmingham Post Shakespeare Quatercentenary Supplement,* 17 April 1964, p. xxi.

Reviews a half-century of ways of "re-creating poetic imagery on the screen," and concludes that while "filmed Shakespeare will always remain something different from . . . Shakespeare staged or read . . . it *has* extended the range of interpretation."

Brace, Keith. **"Spectacular 'Realism' a Heresy."** *Birmingham Post Shakespeare Quatercentenary Supplement,* 17 April 1964, p. xx.

Argues that "the pictorial, realistic, spectacular treatment of Shakespeare is a heresy if regarded as superior to the straight-forward stage presentation of text and action."

Braudy, Leo. **"Acting: Stage vs. Screen."** In his *The World in a Frame,* pp. 191–201. New York: Anchor, 1977.

Includes a comment on the approaches of Olivier and Welles.

Brinson, Peter. **"The Real Interpreter."** *Films and Filming* (London) 1 (April 1955): 4–5.

Browning, Wendy, and Pitcher, Jane, eds. **Audio-Visual Materials on Drama 1978.** 2d ed. London: British Universities Film Council, 1978.

A useful compilation that excludes Shakespeare films.

Camp, Gerald. **"Shakespeare on Film."** *Journal of Aesthetic Education* 3 (January 1969): 107–20.

Discusses the difficulties of adapting Shakespeare to the screen, focusing on the necessity to deal with Shakespeare's language. Some filmmakers [e.g., Castellani, Mankiewicz] have attempted "to create a new, symbolic world." While Olivier's *R3* acknowledges its own artificiality, only *H5* "deals directly with the relationship between action on a stage and the same action as reflected in the imagination of the playgoer."

Camp, Gerald. **"Shakespeare Live."** *Media and Methods* 5 (October 1968): 42–45.

Sees value in films because they demonstrate for students that Shakespeare's plays are "alive" and they present an interpretation of the play.

Chiarini, Luigi. **"Spettacolo e Film."** *Belfagor* (Florence) 7 (1952): 129–43.

Clayton, Thomas. **"Aristotle on the Shakespearean Film: or, Dam Thee, William, Thou Art Translated."** *Literature/Film Quarterly* 2 (Spring 1974): 183–89.

Identifies four kinds of film and play "texts."

Condee, Ralph W. **"Goneril Without a Beard."** *Shakespeare on Film Newsletter* 1 (December 1976): 1, 5, 7.

Describes Pennsylvania State University's Shakespeare film program.

Condee, Ralph W. **A Handbook of Shakespearean Films and Tapes for Instructional Use at the Pennsylvania State University.** University Park: Pennsylvania State University, 1976.

A forty-nine page guide to eight films, including observations on the use of films in undergraduate courses and in adult education.

Crowther, Bosley. **"Stage *Hamlet* with Richard Burton."** New York Times, 24 September 1964, p. 46.

Observes that the production has all the mechanical transmission problems of a filmed play and few of the virtues of the stage production.

D., M. B. **"Films: A Dialogue, Almost True to Life, between a Film-critic and the Editor."** *Shakespeare Quarterly* (London) 1 (Summer 1947): 116–18.

General comments and discussion of *Henry V.*

Davies, Brenda. **Review.** *Monthly Film Bulletin* 41 (September 1974): 210.

On reissue of Taylor's 1929 *Taming of the Shrew* for modern screen, observes how "much of the spirit of the original has been captured, and the performances of the two stars [Mary Pickford and Douglas Fairbanks] do not suffer by comparison with later versions."

Dehn, Paul **"The Filming of Shakespeare."** In *Talking of Shakespeare,* edited by John Garrett, pp. 49–72. London: Hodder & Stoughton, 1954. Reprinted in Dehn's *For Love of Money,* pp. 50–77. New York: Vanguard Press, 1957. London: Max Reinhardt, 1956.

Argues that students should see a live performance of Shakespeare or a film version and then write about it critically. Olivier's *H5* and *Hamlet,* Mankiewicz's *JC,* and other films are discussed.

Duey, Helen. **"Shakespeare in the Films."** *Woman's Home Companion* 43 (June 1916): 8.

In an interview Sir H. Beerbohm Tree contends that "Shakespeare has proved a good film scenario writer," and asks "who can say that the screen Shakespeare may not only renew one's acquaintance with the printed words, but give to them a deeper, grander meaning?"

Duffy, R. **"Gade, Olivier, Richardson: Visual Strategy in *Hamlet* Adaptation."** *Literature/Film Quarterly* 4 (Spring 1976): 141–52.

Examines visual techniques to illustrate the range of strategies used to transpose the play to film.

Durgnat, Raymond. **A Mirror for England: British Movies from Austerity to Affluence.** London: Faber & Faber, 1970.

Discusses (pp. 109–11) Olivier's films: *Hamlet* and *R3* are both acted and spoken but other effects do not reflect the play; *H5* "remains interesting as a series of visual and verbal set pieces."

Dworkin, Martin S. **"'Stay Illusion!' Having Words About Shakespeare on Screen."** *Wascana Review* 11 (1976): 83–93; and *Journal of Aesthetic Education* 11 (January 1977): 51–61.

Contends that because cinema tends to emphasize plot and subordinate poetry, to perform Shakespeare primarily for the story is "to denigrate the whole," especially if done to pursue "some notion of topicality of fashionable 'relevance'." Thus Richardson's *Hamlet* and Zeffirelli's *Rom* warp meaning in their effort to be topical.

Eckert, Charles W., ed. **Focus on Shakespearean Films.** Englewood Cliffs, N.J.. Prentice-Hall, 1972.

Useful anthology and filmography that provides a detailed listing of Shakespeare films, arranged play by play.

"Family Movie Guide: Should Children See the Tragedies of William Shakespeare?" *Parents Magazine and Better Family Living* 23 (September 1948): 13.

Felheim, Marvin. **"Criticism and the Films of Shakespeare's Plays."** *Comparative Drama* 9 (Summer 1975): 147–55.

Discusses film theory and recent criticism; emphasizes that critics tend more often to be Shakespeareans rather than film critics.

Foreman, Joel. **"Reel Shakespeare."** *Shakespeare Newsletter* 27 (May 1977): 21.

Disagrees with Roemer that films make Shakespeare "unreal." See also, in this section, Roemer.

Forrest, Mark. **"Shakespeare on the Screen."** *The Saturday Review* (London), 19 October 1935, p. 352.

Observes that on screen, Shakespeare's speeches "are going to be cut to ribbons to make room for cinematic action, or there is going to be little or no cinematic action."

Fuegi, John. **"Exploration in No Man's Land: Shakespeare's Poetry as Theatrical Film."** *Shakespeare Quarterly* 23 (1972): 37–49.

Discusses the gulf between film criticism and Shakespearean criticism. Filmmakers, concerned with practical problems of adapting plays, should go beyond realism as Olivier did in *Henry V.*

Fukuhara, Rintaro. **Ars Longa.** Tokyo: Tarumizu Shobo, 1956.

Gaertner, Johannes A. **"On Costuming in Shakespeare Films."** *Shakespeare on Film Newsletter* 2 (April 1978): 5.

Argues that historical dress and setting are best for film.

Giannetti, Louis D. **"Drama."** In his *Understanding Movies.* 2d ed., pp. 266–310. Englewood Cliffs, N.J.: Prentice-Hall, 1976.

Discusses the similarities and differences between film and theater, and includes illustrations from films by Polanski (*Macbeth*), Zeffirelli (*Rom*), Olivier (*R3*), Cukor (*Rom*), and Reinhardt (*MND*).

Giesler, Rodney. **"Shakespeare and the Screen."** *Films and Filming* (London) 2 (July 1956): 7.

Gowda, H. H. Anniah. **"Shakespeare on the Screen."** *Literary Criterion* (Bombay) 2 (1953).

Griffin, Alice. **"Shakespeare Through the Camera's Eye: III."** *Shakespeare Quarterly* 7 (1956): 235–40.

Considers effectiveness of Welles's *Othello,* Castellani's *Rom,* and Olivier's *R3* in interpreting Shakespeare on film. Only Olivier's film is considered "an artistic success."

Griffin, Alice. **"Shakespeare Through the Camera's Eye—*Julius Caesar* in Motion Pictures; *Hamlet* and *Othello* on Television."** *Shakespeare Quarterly* 4 (1953): 331–36.

These productions utilize the advantages of the camera in telling a story and revealing character in a visual medium. *Julius Caesar* is "the best Shakespeare film Hollywood has made."

Gross, Sheryl W. **"Olivier's Shakespearean Films: A Selected Bibliography, Part II."** *Shakespeare on Film Newsletter* 2 (December 1977): 1–3.

Includes material on Olivier's *Hamlet, R3,* and recordings.

Gross, Sheryl W. **"Olivier's Shakespearean Films: A Selected Bibliography, Part I."** *Shakespeare on Film Newsletter* 1 (April 1977): 5–6.

Lists biographical studies, interviews, and general studies. Olivier's *Henry V* is highlighted.

Haas, Willy. **"Shakespeare und Shakespeare-Verfilmung."** *Shakespeare Jahrbuch* (Heidelberg) 91 (1955): 278–86.

Argues that film is not the proper medium for the interpretation of Shakespeare; too much of his language is sacrificed.

Halio, Jay L. **"Three Filmed *Hamlets.*"** *Literature/Film Quarterly* 1 (Fall 1973): 316–20.

Compares versions of *Hamlet* by Olivier, Burton, and Chamberlain to "get a clearer notion . . . of how Shakespeare translates into the medium of film."

Hamisch, S. **"Der Film und Shakespeare zum Problem der modernen Dramenverfilmung."** *Deutschunterricht* (Berlin) 17 (1964): 681–84.

Hart, Henry. **"Laurence Olivier."** *Films in Review* 18 (December 1967): 593–617.

Surveys Olivier's film career and mentions his role in Shakespeare films.

Hayman, Ronald. **"Shakespeare on the Screen."** *Times Literary Supplement* (London), 26 September 1968, pp. 1081–82.

Examines various adaptations of Shakespeare's plays into film.

Hellberg, Martin. **"Warum heute Shakespeare?"** In his *Bühne und Film; Reden Aufsätze aus der Praxis.* Berlin: Henschel, 1955.

Herring, Robert. **"Shakespeare on the Screen."** *Life and Letters Today* 16 no. 7 (1937): 125–30.

Hogdon, Barbara. **"Shakespeare on Film: Taking Another Look."** *Shakespeare Newsletter* 26 (May 1976): 26.

Compare Shakespeare films to other films, not to stage productions.

Homan, Sidney. **"Criticism for the Filmed Shakespeare."** *Literature/Film Quarterly* 5 (Fall 1977): 282–90.

A provocative assessment of the "state of the art" that describes five categories of films and several problems common to all Shakespearean film criticism.

Homan, Sidney. **"A Cinema for Shakespeare."** *Literature/Film Quarterly* 4 (Spring 1976): 176–86.

Discusses classroom experience in teaching Shakespearean films.

Houseman, John. **Run-Through: A Memoir.** New York: Simon & Schuster, 1972.

Recounts Welles's involvement with producing Shakespeare at the Mercury Theater (pp. 296–325) and an all-black production of *Macbeth* (pp. 185–204).

Hurtgen, Charles. **"The Operatic Character of Background Music in Film Adaptations of Shakespeare."** *Shakespeare Quarterly* 20 (1969): 53–64.

Ingebar, Nahman, ed. **Shakespeare ba-Kolno'ah [Shakespeare on Film].** Tel Aviv, 1967.

Jackson, Peter. **"Shakespeare: Stage v. Screen."** *Plays and Players* (London) 6 (December 1958): 8–9.

"Shakespeare is always good cinema, but only occasionally is cinema good Shakespeare."

Johnson, Ian. **"Merely players—400 Years of Shakespeare."** *Films and Filming* (London) 11 (April 1964): 41–48. Reprinted in *Focus on Shakespearean Films,* edited by Charles W. Eckert, pp. 7–26. Englewood Cliffs, N.J.: Prentice-Hall, 1972.

An important survey of film adaptations of Shakespeare.

Jordon, William E., and Jordon, Mildred R. **"Post-production Notes on the Film [*Shakespeare's Theater: The Globe Playhouse*]."** *Film Quarterly* 8 (Winter 1953): 350–55.

Reviews the criteria used in planning and producing the film on the principle "that films with a specific purpose aimed at a particular audience are made only through the use of a carefully prepared script and intelligent preplanning as blueprints for production."

Jorgens, Jack J. **Shakespeare on Film.** Bloomington: Indiana University Press, 1977.

An important detailed analysis of sixteen major films listed separately. Reviewed by K. Rothwell, *Literature/Film Quarterly* 5 (Fall 1977): 365–67; by Sidney Homan, *Shakespeare on Film Newsletter* 2 (December 1977): 7; and by A. McLean, *Shakespeare Quarterly* 29 (Spring 1978): 315–20.

Jorgens, Jack J. **"Shakespeare at the Movies."** *Washingtonian* 11 (May 1976): 272–77.

Outlines the problems and possibilities of filming Shakespeare.

Jorgens, Jack J. **"A Course in Shakespeare on Film."** *Shakespeare Newsletter* 23 (November 1973): 43.

Describes team teaching approach used at University of Massachusetts-Amherst.

Jorgens, Jack J., and Egloff, Christina. **Shakespeare on Stage and Screen: A Bibliography of Criticism.** Bloomington: Indiana University Press, 1979.

Journal of the Society of Film and Television Arts 37 (Autumn 1969).

Special issue edited by Roger Manvell on Shakespearean film.

"Julius Caesar." *Senior Scholastic,* 7 April 1947, p. 20.

Provides stills from the British Information Service's film with Felix Aylmer (Brutus) and Leo Genn (Antony).

Kael, Pauline. **"Is There a Cure for Film Criticism? or: Some Unhappy Thoughts on Sigfried Krackauer's *Nature of Film: The Redemption of Physical Reality.*"** *Sight and Sound* 31 (Spring 1962): 56–64.

Contains comments on Reinhardt's *MND*, Olivier's *H5, Hamlet,* and *R3,* and Castellani's *Rom.*

Kelly, F. M. **Shakespearean Costume for Stage and Screen.** Boston: W. H. Baker, 1938. London: A. and C. Black, 1970.

A classic short guide to period costumes with illustrations.

Kermode, Frank. **"Shakespeare in the Movies."** *New York Review of Books,* 4 May 1972, pp. 18–21. Reprinted in *Film Theory and Criticism,* edited by Gerald Mast and Marshall Cohen, pp. 322–32. New York: Oxford University Press, 1974.

Charleton Heston's *Ant* is "a work of no imagination," Polanski's *Macbeth* "gets better as it goes along," and Brook's *Lear,* considering the problems faced, is "a great film."

Kitchin, Laurence. **"Shakespeare on the Screen."** *Shakespeare Survey* (Cambridge) 18 (1965): 70–74.

Surveys films made from the silent days through 1964.

[Kliman, Bernice]. **"S[hakespeare]/F[ilm] in the Classrooms. A Preliminary Report."** *Shakespeare on Film Newsletter* 2 (April 1978): 4–5, 7.

Partial results of questionnaire on the teaching of Shakespeare with film.

Kozintsev, Grigori. **"*Hamlet* and *King Lear*: Stage and Film."** In *Shakespeare 1971,* edited by Clifford Leech and J. M. R. Margeson, pp. 190–99. Toronto: University of Toronto Press, 1972.

Kozintsev comments on his films.

Lalou, Rene. **"Shakespeare, precurseur du cinéma."** *L'Age Nouveau* (Paris) 109 (April–June 1960): 70–71.

Notes how the 'cinematographic' quality of Shakespeare's plays is illustrated by recent film versions.

Lalou, Rene. **"Shakespeare et le Cinéma."** *Etudes Anglaises* (Paris) 5 (1952): 309–18.

Surveys Shakespeare films and the criticism of major productions.

Lemaitre, Henri. **"Shakespeare, Le Cinéma Imaginaire et le Pre-cinéma."** *Etudes Cinematographiques* 6–7 (1960): 383–96. English translation in *Focus on Shakespearean Films,* edited by Charles W. Eckert, pp. 27–36. Englewood Cliffs, N.J.: Prentice-Hall, 1972.

Concludes by asking "why not see Shakespeare and the lessons he can teach us as the unrealized designs of an imaginary cinema capable, at the least, of impregnating today's works of art?"

Levine, Gail. **"Scenes from Shakespeare—The Histories and Tragedies: A Filmography, II."** *Shakespeare on Film Newsletter* 3 (December 1978): 1, 2, 4, 7.

Lists thirty-one films, distributors, and rental fees.

Levine, Gail. **"Scenes from Shakespeare—The Histories and Tragedies: A Filmography, I."** *Shakespeare on Film Newsletter* 2 (April 1978): 1–2, 4.

Lists thirteen educational films with rental sources.

Levine, Gail. **"Scenes from Shakespeare—The Romances and Comedies: A Filmography."** *Shakespeare on Film Newsletter* 1 (April 1977): 1, 2–3.

A guide to rental sources.

Levine, Gail. **"Shakespeare on Film—for Under $50."** *Shakespeare on Film Newsletter* 1 (December 1976): 1, 2.

Lists twenty-nine available feature films based on Shakespeare's plays.

Lillich, Meredith. **"Shakespeare on the Screen."** *Films in Review* 7 (June-July 1956): 247–60.

Surveys sixty-six films from 1905–1956. See also, in this section, Sewell.

Lipkov, A. I. **"The Joining of the Times: On the Filming of Shakespeare's Works in the World of Film Art."** Dissertation, Moscow Institute for Art History, 1972.

Lippman, Max, ed. **Shakespeare im Film.** Wiesbaden: Saaten-Verlag, 1964.

The most complete filmography available (with some errors in silents entries).

MacGowan, Kenneth. **"Imitating Shakespeare's Technique."** In his *Behind the Screen: The History and Techniques of the Motion Picture,* pp. 415–16. New York: Delacorte Press, 1965.

Moviemakers around 1915 seem to borrow Shakespeare's staging techniques whereby one scene flows into the next with small actions between a character's appearances.

MacGowan, Kenneth. **"The Film Director's Contribution to the Screen."** *English Journal* 40 (March 1951): 127–34.

Informative description of the function and importance of the director with reference to Welles and Olivier.

McLean, Andrew. **"Writing Papers for a Shakespeare Film Course."** *Shakespeare on Film Newsletter* 1 (December 1976): 8.

Lists twenty-one suggestions for student papers.

McLean, Andrew. **"Teaching Shakespeare on Film: A Checklist."** *Teaching Shakespeare: Ideas for the Classroom* 1 (Fall 1976): 6–8.

Annotates forty-nine items.

Majdalany, Fred. *"Joe Macbeth."* *Time & Tide,* 29 October 1955, pp. 1402–03.

Judges Ken Hughes's attempt at creating a Chicago atmosphere and character to be irrelevantly long.

Manchel, Frank. **"Adaptation of the Stage Play."** In his *Film Study: A Resource Guide,* pp. 161–68. Rutherford, N.J.: Fairleigh Dickinson University Press, 1973.

Describes six popular approaches to film appreciation: a representative genre, stereotyping, thematic approach, comparative media, a representative period, and the history of film. A useful guide for the teacher, which also gives appropriate films, books, and articles on Shakespeare.

Manvell, Roger. **Shakespeare and the Film.** New York: Praeger, 1971.

A general critical survey of Shakespearean films with a bibliography and filmography.

Manvell, Roger. **"Shakespeare on the Screen."** *Humanist* 85 (May 1970): 134–36.

Observes how "the techniques of film and television must . . . be modified in favour of the clear reception and understanding of the dramatic verse, and visual spectacle introduced only when it forms an integral part of the significance of the actions." The screen can become an extension of the theatre and introduce Shakespeare's plays to an international audience who may be unable to view good theatrical productions.

Manvell, Roger. **"Shakespeare on the Screen: An Anthology of Film and Television."** *Journal of the Society of Film and Television Arts* 37 (Autumn 1969): 2–6.

Brief comments on various films.

Manvell, Roger. **"Shakespeare as a Scriptwriter: Suitability of Shakespeare's Plays for Film or Television."** *World Review* (Lichtenstein) (May 1952): 56–59.

"Shakespeare . . . would probably have understood the needs of the modern filmmaker and television producer . . . because the needs of his theatre and of his audience were so close to those of our own time." Shakespeare, like today's film producer, "knew the necessity of balancing the budget between art and enterprise," wrote popular plays based on popular stories for the public, and moved his characters freely in space and time.

Marder, Louis. **"Unanswered Questions on Filmed Versions of Shakespeare."** *Shakespeare Newsletter* 26 (1976): 26.

Long list of questions on the validity of filmed Shakespeare as a pedagogical tool.

Mast, Gerald, and Cohen, Marshall, eds. **"Shakespeare and Film."** In their *Film Theory and Criticism,* pp. 316–51. New York: Oxford University Press, 1974.

Reprints articles by Reeves, Kermode, Agee, Bazin, and Blumenthal.

Millard, Barbara C. **"Shakespeare on Film: Towards an Audience Per-**

ceived and Perceiving." *Literature/Film Quarterly* 5 (Fall 1977): 352–57.

Considers Shakespeare films as they are perceived by an audience whose conventional responses come from film and television, rather than the theatre.

Milne, W. S. "Shakespeare: Script Writer." *Canadian Forum* (Toronto) 19 (November 1939): 252.

Asserts that Shakespeare, a natural scenario writer, still awaits the right film treatment.

Morris, Peter. Shakespeare on Film. An Index. Ottawa: Canadian Film Institute, 1964; rev. ed. 1972. Reprinted in *Films in Review* 24 (March 1973): 132–63.

A discursive filmography, 1929–1971, with passages from reviews of major films.

Mullin, Michael. "Guest Editor's Introduction." *Literature/Film Quarterly* 5 (Fall 1977): 280–81.

Asks questions about the use and study of Shakespearean films to introduce this special Shakespeare on Film issue.

Mullin, Michael. "Shakespeare on Film in the Classroom." *Illinois English Bulletin* 63 (October 1975): 16–25.

Offers brief comments on thirteen major Shakespearean films and suggests that students view Shakespeare films to familiarize themselves with Shakespeare.

Mullin, Michael. "*Macbeth* on Film." *Literature/Film Quarterly* 1 (Fall 1973): 332–42.

Discusses versions by Welles, Kurosawa, Schaefer, and Polanski that "offer coherent interpretations of the play."

"Music in Films: A Symposium of Composers." *Films* 1 (Winter 1940): 5–24.

Includes Shostakovich, who wrote scores for Kozintsev films.

Nicoll, Allardyce. "Shakespeare and the Cinema." In his *Film and Theatre,* pp. 1–37. New York: Crowell, 1936.

An important theater historian's provocative observations on the relation of film and theatre. (The discussion of Reinhardt's *Midsummer Night's Dream,* pp. 175–81, is reprinted in *Focus on Shakespearean Films,* edited by Charles W. Eckert, pp. 43–47. Englewood Cliffs,

N.J.: Prentice-Hall, 1972.) Argues that while film and theater have many things in common, they are distinct and separate means of expression. Furthermore, filmmaking has developed, changed, and improved just as Shakespeare did as a writer.

Ohad, Michael. **"*Macbeth* on the Screen."** *ha-Aretz* (Tel Aviv), 28 July 1972, pp. 18–21.

Surveys various film versions.

Phillips, James E. **"By William Shakespeare—with Additional Dialogue."** *Hollywood Quarterly* 5 (Spring 1951): 224–36.

Objects to film directors' lack of confidence in Shakespeare's text, expecially Welles's *Macbeth* (pp. 229–36) and Olivier's *Hamlet* (pp. 225–29). Concludes from an analysis of changes and interpretations in film versions that cutting and rearranging is often necessary but that Shakespeare's sense of drama is hard to improve on.

Pierce, Margery M. **"*Julius Caesar* and the Movies."** *English Journal* 26 (April 1937): 322–24.

Suggests that students relate parts of the play to the movies by comparing the plots.

Poague, Leland A. **"*As You Like It* and *It Happened One Night:* The Generic Pattern of Comedy."** *Literature/Film Quarterly* 5 (Fall 1977): 346–50.

Analyzes structural analogies that link the play and Frank Capra's film.

Raynor, Henry. **"Shakespeare Filmed."** *Sight and Sound* (London) 22 (July–September 1952): 10–15.

Evaluates adaptations of Shakespeare to the screen, dealing especially with Olivier's *H5* and *Hamlet* and Welles's *Macbeth.*

Redi, Riccardo. **"Contributo a una bibliografia."** *Bianco e Nero* (Rome) 18 (January 1957): 80–91.

An annotated entry for Olivier's *H5, Hamlet,* Welles's *Macbeth, Othello,* and selected other films.

Redi, Riccardo, and Chiti, Roberto. **"Shakespeare e il Cinema: Filmografia."** *Bianco e Nero* (Rome) 18 (January 1957): 70–91.

A filmography of silent and sound films.

Reeves, Geoffrey. **"Finding Shakespeare on Film: From an Interview with Peter Brook."** *Tulane Drama Review* 11 (Fall 1966): 117–21. Reprinted in *Focus on Shakespearean Films,* edited by Charles W. Eckert, pp. 37–41. Englewood Cliffs, N.J.: Prentice-Hall, 1972; and in *Film Theory and Criticism,* edited by Gerald Mast and Marshall Cohen, pp. 316–21. New York: Oxford University Press, 1974.

Singles out Kozintsev's *Hamlet* and Kurosawa's *Throne of Blood* for special attention.

Reeves, Geoffrey. **"Shakespeare on Three Screens."** *Sight and Sound* (London) 34 (Spring 1965): 66–70.

Interview with Peter Brook, who comments on Shakespeare on film.

Richmond, Hugh M. **"The Synergistic Use of Shakespearean Film and Videotape."** *Literature/Film Quarterly* 5 (Fall 1977): 362–64.

Reports on course that utilizes various modes of instruction—lectures, discussion groups, films, videotapes, student acting—culminating in residential courses at Ashland's Shakespeare Festival.

Richter, Jean-Jose. **"L'Affaire Cesar."** *Cahiers du Cinema* (Paris) no. 29 (December 1953): 45–49.

Comments on versions by Mankiewicz and Bradley.

Ritzau, Tue. **"Film forfattaren Shakespeare [Shakespeare as an author for the cinema]."** *Chaplin* (Stockholm) 1 (4 October 1959): 80–85.

Roemer, Michael. **"Shakespeare on Film: A Filmmaker's View."** *Shakespeare Newsletter* 26 (May 1976): 26.

Shakespearean films are "unreal" because they shift focus from the aural to the visual while theatrical performance is more inclusive and "real." See also, in this section, Foreman.

Sargeant, Seymour H. **"*Julius Caesar* and the Historical Film."** *English Journal* 61 (February 1972): 230–33, 245.

Compares Shakespearean dramatic techniques with those of the historical film.

Schwarz, Daniel. **"The Present and Future of Shakespeare."** *The New York Times Magazine,* 12 May 1946, pp. 22–23, 58.

An interview with Laurence Olivier, giving some of his views on the filming of Shakespeare.

Schwindt, John. **"English 323: Testing a Theory About Filmed Shakespeare."** *Shakespeare on Film Newsletter* 1 (April 1977): 2, 7.

Briefly describes course based on a theory that Shakespearean drama is "suited for film adaptation" and that the best adaptations are "least dependent on Shakespeare."

"Screening Shakespeare at the Cost of Millions." *Literary Digest,* 18 April 1936, p. 23.

Relates that Hollywood spent $3 million filming Reinhardt's *MND* and Cukor's *Rom.*

Sewell, John B. **"Shakespeare on the Screen."** *Films in Review* 20 (August-September 1969): 419–26.

Updates and expands Lillich article, giving brief description of films. See also, in this section, Lillich.

Shafer, Ronald G. **"Film and the Interdisciplinary Shakespeare Course."** *Shakespeare on Film Newsletter* 2 (December 1977): 6.

Reports on Shakespeare/History course designed to put Shakespearean plays in their historical context.

Shakespeare Newsletter 23 (November 1973).

A special Shakespeare on Film issue.

"Shakespeare on Film in Dayton." *Shakespeare on Film Newsletter* 3 (December 1978): 8.

Reports on two-day conference focusing on various film versions of *Macbeth.*

"Shakespeare on the Screen." *World Theatre* 13 (Summer 1964): 132–34.

Provides brief filmography.

Shattuck, Charles H. **"Shakespeare on Film: The Silent Era; The Advent of the Sound Film; Shakespeare Films Since World War II."** In *The Riverside Shakespeare,* edited by G. B. Evans, *et al.,* pp. 1819–25. Boston: Houghton Mifflin, 1974.

Silber, Joan. **"Cinematic Techniques and Interpretations in Film and Television Adaptations of Shakespeare's *Hamlet.*"** *Dissertation Abstracts* 34 (1974): 5370-A.

Analyzes *Hamlet* productions for television or cinema by Kozintsev, Wirth, Saville, Richardson, and Olivier.

Silberstein, Paula E. **"On Film and Filmstrip."** *Scholastic Teacher,* 21 February 1964, pp. 20T–21T.

Surveys various theatrical and educational films and filmstrips available for classroom use.

Skoller, Donald. **"Problems of Transformation in the Adaptation of Shakespeare's Tragedies from Play-Script to Cinema."** Ph.D. dissertation, New York University, 1968.

A sensitive pioneering study discussing each film's speech and visualization, cinematic perspective, camera movement, montage, misc-en-scene, and non-verbal sounds and acting. Studies on Cukor's *Rom* (pp. 175–94), Castellani's *Rom* (pp. 195–220), Bradley's *JC* (pp. 221–48), Mankiewicz's *JC* (pp. 249–82), Olivier's *Hamlet* (pp. 283–305), Kozintsev's *Hamlet* (pp. 306–47), Welles's *Othello* (pp. 348–71), Youtkevich's *Othello* (pp. 372–97), Burge's *Othello* (pp. 398–424), Welles's *Macbeth* (pp. 445–82), Schaefer's *Macbeth* (pp. 483–506) and summaries of critical responses to each film (pp. 507–65).

Smith, Garland Garvey. **"Shakespeare on the Screen."** *Emory University Quarterly* 3 (June 1947): 88–95.

Argues that Shakespeare "as a practical man of the theater certainly would . . . have exploited the advantages offered by the screen," and praises Olivier's *Henry V* as heralding "a new era in recreating Shakespeare for the present generation."

Spaulding, George O. **"The Educational Value of the Motion Picture."** *English Leaflet* 14 (December 1914): 1–6.

Contends that "the adolescent imagination is more effectively stirred and quickened by [a film of *Julius Caesar*] than by the reading either of the 'Commentaries' of Shakespeare's 'Caesar'." "Do not expect from the motion picture the same imaginative appeal that any other art makes, since it is different in its method from all of them; and since it may be the embryonic form of a great new Art, that shall catch man's imagination from a new angle and with a new effectiveness."

Staton, Shirley F. **"Shakespeare Redivivus: Supplementary Techniques for Teaching Shakespeare."** *Literature/Film Quarterly* 5 (Fall 1977): 358–61.

Videotapes and student actors present alternative interpretations of the same scene or play.

Steinlechner, Helga. **"Die filmischen Elemente in den Dramen Shakespeare: Beitrage z. modernen Filmdramaturgie."** Ph.D. dissertation, University of Vienna, 1951.

Taylor, John Russell. **"Shakespeare in Film, Radio, and Television."** In *Shakespeare: A Celebration,* edited by T. J. B. Spencer, pp. 97–113. London: Pelican Books, 1964.

The new media "best calculated to swallow Shakespeare whole . . . are purely aural ones, radio and gramophone records" beause in Shake-spearean drama "the prime accent is on sound rather than sight."

Thorp, Margaret F. **"Shakespeare and the Movies."** *Shakespeare Quarterly* 9 (1958): 357–66.

Speculates on how Shakespeare would have written in an age of cinema, provides a critical look at recent film versions, and generalizations about how best to adapt film to screen.

Thurmann, Irmgard. **"Shakespeare im Film."** *Shakespeare Jahrbuch* (Heidelberg) 76 (1940): 189–98.

Triscoli, Claudio. **"Voci Italiane per Shakespeare Sullo Schermo."** *Bianco e Nero* (Rome) 18 (January 1957): 56–60.

Tucker, Nicholas. **"Shakespeare and Film Technique."** *Use of English* (London) 14 (Winter 1962): 98–104.

Discusses how to teach Shakespeare via film techniques by using plays roughly as film scripts and comparing Shakespeare's artistic conventions with those of the cinema.

"Unique Shakespeare Course at Indiana University of Pa." *Shakespeare Newsletter* 26 (1976): 13–14.

Reports on an interdisciplinary course which utilizes films and invited speakers.

Walker, George Graham. **"Film and Fine Art."** *Sight and Sound* (London) 17 (Winter 1948–1949): 173–74.

Attempts to establish a relationship between the art of the cinema and the art of the painter, using examples from *Henry V,* among other films.

Webb, Chris. **"Shakespeare in the Classroom."** *Visual Education* (March 1972): 31, 33–34.

Offers a survey of audio-visual materials available in Great Britain.

Webster, Margaret. **"Interpretation of Shakespeare Today."** *Wisdom* (July 1956): 23–35.

Includes pictures from Olivier's films.

Welles, Orson. **"The Third Audience."** *Sight and Sound* (London) 23 (January–March 1954): 120–22.

Text of an Edinburgh Festival lecture that includes comments on his work filming Shakespeare: "I do not know whether a happy marriage can exist between Shakespeare and the screen."

Welles, Orson. **"Shakespeare et la Tradition."** *Nouvelles Littéraires* (Paris) 31 no. 1288 (1952): 1, 8.

Argues that no interpreter of Shakespeare can claim to be part of a tradition old enough to impose its authority.

Welsh, James M. **"The Sound of Silents: An Early *Shrew.*"** *English Journal* 62 (May 1973): 754-69.

Sam Taylor's *Taming of the Shrew* is a "great" movie because of the presence of Mary Pickford and Douglas Fairbanks.

Whitehead, Peter, and Bean, Robin. **Olivier—Shakespeare.** London: Lorrimer Films, 1966.

Contains Olivier's filmography—including screen roles—through *Khartoum* (1966). Well illustrated.

Willson, Robert F. **"Shakespeare in *The Goodbye Girl.*"** *Shakespeare on Film Newsletter* 2 (April 1978): 1, 3-4.

Suggests Simon uses *Richard III* as a play within the play.

Yetman, C. Duncan. **"Motion-Picture Appreciation and School Composition."** *English Journal* 41 (November 1952): 488-91.

Compares Rome of *Julius Caesar* with that of the film *Quo Vadis.*

Yutkevitch, Sergei. **Shekspir I Kino (Shakespeare on Film).** Moscow, 1973.

Includes essays on major film versions and includes many stills.

Individual Feature Films

As You Like It *(1936). Directed by Paul Czinner.*

Agate, James. **Review.** *The Tatler* (12 September 1936). Reprinted as "Bergner as Rosalind," in his *Around Cinemas,* pp. 173-77. London: Home & Van Thal, 1946.

Czinner preserves spirit of the text but Bergner's acting is inappropriate.

Agate, James. **Review.** *The Tatler* (1935). Reprinted as "Shyer and Shyer," in *Around Cinemas.* 2d series, pp. 124-26. London: Home & Van Thal, 1948.

Bergner doesn't live up to her reputation as a great actress.

Greene, Graham. **Review.** *The Spectator,* 11 September 1936. Reprinted in his *Graham Greene on Film,* pp. 98, 100. New York: Simon & Schuster, 1972.

"A respectful film[;] it is a better production than you will often see on the stage . . . [but] as a film [it] is less satisfactory."

"Norma Shearer's Juliet Matches Best on Modern Stage." *Newsweek,* 22 August 1936, pp. 28–29.

Discusses the painstaking care taken by Cukor to have script, costumes, and cast proper and prepared.

Chimes at Midnight, *or* Falstaff *(1966). Directed by Orson Welles.*

Archer, Eugene. **"Welles Captures Cannes."** *Saturday Review,* 23 July 1966, pp. 62–63.

While the film was competitive at the Cannes Festival, it is no lasting masterpiece.

"Body English." *Time,* 24 March 1967, p. 89.

"In this film there flickers the glitter of authentic genius, along with great story stretches of dullness and incoherence."

Bessy, Maurice. **"Falstaff: The Joy of Goodness."** In his *Orson Welles,* pp. 101–05. New York: Crown, 1971.

The film is not a period piece, "but rather a great documentary" in which Welles/Falstaff "complete each other."

Billard, Pierre. *"Chimes at Midnight."* *Sight and Sound* (London) 34 (Spring 1965): 64–65. Reprinted in *Focus on Shakespearean Films,* edited by Charles W. Eckert, pp. 162–64. Englewood Cliffs, N. J.: Prentice-Hall, 1972.

Provides background material on the film.

Birstein, Ann. *"Falstaff,* 'a curiously mixed bag'." *Vogue,* 1 January 1967, p. 53.

While Welles is often successful in portraying "the pathos that can only come of dignity," the film sheds more light on Prince Hal than on Falstaff.

Cobos, Juan. **"Falstaff sur le vif."** *Cahiers du Cinema* (Paris) no. 165 (April 1965): 29–30.

Cobos, Juan, and Rubio, Miguel. **"Welles and Falstaff: An Interview."** *Sight and Sound* (London) 35 (Autumn 1966): 158–63.

Offers some candid comments by Welles about one of his most "personal" films.

Cobos, Juan; Rubio, Miguel; and Pruneda, J. A. **"A Trip to Don Quixoteland: Conversation with Orson Welles."** *Cahiers du Cinema in English* 5 (June 1966): 35–47.

Includes brief comments on *Falstaff* and *Othello*. Originally in *Cahiers du Cinema* no. 165 (April 1965): 8–22.

Comolli, Jean-Louis. **"Jack le Fataliste."** *Cahiers du Cinema* (Paris) no. 181 (August 1966): 31–32.

The film encompasses two distinct orders: heaviness of bodies, slowness, armor, and even the way the film is edited *vs.* Falstaff, the power of words and minimal gestures.

Cook, Page. **"The Sound Track."** *Films in Review* 18 (May 1967): 301.

Finds the variety of musical textures in Lavagnino's score interesting.

Cowie, Peter. **"The Study of Good Companionship: *Chimes at Midnight/ Falstaff."*** In his *A Ribbon of Dreams: The Cinema of Orson Welles,* pp. 178–93. New York: A. S. Barnes; London: Tantivy, 1973.

"Critics who complain that Falstaff and the film are not sufficiently rumbustious have a superficial notion of one of Shakespeare's most tragic figures." Well argued and well illustrated.

Crist, Judith. **The Private Eye, the Cowboy and the Very Naked Girl.** Chicago: Holt, Rinehart & Winston, 1968.

Calls the film a testament to Welles's genius as a screenwriter, director, and actor (p. 260).

Crowther, Bosley. **"Falstaff."** *New York Times,* 20 March 1967, sec. 2, p. 26.

"A big, squashy, tatterdemalion show" which "had no business intruding brashly in the serious Shakespearean affairs of the Lancasters, the Percys, and the Mortimers. . . ."

Crowther, Bosley. **"Cannes of Worms?"** *New York Times,* 29 May 1966, sec. 2, p. 1.

Crowther, Bosley. **"Cannes Film Festival."** *New York Times,* 12 May 1966, p. 54.

Daney, Serge. **"Welles au Pouvoir."** *Cahiers du Cinema* (Paris) no. 181 (August 1966): 27–28.

Welles's films concern men who misuse power and are rich in abuses of confidence. Falstaff lives in his past—the entropy of a deliberately spoiled freedom while Hal needs to learn how to make power usable.

Duboeuf, Pierre. **"L'autre face."** *Cahiers du Cinema* (Paris) no. 181 (August 1966): 28, 31.

Falstaff is special in the totality of Welles's work; a marginal film in which values are reversed as if to make explicit the rest of the work by illuminating it in a different light.

Gill, Brendan. **Review.** *The New Yorker,* 25 March 1967, p. 152.

Welles has taken bits and pieces from four plays and made "a coherent whole," imposing on the scrappy and sometimes contradictory actions of Sir John's life previously unnoticed dramatic integrity.

Higham, Charles. *"Chimes at Midnight."* In his *The Films of Orson Welles,* pp. 167–77. Berkeley: University of California Press, 1970.

Provides comments on production problems and a good analysis of the film as "a long lament for Merrie England, symbolized by Falstaff himself."

Houston, Penelope. **"Festival 66: Cannes."** *Sight and Sound* (London) 35 (Summer 1966): 125–27.

Praises the camera work.

Johnson, William. **"Orson Welles: Of Time and Loss."** *Film Quarterly* 21 (Fall 1967): 13–24.

Makes positive comments in passing.

Jorgens, Jack. J. **"Orson Welles's** *Chimes at Midnight* **(Falstaff)."** In his *Shakespeare on Film,* pp. 106–21. Bloomington: Indiana University Press, 1977.

A difficult film because of "its oblique casting and unsettling characterizations, . . . its incredible unevenness." Yet in focusing on the triangle of Hal, Henry IV, and Falstaff, Welles "has still managed to render powerfully the personal, political, and mythical dimensions of the original plays."

Kael, Pauline. **"Orson Welles: There Ain't No Way."** *New Republic,* 24 June 1967, pp. 27–32. Reprinted in her *Kiss Kiss Bang Bang,* pp. 197–202. Boston: Little, Brown, 1968.

Another Welles near masterpiece that cannot reach a large public "because of technical defects due to poverty."

Kaufmann, Stanley. **"Falstaff."** In his *Figures of Light,* pp. 4–5. New

York: Harper and Row, 1971.

"A talented disaster" caused by Welles's "laziness as an actor."

McBride, Joseph. *"Chimes at Midnight."* In his *Orson Welles,* pp. 148–58. London: Secker & Warburg; New York: Viking, 1972. Reprinted in *Focus on Orson Welles,* edited by Ronald Gottesman, pp. 178–86. Englewood Cliffs, N.J.: Prentice-Hall, 1976. See also *Film Quarterly* 23 (Fall 1969): 11–20.

A balanced discussion of Welles's intention, his liberties with the text, and the Bradleyean nature of tragedy.

Morgenstern, Joseph. "Falstaff: Antic Giant." In *Film 67/68,* edited by Richard Schickel and John Simon, pp. 69–72. New York: Simon & Schuster, 1968.

Reprints a review from *Newsweek* emphasizing likenesses between Welles and Falstaff.

Narboni, Jean. "Sacher et Masoch." *Cahiers du Cinema* (Paris) no. 181 (August 1966): 32.

Discusses Welles's progression from the affirmation of his own ego to the fear of no longer being someone, but everything and no one.

Price, James. **Review.** *Sight and Sound* (London) 36 (Summer 1967): 146–47.

Welles's famous visual style "seems to have become not so much a *means* of expression as an *accompaniment* to expression."

Prokosch, Mike. "Orson Welles." *Film Comment* 7 (Summer 1971): 28–37.

Focuses on the atmosphere selected for sequences and provides notes on camera work.

Sarris, Andrew. "Humpty-Dumpty from Wisconsin." In *Film 67/68,* edited by Richard Schickel and John Simon, pp. 72–74. New York: Simon & Schuster, 1968. Reprinted as "Falstaff" in his *Confessions of a Cultist,* pp. 292–94. New York: Simon & Schuster, 1970.

Observes how Welles feels Falstaff from inside out to give Shakespeare a distinct size and shape.

Schickel, Richard, and Simon, John. **Films 67/68.** New York: Simon & Schuster, 1968.

Reprints reviews by J. Morgenstern, A. Sarris, S. Kaufmann, P. Kael, and J. Simon.

Simon, John. **"Falstaff."** In *Films 67/68,* edited by Richard Schickel and
John Simon, pp. 83–85. New York: Simon & Schuster, 1968; and in his
Movies into Film, pp. 30–31. New York: Dell, 1971.

"Ridiculous is the word for the whole enterprise."

Sylvano, John B. **"Orson Welles's** *Falstaff:* **A Selected Bibliography."**
Shakespeare on Film Newsletter 2 (April 1978): 3, 8.

Lists twenty-four annotated entries.

Tynan, Kenneth. **"Interview: Orson Welles."** *Playboy* 14 (March 1967):
53–64.

Includes discussion of *Falstaff.*

Welles, Orson. *"Chimes at Midnight."* *Cahiers du Cinema* (Paris) no. 179
(June 1966): 28–31.

Interview.

Zimmerman, Paul D. **"Falstaff as Orson Welles."** *Newsweek,* 27 March
1967, pp. 96–103.

A brief account of Welles's films with praise for his portrayal of
Falstaff.

Hamlet *(1948). Directed by Laurence Olivier.*

Agee, James. **"Olivier's** *Hamlet."* *Time,* 28 June 1948, pp. 54–56, 59–60.
Reprinted in his *Agee on Film,* pp. 388–96. New York: Grosset &
Dunlap, 1976.

A lengthy review that contains much background information along
with his speculations about Olivier's intentions.

Alexander, Peter. **Hamlet, Father and Son.** Oxford: Clarendon Press, 1955.

A Shakespeare scholar's strong reaction to the film's prologue and
Olivier's interpretation.

Ashworth, John. **"Olivier, Freud and Hamlet."** *Atlantic Monthly* 183
(May 1949): 30–33.

Argues against Olivier's Oedipal reading of play. See also, in this
section, Lesser.

"At Elsinore." *Detroit Free Press,* 27 February 1948.

Babcock, R. W. **"George Lyman Kittredge, Olivier, and the Historical
Hamlet."** *College English* 11 (February 1950): 256–65.

Suggests that Kittredge's 1916 development of Hamlet is followed by Olivier.

Barbarow, George. *"Hamlet* **Through a Telescope."** *Hudson Review* 2 (Spring 1949): 98–117.

The design of *Hamlet* is distorted out of all proportion.

Barnes, Howard. **Review.** *New York Herald-Tribune,* 30 September 1948.

"Scholars may scoff, but the general public will find a transcendent motion picture in *Hamlet."*

Bayley, John. **"Hamlet as a Film."** *National Review* 131 (December 1948): 603–06.

The film allows the reader to feel the swiftness and tension of the story; sees in the film the possibility of a drama renaissance.

Brown, John Mason. **"Seeing Things: Olivier's** *Hamlet."* *Saturday Review of Literature,* 2 October 1948, pp. 26–27. Reprinted in his *Still Seeing Things,* pp. 145–53. New York: McGraw-Hill, 1950.

Criticizes the amount of camera movement.

Cardim, Luiz. **Os Problemas do Hamlet e as Suas Dificuladades CENICAS.** Lisbon, 1949.

Discusses Olivier's and film's difficulties.

"Better than the Play?" *Time,* 17 May 1948, p. 100.

Offers excerpts from English critics' praise of Olivier and Jean Simmons (Ophelia); comments that the cuts make the film more tightly knit than the play.

"Boston Saw *Hamlet* **American Premiere."** *Detroit Free Press,* 22 August 1948.

Carrick, Edward. **"Roger Furse."** In his *Art and Design in the British Film,* pp. 61–63. London: Dobson, 1948.

Short comment on the production designer with four sketches of the set.

Chappell, Connery. **"Olivier's** *Hamlet."* *Kinematograph Weekly,* 6 May 1948.

While critical of film's melodramatic atmosphere, acknowledges that it still catches something not found in any previous Shakespeare films.

"Citizen Dane." *Harper's Magazine,* September 1948, pp. 116–17.

The film is "big, bold and brassy" but a disappointment: it is too long. Constant camera movement isolates characters from one another, and the "geography" of the set is confusing.

Clay, James, and Krempel, Daniel. **"Olivier's *Hamlet.*"** In his *The Theatrical Image,* pp. 247–54. New York: McGraw-Hill, 1967.

Argues that despite many excellent qualities, this film creates "some very troublesome distortions and cannot be regarded as a completely successful translation for modern audiences of Shakespeare's intent."

Cook, Alton. **"Olivier's *Hamlet.*"** *New York World-Telegram,* 30 September 1948.

Cook, D. **Review.** *New York Herald-Tribune,* 9 May 1948, sec. V., pp. 1, 2.

Cross, Brenda, ed. **The Film "Hamlet": A Record of Its Production.** London: Saturn Press, 1948.

Brief essays by fifteen members of the cast and crew including Olivier.

Crowther, Bosley. **"Discussing *Hamlet*: Mr. Olivier's Film Draws Objections and Replies."** *New York Times,* 7 November 1948, sec. II, p. 4.

While most people writing to the newspaper praise the film, those who object focus on dissatisfaction with Olivier's performance.

Crowther, Bosley. **"Olivier's *Hamlet*: Hailing a Shakespearean Tragedy as a Hit, a Very Palpable Hit."** *New York Times,* 3 October 1948, sec. II, p. 1.

The film should be one of the "great popular pictures of our times."

Crowther, Bosley. **"A Trio of Newcomers Arrive: Laurence Olivier's *Hamlet* Bows at the Park Avenue Theatre—'Saxon Charm' Seen."** *New York Times,* 30 September 1948, p. 32.

The film "gives absolute proof that these classics are magnificently suited to the screen. . . . An uncommonly galvanic film."

Dent, Alan, ed. *Hamlet*: **The Film and the Play.** London: World Film Publications, 1948.

Includes a foreword by Olivier, a discussion by Dent of "Text-Editing Shakespeare with particular reference to *Hamlet,*" and the complete text of the play with cuts made for the film enclosed in red brackets.

Dent, Alan. **"Hamlet and Caligari."** *Illustrated London News,* 15 May 1948, p. 562.

Olivier's best moments are in the "to be, or not to be," in the Closet

Scene, and by Ophelia's grave. Herlie is too young to be Olivier's mother.

"Dreimal *Hamlet*." *Der Monat* (Hamburg) 1 (1948/49), II: 96–101.

Includes: Olivier, "Passt die Gebärde dem Wort, das Wort der Gebärde an"; Claude Mauriac, "Welch ein Meisterwerk . . ."; and Robert Herring, "O Hamlet, welch ein Abfall."

Durgnat, Raymond. **Films and Feelings.** Cambridge: Massachusetts Institute of Technology Press, 1967.

Criticizes Olivier's *Hamlet* for its banal visual style with barn-size sets and deep focus compositions (p. 49).

"Excerpts from Letters about *Hamlet*." *New York Times,* 7 November 1948, p. 4X.

Excerpts from letters for and against the film and the *New York Times* criticism of it.

Farbman, N. R. *"Hamlet." Life,* 15 March 1948, pp. 117–27.

Cover story on Olivier is well illustrated.

Flatter, Richard. *"Hamlet* als Film." *Shakespeare Jahrbuch* (Heidelberg) 87/88 (1952): 58–60.

Olivier so completely takes over the character of Hamlet that when Hamlet speaks, the audience sees and hears Olivier and not the character Hamlet.

Fowler, Roy A. **"Notes sur Hamlet."** *Revue du Cinema* (Paris) 3 (August 1948): 58 66.

Olivier doesn't remain true to his stated purpose of showing the tragedy of an irresolute man; yet the film will reach a large public.

Gross, Sheryl W. **"Poetic Realism in Olivier's Hamlet."** *Shakespeare on Film Newsletter* 3 (December 1978): 6.

Abstracts a paper which argues that deep focus photography blends poetic and realistic tendencies in the film.

"*Hamlet* by William Shakespeare." *Sight and Sound* (London) 17 (Spring 1948): 10–11.

A picture story that includes four illustrations from the film (Ophelia is the cover photo).

"*Hamlet*: The Play and the Screenplay." *Hollywood Quarterly* 3 (Spring 1948): 293–300.

Presents parallel excerpts from the "Nunnery Scene" and a biographical sketch of Olivier.

"Hamlet **Triumph."** *Newsweek,* 27 September 1948, pp. 87–88.

"A compelling performance—subtle, eloquent, and illuminated by the perfected craftsmanship of one of the finest actors on stage or screen."

H[art], H[enry]. *"Hamlet* **(Revisited)."** *Films in Review* 5 (March 1954): 144–45.

Comments on the film's reissue for wide screens and speculates on how future Shakespearean films will allow us to compare great actors with each other.

Hartung, Philip. **Review.** *Commonweal,* 1 October 1948, p. 596.

Hatch, Robert. **Review.** *New Republic,* 4 October 1948, pp. 28–30.

Herring. R. *"Hamlet,* **Sir Laurence Olivier's Picture."** *Life and Letters* (London) 57 (June 1948): 183–92.

Maintains that "The film fails because Sir Laurence's use of the medium is not, fundamentally, cinematic." Also critical of the "peculiarly insensitive rearrangement" of the final scene and says "the age-grouping of the casting defies analysis."

Hift, Fred. **"Honors for *Hamlet."*** *New York Times,* 14 May 1950, p. X5.

Discusses the honors awarded the film throughout the world, which countries it has played in, and who has translated it where.

Homan, Sidney. **"Visual Failure and Visual Success: *Hamlet,* Fellini's *Satyricon,* and Filmed Versions of the Play."** *Shakespeare on Film Newsletter* 3 (December 1978): 6.

Abstracts a paper which suggests Olivier and (more so) Kozintsev are closest to Shakespeare's own perspective of Hamlet.

Hopkins, Arthur. **"Hamlet and Olivier."** *Theatre Arts* 32 (August-September 1948): 30–31.

"The tragedy of Hamlet in this picture version is persistent misconception that reduces both Shakespeare and Olivier to proportions of little tragic impact."

Huntley, John. **"The Music of *Hamlet."*** *Penguin Film Review No. 8.* London: Penguin Books, 1949.

Jorgens, Jack J. **"Teaching Manual, *Hamlet* (Olivier Version)."** Audio Brandon Films, 1978.

Part of the "Literature and Film" series, includes a critical interpretation, film outline, critic's round table, activities for students, and bibliography.

Jorgens, Jack J. **"Laurence Olivier's *Hamlet*."** In his *Shakespeare on Film,* pp. 207–17. Bloomington: Indiana University Press, 1977.

A "dreamy, lyrical film with its misty ramparts, dissolves, and gliding camera," which "captures the *inner* Hamlet."

Kael, Pauline. **"Olivier's *Hamlet*."** In her *I Lost It at the Movies,* p. 280. Boston: Little, Brown, 1965.

Defends the additional perspective that filmmaking can offer a play.

Kliman, Bernice W. **"Olivier's *Hamlet*: A Film-Infused Play."** *Literature/ Film Quarterly* 5 (Fall 1977): 305–14.

Discusses the combination of cinematic and theatrical strategies in the film.

Klitscher, Hermann. **"Über Sir Laurence Olivier's *Hamlet-Film*."** In his *Shakespeare-Studien, Festschrift für Heinrich Mutschmann,* pp. 107–14. Marburg: N. G. Elwert, 1951.

Kobler, John. **"Sir Laurence Olivier."** *Life,* 18 October 1948, pp. 128–37.

Offers general comments on the film and Olivier's career.

Lejeune, C. A. **"London Begins a Busy Film Schedule."** *New York Times,* 1 June 1947.

Provides gossip about Olivier filming behind the iron curtain.

Lesser, Simon O. **"Freud and *Hamlet* Again."** *American Imago* 12 (1955): 207–20.

Answers Ashworth. See also, in this section, Ashworth.

McCarten, John. **"Olivier's *Hamlet*."** *The New Yorker,* 2 October 1948, pp. 90–91.

Finds that Olivier is hard put "to avoid static scenes," which his camera movement does not overcome.

McCarthy, Mary. **"A Prince of Shreds and Patches."** In her *Sights and Spectacles,* pp. 141–45. New York: Farrar, Strauss, 1956. Reprinted in *Focus on Shakespearean Films,* edited by Charles W. Eckert, pp. 64–67. Englewood Cliffs, N.J.: Prentice-Hall, 1972.

A perceptive discussion of Olivier's interpretation.

McManaway, James. **"Laurence Olivier's *Hamlet.*"** *Shakespeare Association of America Bulletin* 24 (January 1949): 3–11.

A thorough study of Olivier's interpretation.

Manvell, Roger. **"The Film of *Hamlet.*"** *Penguin Film Review* 8 (January 1949): 16–24.

While Olivier made many mistakes filming the play, "nevertheless, there is a nobility in the production."

Marshall, Margaret. **"Notes By The Way."** *Nation,* 23 October 1948, p. 468.

Finds the interpretation of Ophelia is fresh and exciting, but considers Olivier's Hamlet "competent and faithful and a little shallow."

"The New Play *Hamlet.*" *Vogue,* 15 September 1948, p. 158.

"Olivier Explains His Cinematic Approach to *Hamlet.*" *New York Times,* 19 September 1948, p. X5.

Excerpts Olivier's introduction to Dent's *Hamlet,* in which he comments on the difficulty of filming the world's best known play.

"Olivier Film *Hamlet* Acclaimed in London." *New York Times,* 5 May 1948, p. 29.

Excerpts favorable London reviews.

"Olivier's *Hamlet.*" *Time,* 29 June 1948, pp. 54–62.

Argues that the film proves Shakespeare can be filmed. "It is worked out with intelligence, sensitivity, thoroughness and beauty; . . . it has everything which high ambition, deep sobriety and exquisite skill can give it."

"Oops! Wrong Hamlet." *Saturday Review,* 16 May 1953, p. 19.

Powell, D. **"*Hamlet* on the Screen."** *Britain Today* 147 (July 1948): 18–21.

Contains illustrations.

Ramsaye, Terry. **"Britain's *Hamlet* is Presented to American Reviewers."** *Motion Picture Herald,* 3 July 1948.

"Scenes from the Olivier Production of *Hamlet.*" *Life,* 15 March 1948, pp. 117–27.

Pictures from film.

"*Hamlet*: The Play and the Screenplay." *Film Quarterly* 3 (Spring 1948): 293–300.

Reprints parallel texts of the "get thee to a nunnery" scene from play and screenplay.

Simon, John. **"Olivier's *Hamlet*."** In his *Private Screenings,* pp. 210–14. New York: Berkeley Publishing Corporation, 1971.

"Speaking of Pictures." *Life,* 24 November 1947, pp. 18–19.

Pictures of Olivier directing *Hamlet.*

Sullivan, Kay. **"Great Tragedy Superbly Done."** *Parade,* 1 August 1948, p. 23.

Tyler, Parker. **"Olivier's *Hamlet*."** In his *Classics of the Foreign Film,* pp. 176–77. New York: Citadel Press, 1962.

Praises Olivier's performance and the clarity of Shakespeare's language on film.

Tyler, Parker. **"*Hamlet* and Documentary."** *Kenyon Review* 11 (Summer 1949): 527–32.

Complains that Olivier has produced "traditional cinema" as a pseudo-documentary form in attempting to make *Hamlet* "cinematic"; his documentary approach displaces the view of Hamlet as a suffering individual.

Vesselo, Arthur. **"British Films of the Quarter."** *Sight and Sound* (London) 17 (Summer 1948): 99–100.

Reviews film and comments on how to film Shakespeare.

"William Shakespeare, Esq." *Saturday Review,* 16 May 1953, pp. 33–34.

Winnington, Richard. **"*Hamlet*."** In his *Drawn and Quartered,* pp. 112–14. London: Saturn Press, 1948.

"Olivier has made in *Hamlet* no contribution to the evolution of the cinema or to appreciation of Shakespeare."

Wyatt, Euphemia. **Review.** *The Catholic World* 168 (December 1948): 243–44.

See also, in General section, Bazin, Dehn, Duffy, Durgnat, Halio, Kael, Phillips, Raynor, Silber, Skoller.

Hamlet *(1960). Directed by Franz Peter Wirth.*

"Schell's Hamlet." *Newsweek,* 19 August 1968, p. 90.

Notes controversy in Germany because Schell's Hamlet is "something of a student activist," and his disillusionments are political.

Schumach, Murray. **"Hollywood Dubbing: Schell Plays Hamlet with German Accent."** *New York Times,* 14 October 1962, sec. II, p. 9.

Laments poor dubbing into English.

Tourtelot, Madeline. **"San Francisco's 6th Festival."** *Films in Review* 13 (December 1962): 618.

The film "has such an inadequate supporting cast and such inferior sets and costuming, that everyone felt it was a great mistake."

Wilds, Lillian. **"On Film: Maximillian Schell's Most Royal Hamlet."** *Literature/Film Quarterly* 4 (Spring 1976): 134-40.

Presents a list of the film's "faults and beauties" with emphasis on the latter.

Hamlet *(1964). Directed by Grigori Kozintsev.*

Brugiere. B. **"*Hamlet,* film de G. Kozintsev transposition fidele e hardie de *Hamlet.*"** *Mercure de France* (Paris) 359 (July-August 1965): 623-25.

Cook, Page. **"The Sound Track."** *Films in Review* 17 (May 1966): 306-07.

Discusses Shostakovich's score which has, like the film script, "multi-shaded intricacies which shroud, rather than adorn, the tragedy."

Cowie, Peter. **Review.** *Films and Filming* (London) (February 1965): 29.

"The finest film version of *Hamlet* ever made."

Crist, Judith. **"The *Hamlet* from Russia—Old-Fashioned, Unexciting."** *New York Herald-Tribune,* 15 September 1964.

Crowther, Bosley. **"Shakespeare on Film—Again?"** *New York Times,* 20 March 1966.

Using Kozintsev's *Hamlet* as the example, argues that Shakespeare can be filmed.

Crowther, Bosley. **"Russians Present a Powerful *Hamlet.*"** *New York Times,* 16 March 1966, p. 48.

"An essentially graphic film, . . . a vibrant, manly Hamlet."

Crowther, Bosley. **"Film Festival: Regal Soviet *Hamlet.*"** *New York Times,* 15 September 1964, p. 32.

"This *Hamlet* is a vast and regal show of strong cinematographic values."

Georgi, Renate. **"Hamlet in filmischer Poesie."** *Shakespeare Jahrbuch* (Weimar) 106 (1970): 176–201.

Kozintsev's film illustrates the transformation of a literary model into a film that becomes an independent work of art. A good discussion of Pasternak's prose translation, music, etc.

Gill, Brendan. **"Shakespeare and After."** *New Yorker,* 26 March 1966, pp. 125–26.

"In this production the emphasis is quite properly on the manifestation in solid, physical terms of whatever of the morbid and bizarre is conveyed in poetical terms in the play."

Guidry, Frederick H. **"Estonian Castle Setting: Soviet *Hamlet.*"** *Christian Science Monitor,* 10 October 1966.

Hartung, Philip T. **Review.** *Commonweal,* 25 February 1966, p. 615.

Enjoys photography, setting, and cast but wishes there were more Shakespearean lines.

Hayman, Ronald. **"Shakespeare on the Screen."** *Times Literary Supplement* (London), 26 September 1968, pp. 1081–82.

Thinks Kozintsev's film is the most imaginative of screen versions; singles out successful incorporation of images of sea and sky, which are merely background additions in Olivier's film.

H[art], H[enry]. *"Hamlet."* *Films in Review* 17 (April 1966): 251–52.

Finds the film an ideological and cinematic confusion; says the acting is mediocre and the English sub-titles are poorly done.

Hatch, Robert. **Review.** *Nation,* 28 September 1964, pp. 175–76.

Kozintsev sees *Hamlet* "as costume melodrama, and clearly he makes his point."

Hodgdon, Barbara. **"'The Mirror Up to Nature': Notes on Kozintsev's *Hamlet.*"** *Comparative Drama* 9 (Winter 1975–1976): 305–17.

Explains how the film "re-invents" Shakespeare's play by expanding the limitations of its stage reality in order to show us a more complete world.

Houston, Penelope. *"Hamlet. U.S.S.R., 1964."* *Monthly Film Bulletin* 32 (February 1965): 19–20.

Recognizes that the "whole line of the film is boldly laid down" in the opening sequence and that "the most effective scenes are often those painted with the boldest brushstrokes" (e.g., Claudius' council speech, Laertes' return, Ophelia).

Jorgens, Jack J. **"Grigori Kozintsev's** *Hamlet.***"** In his *Shakespeare on Film,* pp. 218–34. Bloomington: Indiana University Press, 1977.

Calls film an epic version that captures the "outer" Hamlet and "retains a greater portion of the play's complexity and mystery . . . because the visual texture is denser, the images and connections more consistently meaningful."

Jorgens, Jack J. **"Image and Meaning in the Kozintsev** *Hamlet.***"** *Literature/Film Quarterly* 1 (Fall 1973): 307–15.

Points to the cumulative effect of the juxtaposition or repetitions of powerful images.

Knight, Arthur. **"Shakespeare à la Russe."** *Saturday Review,* 21 May 1966, p. 49.

Praises the director's ability "to discover a proper style" and to choose images that "contribute a poetry of their own."

Koval, Francis. **"Venice 1964."** *Films in Review* 15 (October 1964): 464–65.

Likes the way that Kozintsev has turned "a work overladen with literary and philosophical connotations into a drama of sweeping action."

Kozintsev, Grigori. **Shakespeare: Time and Conscience.** New York: Hill and Wang, 1966.

Useful for long appendix of diary notes (pp. 211–76) on *Hamlet* and for glimpses into the practice and theory of a contemporary filmmaker.

Kozintsev, Grigori. **"The Hamlet Within Me."** *Films and Filming* (London) (September 1962): 20.

Remarks on the film he will make; his task will be "to change the poetical imagery of the work into the visual."

Kustow, Michael. *"Hamlet." Sight and Sound* (London) 33 (Summer 1964): 144–45. Reprinted in *Focus on Shakespearean Films,* edited by Charles W. Eckert, pp. 47–49. Englewood Cliffs, N.J.: Prentice-Hall, 1972.

"Kozintsev's imagination catches fire and he sends his figures hurling across the screen with true Shakespearean energy."

Lordkipandze, Natela. *"Hamlet* **on the Screen."** *Soviet Literature* no. 9 (1964): 170–73.

Macdonald, Dwight. **Review.** *Esquire* (December 1967): 74–76. Reprinted in his *Dwight Macdonald on the Movies,* pp. 271–73. Englewood Cliffs, N.J.: Prentice-Hall, 1969; and *Focus on Shakespearean Films,* edited by Charles W. Eckert, pp. 149–50. Englewood Cliffs, N.J.: Prentice-Hall, 1972.

"A successful though not a great movie," because Hamlet is changed to one who rides and duels more than he reflects. He is too much of a man of action.

"Meeting with Grigori Kozintsev." *Film* (Autumn 1967): 27–29.

Provides background on film.

Regiere, Bernard B. **"***Hamlet,* **film de G. Kozintsev."** *Mercure de France* (Paris) 359 (July–August 1965): 623–25.

Rhode, Eric. **"Screened Culture-Letter from Venice."** *Encounter* 23 (November 1964): 61–65. Excerpted in *Focus on Shakespearean Films,* edited by Charles W. Eckert, pp. 151–52. Englewood Cliffs, N.J.: Prentice-Hall, 1972.

The film "may have been academic, but it had passion."

Rowe, Eleanor. *Hamlet:* **A Window on Russia.** New York: New York University Press, 1976.

Provides interesting discussion of Pasternak-Kozintsev correspondence, published in *Voprosy literatury* (Moscow) 1 (January 1975): 212–23.

"The Russians Film *Hamlet.***"** *Illustrated London News,* 26 December 1964, pp. 1026–27.

Comments on the innovation of portraying Ophelia "almost as a pawn of her own subconscious." Includes five stills from the film.

Shabad, Theodore. **"Moscow Unveils Filmed** *Hamlet.***"** *New York Times,* 14 April 1964, p. 9.

Provides biographical background on director, translator, and cast.

Tynan, Kenneth. **"The Best of Elsinores."** *London Observer,* 10 January 1965.

"The Play's Not the Thing." *Newsweek,* 14 March 1966, pp. 99–100.

Generally critical of film but praises setting.

Hamlet *(1969). Directed by Tony Richardson.*

Alvarez, A. **"Williamson: 'I Hate Intellectual Actors'."** *New York Times,* 27 April 1969, p. 1D.

Interview concerns his stage performance.

Barnes, Clive. **"Stage: Midland's Hamlet."** *New York Times,* 2 May 1969, p. 38.

Williamson's stage performance is exciting and moving but rest of production is bland.

Crist, Judith. **"A Few Bangs, and Many a Whimper."** *New York Magazine,* 22 December 1969, p. 57.

"It is a brisk and pointed production."

"Elsinore of the Mind." *Time,* 12 January 1970, p. 73.

Considers Williamson's Hamlet one of the great performances.

Esslin, Martin. **"Theater in London; A Great Actor—I Mean Great."** *New York Times,* 2 March 1969, p. D3.

Considers this "the most intelligent Hamlet I have ever seen, the only one who quite obviously understands every word he is saying . . . a great and revolutionary Hamlet."

Frederick, Robert B. **"Nicol Williamson at Film Confab Shows Heart's with Legit."** *Variety,* 14 May 1969, p. 18.

Greenspun, Roger. **"Williamson as Hamlet: Richardson Film Based on Debated Version."** *New York Times,* 22 December 1969, p. L43.

Because the text "has been cut to ribbons . . . Hamlet's presence is magnified out of all proper relationship to the world around him."

"*Hamlet* (British—Color)." *Variety,* 17 December 1969.

"*Hamlet* Film: A Piercing Experience." *Christian Science Monitor,* 3 January 1970.

Haskell, Molly. **"*Hamlet.*"** *Village Voice,* 8 January 1970, pp. 53–54.

Calls the film "a mirror of the cosmically bereft times we live in"; its effect is "one of fragmented introversion" void of tragic framework.

Hewes, Henry. **"A Fresh Hamlet."** *Saturday Review,* 12 April 1969, p. 58.

Reviews London production from which film was made, finding Williamson ignoring the meter of the verse and attempting "to give us a smaller and more human Hamlet."

Jorgens, Jack J. **"Teaching Manual, *Hamlet* (Richardson Version)."** Audio Brandon Films, 1978.

Part of the "Literature and Film" series, includes a critical interpretation, film outline, critic's round table, activities, and bibliography.

Kael, Pauline. **"The Current Cinema: English Bull."** *New Yorker,* 17 January 1970, pp. 66–71. Reprinted in her *Deeper Into Movies,* pp. 88–91. Boston: Little, Brown, 1973.

"The play collapses not only as drama, but as poetic drama. Williamson's morose, self-pitying Hamlet lacks heroism, and Hamlet's speeches, as Williamson delivers them, lack beauty."

Kerr, Walter. **"Oliver Twist as Hamlet."** *New York Times,* 11 May 1969, p. 1D.

"Williamson's performance is without physical tension of any kind . . . he stands at one side of the stage, readying his next thought, while no play goes on without it."

Knight, Arthur. **"Still There, Old Mole?"** *Saturday Review,* 17 January 1970, p. 44.

While not destined to go down in the history books, Richardson's *Hamlet* is memorable and presents a fresh, controversial interpretation.

Litton, Glenn. **"Diseased Beauty in Tony Richardson's *Hamlet.*"** *Literature/Film Quarterly* 4 (Spring 1976): 108–22.

Argues that every shot "is designed to express metaphorically Elsinore's diseased beauty" by means that "do not draw attention to themselves."

Mullin, Michael. **"Tony Richardson's *Hamlet*: Script and Screen."** *Literature/Film Quarterly* 4 (Spring 1976): 123–30.

Explores the unconventional production as conceived for both stage and screen.

"Salute of the Week: Nicol Williamson." *Cue,* 17 May 1969.

Simon, John. **"My Throat's in the Midlands."** *New York Magazine,* 19 May 1969, p. 56.

Objects to Williamson's accent and appearance, praises the Play Scene, observes that the "Hamlet-Ophelia scenes substitute sexual horseplay for authentic feeling," finds that the portrayal of the Ghost is "worst of all," and thinks that "the supporting performances are quite unsupportable."

"Theater Abroad: Member of the Company." *Time,* 28 February 1969, p. 74.

Praises Williamson's performance.

Tynan, Kenneth. **"Nicol Williamson: the Road to the White House."** In his

The Sound of Two Hands Clapping, pp. 13–57. New York: Holt, Rinehart & Winston, 1975.

A delightful personal account of Williamson's preparation to perform Shakespeare at the White House; also mentions stage *Hamlet.*

Walsh, Moira. **Review.** *America,* 14 February 1970, p. 170.

"I have severe problems with Williamson's interpretation (strong in sardonic humor but weak on poetry and grandeur), as well as with the odd way the text was cut and the claustrophobically close-up photography."

Wardle, Irving. **"Tony Richardson Courts Young Theater Audience."** *New York Times,* 19 February 1969, p. 38.

Williamson "flouts the character's nobility and irresolution, and presents a blisteringly sardonic man of action."

See also, in General section, Duffy, Dworkin, Halio, Silber.

Henry V *(1944). Directed by Laurence Olivier.*

Agate, James. **Review.** *The Times* (London), 3 December 1944.

Agee, James. *"Henry V." Time,* 8 April 1946, p. 58. Reprinted in his *Agee on Film,* pp. 209–12. New York: Grosset & Dunlap, 1958; in *Focus on Shakespearean Films,* edited by Charles W. Eckert, pp. 54–56. Englewood Cliffs, N.J.: Prentice-Hall, 1972; and in *Film Theory and Criticism,* edited by Gerald Mast and Marshall Cohen, pp. 333–36. New York: Oxford University Press, 1974.

Praises Olivier's achievement and the language of the film.

B., G. **"The Film of *Henry V."*** *English* 5 (1945): 107–08.

"The picture is not only a fine achievement in itself but gives promise of infinite possibilities in respect of filming further plays" by Shakespeare.

Brown, John Mason. **"Seeing Things: The Old Vic and *Henry V."*** *Saturday Review of Literature,* 25 May 1946, pp. 24–26, 28.

Reviews Old Vic Broadway production of *1 & 2 H4* and Olivier film, missing in stage production "what the screen can do . . . those qualities of physical freedom of the chronicle—history uncaged and sent soaring skyward, which makes *Henry V* by all odds, the finest movie I have ever seen, and one of the most enthralling and stirring Shakespearean performances I ever hope to see."

Crowther, Bosley. **Review.** *New York Times,* 18 June 1946, p. 30. Reprinted in his *The Great Films: Fifty Years of Motion Pictures,* pp. 165–68. New York: G. P. Putnam's Sons, 1967, and in *Focus on Shakespearean Films,* edited by Charles W. Eckert, pp. 57–62. Englewood Cliffs, N.J.: Prentice-Hall, 1972.

Thoughtful and enthusiastic praise.

Farber, Manny. **Review.** *New Republic,* 8 July 1946, p. 14.

"A film that is always as exciting, sometimes more so, than the Shakespeare play."

Geduld, Harry. **Filmguide to *Henry V.*** Bloomington: Indiana University Press, 1973.

An excellent guide through the film which includes bibliography. Reviewed by A. McLean in *Literature/Film Quarterly* 1 (Fall 1973): 377–80.

"Great King Henry." *Newsweek,* 17 June 1946, p. 102.

Finds the production "magnificent."

Hartung, Philip T. **Review.** *Commonweal,* 21 June 1946, pp. 238–39.

"Technically, except for its static opening, it is an excellent job."

"Henry V." *Clearing House* 33 (September 1958): 59.

Brief study guide lists ten questions for student discussion.

"Henry V." *Senior Scholastic,* 21 October 1946, pp. 22–23.

A picture story with the comment that "the whole production is a thrilling and imaginative version of motion picture art."

Huntley, John. *"Henry V."* In *British Film Music,* edited by John Huntley, pp. 74–76. London: Robinson, 1947. Reprinted New York: Arno Press, 1972.

Records impressions of the film by composer Hubert Clifford.

Hutton, C. Clayton. **The Making of *Henry V.*** London: Ernest J. Day, 1945.

Jorgens, Jack J. **"Laurence Olivier's *Henry V.*"** In his *Shakespeare on Film,* pp. 122–35. Bloomington: Indiana University Press, 1977.

"A classic among Shakespeare films . . . it is a unique blend of realism and artifice."

Lejeune, Caroline A. **Review.** *The Observer,* 26 November 1944. Revised and reprinted as "The Wider Cockpit: Henry the Fifth," in her *Chestnuts* *in Her Lap, 1936–46,* pp. 134–35. London: Phoenix House, 1947; and as "Two English Films," in *Theatre Arts Anthology,* edited by Rosamond Gilder, et al., pp. 564–69. New York: Theatre Arts Books, 1950.

Recognizes Olivier for catching Shakespeare's "salute to high adventure . . . [and] a kind of boyish exaltation of man's grim work."

Life, 20 May 1946, pp. 38–42.

Provides background of film.

McCarten, John. **Review.** *The New Yorker,* 22 June 1946, pp. 40–42.

"There is no air of pedantry about the film. . . . On the strength of *Henry V* . . . [Olivier] has emerged as the most imaginative film-maker around."

McConnell, Stanlie. *"Henry V:* **An American Analysis of the Score."** In *British Film Music,* edited by John Huntley, pp. 171–76. London: Robinson, 1947. Reprinted New York: Arno Press, 1972.

A succinct commentary on aspects of the score.

McCreadie, Marsha. *"Henry V:* **Onstage and On Film."** *Literature/Film Quarterly* 5 (Fall 1977): 316–21.

Compares film with recent theatrical productions.

Manvell, Roger. *"Henry V* **on the Films."** *Britain Today,* March 1945, pp. 25–26.

Manvell, Roger, and Huntley, John. **The Technique of Film Music.** New York: Hastings House, 1975, rev. and enlarged by Richard Arnell and Peter Day.

Contains an analysis of the music for the Agincourt sequence with stills and musical score reproduced (pp. 96–107), a discussion of the "music and action" (pp. 90–95), the opening score (pp. 126–27), and the use of music to underlie speech as in Falstaff's death scene (p. 165).

Merton, James. **"Shakespeare Comes to the Films."** *Christian Science Monitor,* 30 March 1946, p. 7.

"The production . . . follows the original text more closely than any of the many stage productions."

Mosdell, D. **Review.** *Canadian Forum* (Toronto) 26 (October 1946): 161.

Norton, Elliott. **"Drama and Politics Mingled Expertly in Film** *Henry V.*" *Boston Post,* 7 April 1946.

"I have rarely ever seen Shakespeare done with such magnificent success or British propaganda presented with such pushing insistence."

Herzberg, M. **"Olivier as *Henry V.*"** *Scholastic Teacher,* 14 October 1946, p. 6T.

"Olivier Found England at War No Place to Film Battle of 1415." *New York Herald-Tribune,* 2 June 1946, p. 3.

Olivier, Laurence, and Beck, Reginald. **"Screenplay for *Henry V.*"** In *Film Scripts One,* edited by G. P. Garrett, O. B. Hardison, Jr., and Jane R. Gelfman. New York: Appleton-Century-Crofts, 1971.

Presents scenario text used for the film.

Phillips, James E. **"Adapted from a Play by Shakespeare."** *Hollywood Quarterly* 2 (October 1946): 82–90.

Analysis of cuts made in the film.

Powell, Dilys. **Review.** *The Times* (London), 26 November 1944.

"A production finely felt and finely played. . . ."

"Recreates Medieval Paintings." *Vogue,* 1 September 1946, pp. 218–19.

Wyatt, Euphemia. **Review.** *The Catholic World* 163 (August 1946): 457.

See also, in General section, Camp, D., Dehn, Durgnat, Fuegi, Kael, Raynor, Smith, Walker.

Julius Caesar *(1950). Directed by David Bradley.*

Foy, Ted. **"A Non-Shakespearean Anachronism in Bradley's *Julius Caesar.*"** *Shakespeare on Film Newsletter* 2 (December 1977): 8.

Notes that in the Lupercal frames, a taxi can be seen through the grill behind Caesar.

Huff, Theodore. **Review.** *Films in Review* 4 (January 1953): 38.

"A very ingenious movie," more cinematic than Olivier's films; also has enthusiasm, vigor, and freshness.

Review. *Saturday Review,* 13 December 1952, p. 28.

Review. *Scholastic Teacher,* 2 April 1952, p. 13T.

Seton, Marie. **"Ancient Rome in Gangster Town."** *Sight and Sound* (London) 19 (June 1950): 176–77.

A low budget ($10,000) compelled Bradley to use his imagination to produce "the most essentially 'filmic' production of Shakespeare."

See also, in General section, Richter, Skoller.

Julius Caesar *(1953). Directed by Joseph Mankiewicz.*

Bentley, Eric. *"Julius Caesar,* **1953."** *New Republic,* 3 August 1953, pp. 20–21.

While Gielgud and O'Brien play their roles well, Mason and Brando do not. "The actual filming of Shakespeare never fails to remind me how utterly he belongs to the stage."

Bernard, M. A. *"Julius Caesar* in Hollywood." *Philippine Studies* (Manila) 2 (1954): 286–90.

Analysis of the film's success and its impact on the Philippines.

Bontemps, Jacques, and Overstreet, Richard. **"Mesure pour Mesure: Entretien avec Joseph L. Mankiewicz."** *Cahiers du Cinema* (Paris) no. 178 (May 1966): 36–50.

Interview covers much of Mankiewicz's work and includes a filmography; Mankiewicz says "je ne connais pas d'auteur dramatique plus vivant que M. Shakespeare."

Crowther, Bosley. **Review.** *New York Times,* 5 June 1953.

Praises director's ability to cope with the theatrical modes of the text.

Doeckel, Ken. **"Miklos Rozsa."** *Films in Review* 16 (November 1965): 536–48.

Rozsa decided "to regard the film as a drama about the eternal problem of dictators. I wrote the music I would have written for a modern stage representation: interpretive, incidental music, expressing, with my own musical language for a modern audience, what Shakespeare expressed with his own language for his own audience . . ." (p. 544).

"Et tu, Brando?" *Time,* 27 October 1952, p. 87.

Announces the cast and comments on treatment of Shakespearean dialogue.

Guernsey, Otis. **Review.** *New York Herald-Tribune,* 5 June 1953.

A powerful film with excellent dialogue.

Hart, Henry. **"1953's Ten Best."** *Films in Review* 5 (January 1954): 1–2.

The film is "not only an able transfer to the screen of a great Shake-spearean classic, . . . it is also an unusually skillful use of cinematic means for vivifying truths about political power. . . . No production of *Julius Caesar* has been infused with more *contemporaneity.* . . ."

Hatch, Robert. **"Joe Mankiewicz and the Capitoline Hill Mob."** *The Reporter,* 21 July 1953, pp. 35–36.

"The picture is bold, immediate, and passtionate; . . . As film workman-ship it is exemplary." Yet, regards the play as filmed too much a Roman contest of strength and too little an Elizabethan tragedy of psychological weakness.

"Holl." **Review.** *Variety,* 3 June 1953.

Sees setting as "stylized" but appropriate.

Hope-Wallace, Philip. **Review.** *Sight and Sound* (London) 21 (August-September 1951): 22–23.

Houseman, John. *"Julius Caesar***: Mr. Mankiewicz's Shooting Script."** *Film Quarterly* 8 (Winter 1953): 109–24.

Presents two fragments of the screenplay: the moments preceding and following Caesar's death and the Forum sequence.

Houseman, John. **"Filming** *Julius Caesar."* *Sight and Sound* (London) 23 (July-September 1953): 24–27.

Houseman, John. **"This Our Lofty Stage."** *Theatre Arts* 37 (May 1953): 26–28.

Discusses conceptions behind casting, sets, etc.

Houseman, John. **"On Filming** *Julius Caesar***: The Problem Was to Present Shakespeare's Words in a Medium Primarily Visual."** *Films in Review* 4 (April 1953): 184–88.

Explains choice of black and white over color, consciousness of recent historical parallels, and need "to secure a perfect final voicetrack in the set during shooting."

Houston, Penelope. **"Interview with John Houseman."** *Sight and Sound* (London) 31 (Autumn 1962): 160–65, 207. Translated: "Entretien avec John Houseman." *Cahiers du Cinema* (Paris) no. 142 (April 1963), references to *Julius Caesar,* pp. 28–29.

Jorgens, Jack J. **"Joseph Mankiewicz's** *Julius Caesar."* In his *Shakespeare on Film,* pp. 92–105. Bloomington: Indiana University Press, 1977.

Notes that film refuses "to sentimentalize, popularize, or oversimplify" although it is visually disappointing.

Kass, Robert. *"Julius Caesar." Films in Review* 4 (May 1953): 237–39.

Praises film because it "is cinema Shakespeare at its most sincere, its most distinguished, and its most polished."

Kass, Robert. **Review.** *The Catholic World* 177 (July 1953): 303.

Applauds film because it "is quite near to being a filmed play. . . . one of the best samples . . . of pure Bard on film."

Lambert, Gavin. **Review.** *Sight and Sound* (London) 23 (October–December 1953): 89–90.

Praises faithfulness to the text and finds that the production "has an austerity, a dynamic inner force, an absence of externals," and good acting which make it an effective film.

Lewin, William, and Frazier, A. **Standards of Photoplay Appreciation.** Summit, N.J.: Educational and Recreational Guides, 1957.

Final section (pp. 122–60) gives guide for class discussion of Mankiewicz's *Julius Caesar*.

McCarten, John. **"Et Tu, Mankiewicz."** *The New Yorker,* 13 June 1953, p. 60.

". . . there are some extremely apt demonstrations of the art of elocution but little to indicate that the movie commands visual resources that Shakespeare never dreamed of."

Pasinetti, P. M. *"Julius Caesar*: **The Role of the Technical Advisor."** *Quarterly of Film, Radio and Television* 8 (Winter 1953): 131–38. Excerpted in *Focus on Shakespearean Films,* edited by Charles W. Eckert, pp. 102–06. Englewood Cliffs, N.J.: Prentice-Hall, 1972.

Offers interesting observations about the historical accuracy in the filming of the play.

Phillips, James E. *"Julius Caesar*: **Shakespeare as a Screen Writer."** *Film Quarterly* 8 (Winter 1953): 125–30.

Discusses the cutting of the play for the film.

Review. *Newsweek,* 8 June 1953, p. 101.

"An impressive and highly faithful treatment of Shakespeare."

Review. *Time,* 1 June 1953, pp. 94, 96.

Praises the polished and lavish production that "is the best Shakespeare Hollywood has yet produced."

"Speaking of Pictures . . ." *Life,* 2 February 1953, pp. 8–9.

Shows in pictures how actors prepare props and costumes to make the set appear "Roman."

Tyler, Parker. **"Et Tu, Mankiewicz."** *Theatre Arts* 37 (June 1953): 84, 86.

Sees film lacks "heroic proportions" but notes it is well spoken by a star-studded cast.

Walker, Roy. **"Look Upon Caesar."** *Twentieth Century* 154 (1953): 469–74.

Wyatt, Euphemia. **Review.** *The Catholic World* 177 (July 1953): 303.

See also, in General section, Alpert, Dehn, Griffin, Richter, Skoller.

Julius Caesar *(1970). Directed by Stuart Burge.*

Costner, Tom. **Review.** *Village Voice,* 25 February 1971, p. 57.

Jorgens, Jack J. **"Teaching Manual, *Julius Caesar* (Burge)."** Audio Brandon Films, 1979.

Part of the "Literature and Film" series, includes a critical interpretation, film outline, critic's comments, questions for students, and bibliography.

Review. *Cue,* 6 February 1971, p. 64.

Review. *Look,* 9 March 1971, p. 31.

Review. *Media and Methods* 7 (September 1970): 30.

Review. *Senior Scholastic,* 28 September 1970, p. 25.

Review. *Variety,* 10 June 1970, p. 26.

Tiruchelvam, Sharmini. **Review.** *Daily Telegraph Magazine* (London), 6 February 1970, pp. 14–22.

King Lear *(1969). Directed by Peter Brook.*

Andrews, Nigel. **Review.** *Sight and Sound* (London) 40 (Autumn 1971): 223–24.

"A quintessential Dark Ages vision of *Lear* . . . an extension of his fur, leather and steel production at Stratford in 1962 . . . and a further attempt to embody the play's classic antitheses—hard/soft, nature/nurture, natural/unnatural, madness/reason—in terms of palpable, corporeal images."

Berlin, Norman. **"Peter Brook's Interpretation of** *King Lear*: 'Nothing Will Come of Nothing'." *Literature/Film Quarterly* 5 (Fall 1977): 299–303.

Attacks film as untrue to the "spirit of the play" because it ignores play's warmth.

Birkett, Michael. **"King Lear: From Page to Screen: Michael Birkett talks to Roger Manvell."** *Journal of the Society of Film and Television Arts* 37 (Autumn 1969): 15–21.

Discusses various aspects of developing the text, scene, and cast.

Braucourt, Guy. **"Lear a deux voix."** *Nouvelles Littéraires,* 11 March 1974, pp. 20–21.

Compares the Brook and Kozintsev films of *Lear.*

Braun, Eric. **Review.** *Films and Filming* (London) 18 (October 1971): 54–56.

Brook, Peter. **"Entre l'humain et l'epique."** *Nouvelles Littéraires,* 11 March 1974, p. 20.

Brook comments on his film of *Lear.*

Chaplin, William. **"Our Darker Purpose: Peter Brook's** *King Lear."* *Arion* n.s. 1 (Spring 1973): 168–87.

Argues that the film "challenges us to rethink the play," and allowed the director "to explore the scope of cruelty."

Eidsvik, Charles. *"King Lear* **and the Theater of Cruelty."** In his *Cineliteracy: Film Among the Arts,* pp. 257–62. New York: Random House, 1978.

Argues this is an "impersonalized film" in which both Lear and the viewer "become involved in trying to comprehend the incomprehensible."

Johnson, William. **Review.** *Film Quarterly* 25 (Spring 1972): 41–48.

Recognizes a thoughtful exploration of "the confusion of realism and absurdity which persists throughout the film"; also discusses Polanski's *Macbeth* and the influence of Jan Kott.

Jorgens, Jack J. **"Teaching Manual,** *King Lear* **(Brook Version)."** Audio Brandon Films, 1978.

Part of the "Literature and Film" series, includes a critical interpretation, selection from a draft shooting script, film outline, critic's round table, activities, and a bibliography.

Jorgens, Jack J. *"King Lear*: Peter Brook and Grigori Kozintsev." In his *Shakespeare on Film,* pp. 235–51. Bloomington: Indiana University Press, 1977.

Contrasts Kozintsev's "Christian-Marxist story of redemption and social renewal" with Brook's "bleak, existential tale of meaningless violence in a cold, empty universe."

Kael, Pauline. **"Peter Brook's 'Night of the Living Dead'."** In her *Deeper into Movies,* pp. 354–57. Boston: Little, Brown, 1973.

"I didn't just dislike this production—I hated it."

"Kell." **Review.** *Variety,* 17 February 1971, p. 18.

Thinks that lack of color in madness sequences is "disastrous;" and that film remains "very much a stage play."

Knoll, Robert F. **Review.** *Western Humanities Review* 27 (Winter 1973): 85–89.

Emphasizes that Brook "anchors his characters in . . . a medieval world which still shows its links to the Iron Age."

Reilly, Charles P. **Review.** *Films in Review* 22 (December 1971): 627–38.

Calls the film "a mixed bag." "Scofield's portrayal of Lear is one of the great screen performances of the decade." Disparages Brook's attempts "to demonstrate Lear's madness via camera distortion, blurring and off-focusing" as not convincing.

Review. *Catholic Film Newsletter,* 15 December 1971, p. 117.

"A brilliant, stunning production" with powerful performances.

Review. *Filmmakers* 5 (December 1971): 56.

Wilds, Lillian. **"One *King Lear* for Our Time: A Bleak Film Vision by Peter Brook."** *Literature/Film Quarterly* 4 (Spring 1976): 159–64.

Argues that Brook's "interpretation is marvellously realized, that the great strength of the film comes from its carefully articulated design, and that the 'faults' . . . are indeed deliberate and work positively" to support Brook's vision of the play.

Wolf, William. **Review.** *Cue,* 27 November 1971, p. 76.

While admitting Brook "goes overboard" in the storm sequence, calls the film a basically "intelligent, gripping, and commendable adaptation."

See also, in General section, Kermode.

Karol Lir/ King Lear *(1971). Directed by Grigori Kozintsev.*

Adling, Wilfried. **"Historizität und Actualität in Kosinzews Film *König Lear.*"** *Shakespeare Jahrbuch* (Weimar) 109 (1973): 101–02.

Sees Kozintsev's Lear as relevant to our time and reality because it does not copy every detail exactly as it is in the play.

Andrews, Nigel. **Review.** *Sight and Sound* (London) 41 (Summer 1972): 171–72.

"Kozintsev . . . has brought Shakespeare's play fully and idiosyncratically to life without any strenuous reshaping of the original."

Anikst, A. **"G. Kozintsev's *Lear.*"** *Soviet Literature* no. 6 (1971): 176–82.

Reviews comments by Soviet critics who emphasize "the deep humanism" of the film.

Dolinsky, M. **"From Hamlet to Lear." Literaturnaya zageta** (Moscow) 37 (1969): 8.

Concerns the shooting of the film.

Fischer-Weimann, Waltraud. **"Der Film *König Lear*: Aufgaben und Probleme der deutschsprachigen Synchronisation."** *Shakespeare Jahrbuch* (Weimar) 109 (1973): 74–80.

Discusses problems of German synchronized version in bringing a synthesis of the original text, Pasternak's Russian translation, and colloquial German. It is difficult to adapt the Shakespearean text to a film text and to fit the words and verse of Shakespeare to the optical elements of film. Film changes drama.

Hodgdon, Barbara. **"Kozintsev's *King Lear*: Filming a Tragic Poem."** *Literature/ Film Quarterly* 5 (Fall 1977): 291–98.

A sensitive reading of the film, explains how the film achieves the director's intentions, and shapes our response.

Kozintsev, Grigori. *King Lear*: **The Space of Tragedy. The Diary of a Film Director.** Berkeley: University of California Press. London: Heinemann, 1977.

The director's day by day record of his meditations on the play and his adaptation of it. Reviewed by D. Robinson, *Sight and Sound* 46

(Summer 1977): 194–95; by J. M. Welsh, *Literature/Film Quarterly* 5 (Fall 1977): 368–69; and by Lindsay Anderson, *The Guardian*, 14 April 1977, p. 9.

Kozintsev, Grigori. **"Ainsi parlait Shakespeare. . . ."** *Nouvelles Littéraires,* (Paris) 11 March 1974, p. 21.

Comments briefly on his *Lear.*

Kozintsev, Grigori. **"Gedanken zum Film *König Lear.*"** *Shakespeare Jahrbuch* (Weimar) 109 (1973): 56–61.

Contents that Lear achieves greatness once he has become an outlawed subject. Also, the film deals with the conflicts resulting from the predominance of a minority over a majority without rights.

Koztinsev, Grigori. **"Aus der Arbeit am Film *König Lear.*"** *Kunst and Literatur* (Berlin) 20 (1972): 409–25.

Kuckhoff, Armin-Gerd. **"Shakespeare und die Schauspielkunst heute."** *Shakespeare Jahrbuch* (Weimar) 109 (1973): 81–87.

The actors in this film demonstrate the extent to which all action is determined by society.

Laud. **Review.** *Variety,* 29 September 1971, p. 18.

Calls the film an impressive drama with cinematic merit.

Millar, Sylvia. *"King Lear/Karol Lir."* *Monthly Film Bulletin* 39 (August 1972): 165.

Sees the film "as a simple folk tale with rather heavily etched political overtones."

Weimann, Robert. **"Lear und das Bild der 'armen nackten Elenden'. Zum spezifischen Gehalt der filmischen Umsetzung von Shakespeare Tragödie."** *Shakespeare Jahrbuch* (Weimar) 109 (1973): 62–73.

Calls attention to the 'poor naked wretches,' whose appearance at decisive moments throughout the film constitutes a leitmotif with Lear's development.

Welsh, James M. **"To See It Feelingly: *King Lear* Through Russian Eyes."** *Literature/Film Quarterly* 4 (Spring 1976): 153–58.

Admires film because the director's approach is "scholarly, pragmatic, and exegetical . . . and translates Shakespeare's poetry into a coherent structure of unforgettable images."

Willson, Robert F., Jr. **"On the Closing of Gloucester's Door in the Kozintsev *Lear.*"** *Shakespeare on Film Newsletter* 2 (December 1977): 3, 5.

Examines director's use of "cinematic synecdoche."

Yacowar, Maurice. *"King Lear."* *Take One* 3 (January/February 1971): 28–29.

Comments on the eye motif in the film and observes that "Kozintsev understands the duties of the adapter, as well as his rights."

Yutkevich, Sergei. **"The Conscience of the King: Kozintsev's *King Lear.*"** *Sight and Sound* (London) 40 (1971): 192–96.

Offers a detailed analysis of film with reference to shooting script.

Macbeth *(1948). Directed by Orson Welles.*

Bessy, Maurice. *"Macbeth."* In his *Orson Welles,* pp. 41–47. New York: Crown, 1971.

"*Macbeth* reflects the bloody horror the world had just been through: the war, the concentration camps; in this way, the individual pasts of Welles's characters participate in the collective past, and point toward an apocalyptic future."

Beylie, Claude. **"*Macbeth* ou la Magic des Profondeurs."** *Etudes Cinematographiques* (Paris) 24–25 (1963): 86–89. English translation in *Focus on Shakespearean Films,* edited by Charles W. Eckert, pp. 72–75. Englewood Cliffs, N.J.: Prentice-Hall, 1972.

"*Macbeth* is great art precisely because Welles refuses the mediocre compromises habitual in attempts at realism."

"Assignment in Hollywood." *Good Housekeeping,* January 1949, pp. 10–11, 100.

"It's all pretty bad."

Clay, James, and Krempel, Daniel. **"Orson Welles' *Macbeth.*"** In their *The Theatrical Image,* pp. 238–46. New York: McGraw-Hill, 1967.

Contends that if "skilled translation of the playwright's intent is to be our gauge, then this *Macbeth* is only an interesting experiment that misfired." Good analysis of how Welles develops the conflict between savage paganism and newly arrived Christianity as leitmotif in film.

Cowie, Peter. **"The Study of Panic: *Macbeth.*"** In his *A Ribbon of Dreams:*

The Cinema of Orson Welles, pp. 108–15. New York: A. S. Barnes; London: Tantivy, 1973.

Despite poverty of the film's production values "and the unsettling rhythm of the dialogue . . . , there are things to praise in *Macbeth*—the outlandish quality of it all, the . . . respect for Scottish accents, the raw authenticity of the costumes . . . , the intelligent use of extras, . . . and the unerring sense of a man's psyche in the process of disintegration."

Goldwasser, Noe. **"Film Diary for a Film Version of Shakespeare's** *Macbeth." Cineaste* 2 (Fall 1968): 9–12.

Spoofs Welles through fictitious recreation of a "director's notebook."

Hatch, Robert. **"Bloody, Bold, and Resolute!"** *New Republic,* 15 January 1951, pp. 30–31.

Welles has lost more of the play than he has preserved, "but that which he does keep he presents with power and a conviction that will make it stick in the mind."

Higham, Charles. *"Macbeth."* In his *The Films of Orson Welles,* pp. 125–34. Berkeley: University of California Press, 1970.

Provides comments on production problems of an "engrossing melodrama" that Welles intended "to bring . . . to the world of the small town."

Hope-Wallace, Philip. *"Macbeth."* *Sight and Sound* (London) 21 (August–September 1951): 22–23.

While film is not a failure, "one cannot help thinking that a more powerful effect might have been achieved if the film, properly, had been silent."

Knight, Arthur. **"Violence on a Low Budget."** *Saturday Review,* 3 February 1951, p. 25.

"There's precious little Shakespeare here."

Leonard, Harold. **"Notes on** *Macbeth." Sight and Sound* (London) 19 (March 1950): 15–17.

Provides production background, Welles's previous involvement with the play, and observes how he seeks "to demonstrate . . . the practical viability of classics-derived films for a less than total movie audience if turned out on a drastically curtailed budget."

"Macbeth." *Senior Scholastic,* 27 October 1948, p. 29.

Praises Welles's conception of the play as a tale of bloodshed but feels the action lacks suspense and interest.

McBride, Joseph. *"Macbeth and Othello."* In his *Orson Welles,* pp. 106–22. London: Secker & Warburg; New York: Viking, 1972.

Discusses Welles's early love of Shakespeare and analyzes camera work and character portrayal (pp. 112–17).

McCarten, John. **"Orson's Cauldron."** *The New Yorker,* 30 December 1950, p. 51.

Production's "slam-bang quality . . . makes for lively going at least part of the time."

Mullin, Michael. **"Orson Welles' Macbeth."** In *Focus on Orson Welles,* edited by Ronald Gottesman, pp. 136–45. Englewood Cliffs, N.J.: Prentice-Hall, 1976.

Presents a detailed analysis of the film.

"Murder! Orson Welles' Macbeth." *Life,* 11 October 1948, pp. 106–08.

Objects to juggling of scenes and interchange of characters' lines.

Naremore, James. **"The Walking Shadow: Welles's Expressionist *Macbeth.*"** *Literature/Film Quarterly* 1 (Fall 1973): 360–66.

Examines film in context of the director's *oeuvre.*

Noble, Peter. **"Macbeth—And Old Worlds to Conquer."** In his *The Fabulous Orson Welles,* pp. 176–83. London: Hutchinson, 1956.

Brief account of events surrounding and following making of the film.

Pechter, William S. **Twenty-four Times a Second: Films and Filmmakers.** New York: Harper and Row, 1971.

Comments on Welles's *Othello* and *Macbeth* (pp. 170–71), the latter film suggesting that adaptation requires radical transformation of the original materials.

Raynor, Henry. **"Shakespeare Filmed."** *Sight and Sound* (London) 22 (July-September 1952): 10–15.

Review. *Time,* 1 November 1948, p. 90.

Finds fault that Welles and Nolan "play their roles . . . at the top of their lungs," but compliments Welles's imaginative camera work.

Rotha, Paul. **"Murder, My Sweet! *Macbeth.*"** In his *Rotha on the Film,* pp. 176–77. London: Faber & Faber, 1958.

Reprints 1 June 1951 review from *Public Opinion* which claims that "the poetry which alone makes this brutal play acceptable has vanished. Nothing worthwhile is put in its place."

"Scotch Broth." *Newsweek,* 18 October 1948, pp. 109–10.

Notes that "the film falls short not so much in production as in conception," and that Macbeth "is a static, two-dimensional creature."

Smeets, Marcel. *"Macbeth.* **Une Adaptation Cinematographique d'Orson Welles."** *Revue des Langues Vivantes* (Brussels) 17 (1951): 58–62.

Focuses on the cinematic technique that captures the Shakespearean essence.

Wilson, Richard. *"Macbeth* **on Film."** *Theatre Arts* 33 (June 1949): 53–55.

An account of the Utah stage production that preceded Welles's film.

See also, in General section, Bazin, Mullin, Ohad, Phillips, Raynor, Skoller.

Kumonosu-Djo/Throne of Blood *(1957). Directed by Akira Kurosawa.*

Anon. **"Un Macbeth Japonais."** *Cahiers du Cinema* (Paris) 73 (July 1957): 30–31.

Additional comment on "Le Trone de Sang" by Andre Bazin appears in *Cahiers du Cinema* (Paris) 75 (October 1957): 38–39.

Barnet, Sylvan. **"A Japanese *Macbeth.*"** In his *A Short Guide to Writing About Literature,* 2nd ed., pp. 163–69. Boston: Little, Brown, 1971.

A student essay, arguing for the film's artistic integrity, illustrates how to organize and write a critical essay on film.

Bazerman, Charles. **"Time in Play and Film: *Macbeth* and *Throne of Blood."*** *Literature/Film Quarterly* 5 (Fall 1977): 333–37.

Compares the handling of time, pace, and rhythm in film and play.

Beckley, Paul. **Review.** *New York Herald-Tribune,* 23 November 1961.

Finds dialogue a bore.

Blumenthal, J. *"Macbeth* **and** *Throne of Blood."* *Sight and Sound* (London) 34 (Autumn 1965): 190–95. Reprinted in *Films and the Liberal Arts,* edited by T. J. Ross, pp. 122–33. New York: Holt, Rinehart & Winston, 1970; in *Renaissance of the Film,* edited by J. Bellone, pp. 289–305. London: Collier Booking, 1970; and in *Film Theory and Criticism,* edited by Gerald Mast and Marshall Cohen, pp. 340–51. New York: Oxford University Press, 1974.

A provocative analysis of Kurosawa's "distillation" of the essence of Macbeth and his world. See also, in this section, Gerlach.

Crowther, Bosley. **Review.** *New York Times,* 23 November 1961.

While certain scenes are moving, film is "grotesquely brutish and barbaric. . . . To our western eyes it looks fantastic and funny."

Gerlach, John. **"Shakespeare, Kurosawa, and** *Macbeth***: A Response to J. Blumenthal."** *Literature/Film Quarterly* 1 (Fall 1973): 352–59.

Charges Blumenthal with obscuring the extent to which Kurosawa has *betrayed* the power of the play but reveals author's own misunderstanding of film. See also, in this section, Blumenthal.

Kinder, Marsha. *"Throne of Blood:* **A Morality Dance."** *Literature/Film Quarterly* 5 (Fall 1977): 339–45.

Analyzes visual symbolism and visual polarities in film.

Koval, Francis. **"Venice 1957."** *Films in Review* 8 (October 1957): 375–82.

"Mifune ranted magnificently through beautifully composed scenes of medieval savagery, in which each shot was a visual feast. But neither Macbeth's tragedy, nor his lady's madness, touches the spectator's heart in this film. At least not the heart of Western spectators."

MacDonald, Dwight. **Review.** *Esquire* 57 (March 1962): 22.

Experiences characters as 'animals' and the film as a game of cops and robbers.

Review. *Time,* 1 December 1961, p. 76.

"Quite the most brilliant and original attempt ever made to put Shakespeare in pictures."

Richie, Donald. **Japanese Cinema: Film Style and National Character.** London: Seeker & Warburg, 1972.

"In this film Kurosawa continued his thesis that power invariably corrupts."

Richie, Donald. *"Throne of Blood."* In his *The Films of Akira Kurosawa,* pp. 115–24. Berkeley: University of California Press, 1965.

An excellent film analysis well illustrated.

Richie, Donald. **"Kurosawa on Kurosawa."** *Sight and Sound* (London) 33

(Autumn 1964): 200–03.

Comments on the film.

"A Japanese *Macbeth*: Kurosawa's *Throne of Blood.*" *Sight and Sound* (London) 26 (Spring 1957): 195–96.

A picture story.

Sato, Tadao. **"Japanese *Macbeth.*"** *Journal of the Society of Film and Television Arts* 3 (Autumn 1969): 6–8.

Interviews Kurosawa about the influence of Noh and significance of film's title.

Tyler, Parker. *"Throne of Blood."* In his *Classics of the Foreign Film: A Pictorial Treasury,* pp. 220–21. New York: Citadel Press, 1962.

"One can hardly imagine a better adaptation from stage to film or nation to nation."

Whitebait, William. *"Macbeth* **as Stag-Beetle."** *New Statesman and Nation,* 10 May 1958, p. 603.

Regards the film as "neither Shakespeare nor best Japanese."

Zambrano, Ana Laura. *"Throne of Blood*: Kurosawa's *Macbeth."* *Literature/Film Quarterly* 2 (Summer 1974): 262–74.

Demonstrates that the adaptation "evolves not in the traditions of Elizabethan theatre but in a purely Japanese context."

Zunser, Jesse. *"Throne of Blood."* *Cue,* 25 November 1961.

By imagination, dramatic photography, and fine performances, the director has "reshaped *Macbeth* into an engrossing Samurai drama."

See also, in General section, Mullin, Ohad, Reeves.

Macbeth *(1960). Directed by George Schaeffer.*

Deihl, Ernest Roderick. **"George Schaeffer and the Hallmark Hall of Fame: A Study of the Producer-Director of a Live Television Drama Series."** Ph.D. dissertation, Ohio State University, 1964.

Gilliatt, Penelope. **Review.** *London Observer,* 28 May 1961.

Film is "scrupulously uninventive, and curiously bathetic."

Gruen, John. **Review.** *N.E. Herald-Tribune,* 3 October 1964.

Impressed with the use of outdoor locations.

Hutton, Clay. **Macbeth: The Making of the Film.** London, 1960.

Promotional booklet.

Johnson, Sydney. **Review.** *Montreal Star,* 12 December 1964.

All students should see this film for its fidelity to Shakespeare.

Jorgens, Jack J. **"Teaching Manual,** *Macbeth* **(Schaeffer Version)."** Audio Brandon Films, 1978.

Part of the "Literature and Film" series, includes critical interpretation, film outline, quotes from critics, study questions, and bibliography.

Kiley, Frederick S. **"Fates Midnight: A Teaching Guide for Macbeth."** *English Journal* 49 (November 1960): 589–92.

Comments on the TV production and provides six questions for discussion.

See also, in General section, Manvell, Mullin, Skoller.

Macbeth *(1971). Directed by Roman Polanski.*

Andrew, Nigel. *"Macbeth." Sight and Sound* (London) 41 (Spring 1972): 108.

Sees the strength of film is that "it works concurrently on both a naturalistic and a psychological plane."

Berlin, Normand. *"Macbeth*: **Polanski and Shakespeare."** *Literature/Film Quarterly* 1 (Fall 1973): 291–98.

Argues how Polanski reads *Macbeth* "indicates the rich suggestiveness of Shakespeare's art; it also indicates Polanski's personal vision of the modern world."

Coursen, H. R. *"Macbeth*: **Polanski's Disastrous Version."** *Shakespeare on Film Newsletter* 3 (December 1978): 2, 4, 5.

Finds the film is themeless, the movie "all surface."

Crowl, Samuel. **"Chain Reaction: A Study of Roman Polanski's** *Macbeth.***"** *Soundings* 59 (Summer 1976): 226–33.

Describes how Polanski has "artfully interwoven his images of the chain of power, the cup of appetite, and the crown of ambition into a moving testament to *Macbeth*'s power to unsettle us still."

Greenspun, Roger. **Review.** *New York Times,* 21 December 1971, p. 51.

Considers the film neither especially rude nor unnecessarily violent.

Violence is what the play is all about.

Grossvogel, David I. **"When the Stain Won't Wash: Polanski's** *Macbeth.***"** *Diacritics* 2 (Summer 1972): 46–51.

Argues that Polanski's film is flat not because of the director's personal views but because of the difficulties of filming any Shakespeare play.

Jorgens, Jack J. **"Roman Polanski's** *Macbeth.***"** In his *Shakespeare on Film,* pp. 161–74. Bloomington: Indiana University Press, 1977.

Polanski projects a darker view of human nature than does the play and his film becomes a melodrama imbued with political cynicism.

Jorgens, Jack J. **"The Opening Scene of Polanski's** *Macbeth.***"** *Literature/ Film Quarterly* 3 (Summer 1975): 277–78.

Points to inaccuracies in Norman Silverstein's correction [*Literature/ Film Quarterly* 2 (Winter 1974): 88–90] of Kenneth Rothwell's review of the film. See also, in this section, Rothwell.

Kael, Pauline. **"Killers and Thieves."** In her *Deeper into Movies,* pp. 399–401. Boston: Little, Brown, 1973.

Knoll, Robert F. **Review.** *Western Humanities Review* 27 (Winter 1973): 85–89.

Polanski "consistently sees *Macbeth* as a tale of prolonged carnage arising from political instability," while the principal actors "offer nothing beyond certain pleasant exteriors in far more demanding roles."

Reilly, Charles P. **Review.** *Films in Review* 23 (February 1972): 111–12.

"A bloody play has been made bloodier, and the essence of it has been lost."

Review. *Variety,* 15 December 1971, pp. 14, 18.

"There is a pervading virility, bawdy and vulgar but noble at the same time."

Review. *Cue,* 25 December 1971, p. 64.

Richardson, Jack. **"'Relevant' Shakespeare."** *Commentary* 53 (April 1972): 85–87.

Contends that the film is far removed from relevance of any sort and that the play itself has vanished from Polanski's version.

Rothwell, Kenneth. **Review.** *Literature/Film Quarterly* 1 (Winter 1973): 72.

The film's setting "is not so much Scotland as Golgotha" and while

Polanski capitalizes on pop culture, and the vogue of sex and violence, the film "is far better than the egregious publicity surrounding it."

Strick, Philip. *"Macbeth." Monthly Film Review* 39 (March 1972): 52.

The Tynan-Polanski text eliminates ambiguities, strengthens dramatic structure, and gives Shakespeare's language new freshness.

Taylor, John Russell. **"Polanski's** *Macbeth." Sight and Sound* (London) 40 (1971): 77–78.

Comments on "the remarkable youth of the cast" and includes observations by script collaborator Kenneth Tynan.

Tynan, Kenneth. **"Magnetic Pole: A Portrait of Polanski."** In his *The Sound of Two Hands Clapping,* pp. 87–105. New York: Holt, Rinehart & Winston, 1975.

Includes diary notes on production, script, and casting and comments on Polanski's use of a single camera.

Young, Vernon. **"Fat Shakespeare, Fat City, Lean Wilderness."** *Hudson Review* 26 (Spring 1974): 170–76.

Regards this film as "all but the worst Shakespeare ever filmed. . . . Polanski's setting is a panoramic slaughterhouse in which the language is only impedimenta unreasonably holding up the 'action'."

See also, in General section, Gianetti, Kermode, Mullin.

A Midsummer Night's Dream *(1935). Directed by Max Reinhardt.*

Agate, James. **Review.** *John O' London Weekly,* 19 October 1935. Reprinted as "To Film or Not to Film," in his *Around Cinemas,* pp. 151–54. London: Home & Van Thal, 1946.

Takes G. B. Harrison to task for praising the film; only the performances of Cagney and Rooney are praiseworthy.

Agate, James. **Review.** *The Tatler* (1935). Reprinted in his *Around Cinemas.* 2d series, pp. 122–24. London: Home & Van Thal, 1948.

Complains that no one in cast knows how to deal with Shakespearean verse. *Midsummer Night's Dream* "was turned into a Reinhardt's Midsummer Nightmare."

Clay, James H., and Krempel, Daniel. **"Max Reinhardt's** *A Midsummer Night's Dream." In their* *The Theatrical Image,* pp. 232–38. New York: McGraw-Hill, 1967.

Argues that Reinhardt's film "looks like Mendelssohn's music sounds," and as an interpretation of the play "it illustrates a carefully organized image that was definitely not a solution to the problem of communicating the author's intent to a particular kind of audience."

Davy, Charles. **Review.** *London Mercury and Bookman* 33 (November 1935): 62–63.

Film suffers from "a confused excess of arbitrary ornament in which the voice of Shakespeare is heard only faintly and at intervals."

Doybe, Neil. **"Olivia de Havilland."** *Films in Review* 13 (February 1962): 72.

Gives background to how she became involved in her first film, repeating the Hermia role she had played in Reinhardt's Hollywood Bowl production.

Ferguson, Otis. **"Shakespeare in Hollywood."** *New Republic,* 16 October 1935, p. 272. Reprinted in *The Film Criticism of Otis Ferguson,* edited by Robert Wilson, pp. 97–98. Philadelphia: Temple University Press, 1971.

Suggests filming of Shakespeare signifies one aspect of the "culture-club" mentality in Hollywood. Special effects are high-lighted and lengthened in the film while the script is downplayed and shortened.

Greene, Graham. **"On *Midsummer Night's Dream.*"** *The Spectator,* 18 October 1935, p. 606. Reprinted in his *Graham Greene on Film,* pp. 28–29. New York: Simon & Schuster, 1972.

Appreciates acting and scenery but criticizes director's techniques "because Herr Reinhardt cannot visualize how his ideas work out on the screen."

Herring, Robert. **Review.** *Life and Letters Today* 13 no. 2 (1935): 187–88.

Hollywood has exceeded "our worst fears with this picture . . . , the opportunities of the cinema have been so mis-used as to make the play clumsier, more drawn-out and more boring than on the stage."

Jouvet, Louis. **"The Profession of the Producer, II."** *Theatre Arts* (January 1937): 61.

Reinhardt comments: "I have set the condition that this work should represent Shakespeare, and nothing but Shakespeare."

Koeppler, Paul. **"Max Reinhardt auf der Probe: Shakespeare-Inszenierungen aus den Jahren 1905–1938."** *Maske und Kothurn* (Vienna) 19 (1973): 143–50.

Provides insights into Reinhardt's personal involvement with productions and his central concern with Shakespeare.

"Play by Shakespeare, Mendelssohn, and Warner Bros." *Newsweek,* 12 October 1935, pp. 28–29.

Provides background information, credits, cost, etc.

Pleville, M. B. **"Shakespeare a l'Ecran."** *La Revue Hebd,* 28 December 1935, pp. 493–97.

Reinhardt, Max. **"Foreword."** *Shakespeare's* A Midsummer Night's Dream. New York: Grosset & Dunlap, 1935.

Comments on a text of Shakespeare's play illustrated with stills from the picture.

Review. *Time,* 21 October 1935, pp. 44–45.

Sees film as both a work of art and an expensive and experimental curiosity. "It compares favorably with any stage production the play is likely to receive."

Van Doren, Mark. **"Shakespeare Without Words."** In his *The Private Reader: Selected Articles and Reviews,* pp. 299–302. New York: Krauss, 1968.

Notes much splendor but little that was Shakespeare's. Credits Cagney with best part as Bottom.

Watts, Richard, Jr. **"Films of a Moonstruck World."** *Yale Review* 25 (December 1935): 311–20. Excerpted in *Focus on Shakespearean Films,* edited by Charles W. Eckert, pp. 47–52. Englewood Cliffs, N.J.: Prentice-Hall, 1972.

Speculates on close relationship of Shakespearean drama and film, using *Midsummer Night's Dream* to illustrate.

Willson, Robert F. **"Ill Met by Moonlight: Reinhardt's *A Midsummer Night's Dream* and Musical Screwball Comedy."** *Journal of Popular Film* 5 (1976): 185–97.

Suggests Warner Bros. tried to capture an audience for the film by using the techniques of successful comedies of the period.

See also, in General section, Gianetti, Kael, Nicoll.

A Midsummer Night's Dream *(1968). Directed by Peter Hall.*

Eidsvik, Charles. **"The Subversion of Space: Peter Hall's *A Midsummer Night's Dream.*"** In his *Cineliteracy: Film Among the Arts,* pp. 237–44.

New York: Random House, 1978.

Hall's film "opens to cinema new possibilities for portraying dreams in visual terms" as the director "stylizes his images and so fragments his montage that the viewer has to rely on language to sustain coherence."

Hall, Peter. **"'On the Dank and Dirty Ground'."** *Journal of the Society of Film and Television Arts* 37 (Autumn 1969): 11–15.

Interviews Hall on the filming of *Midsummer Night's Dream.*

Hall, Peter. **"Why the Fairies Have Dirty Faces."** *Sunday Times,* 26 January 1969.

Jorgens, Jack J. **"Peter Hall's** *A Midsummer Night's Dream."* In his *Shakespeare on Film,* pp. 51–65. Bloomington: Indiana University Press, 1977.

Provides excellent analysis of opening scenes of this bold experiment with cinematic style and Shakespearean meaning.

Mullin, Michael. **"Peter Hall's** *A Midsummer Night's Dream* **on Film."** *Educational Theatre Journal* 27 (December 1975): 529–34.

"An extremely interesting interpretation of the play" with a uniformly excellent cast and experienced director who uses the full text even though this means too much speaking and some redundancy on film.

Review. London *Times,* 30 January 1969.

"Frankly terrible on every conceivable level."

Review. *The Guardian,* 31 January 1969.

"Just damn silly."

Review. *Observer,* 2 February 1969.

"Drab, mundane, and shockingly inept."

Othello *(1951). Directed by Orson Welles.*

Bazin, Andre. **Review.** *Cahiers du Cinema* (Paris) no. 13 (June 1952): 18–19. Reprinted in *Focus on Shakespearean Films,* edited by Charles W. Eckert, pp. 77–78. Englewood Cliffs, N.J.: Prentice-Hall, 1972; and in *Film Theory and Criticism,* edited by Gerald Mast and Marshall Cohen, pp. 337–39. New York: Oxford University Press, 1974.

"An entrancing work . . . profoundly faithful to Shakespeare's poetry."

Bentley, Eric. *"Othello* **on Film and on the Stage."** *New Republic,*

3 October 1955, pp. 21–22. Reprinted as "Orson Welles and Two Othellos" in his *What Is Theatre?*, pp. 68–72. New York: Antheneum, 1968.

Film is a "precise example of formalistic decadence"; dialogue too obviously dubbed and Welles's acting the part of Othello is poorly done.

Bessy, Maurice. *"Othello."* In his *Orson Welles,* pp. 70–71. New York: Crown, 1971.

"Never before or again . . . did Welles bring Shakespeare to the screen with such perfection, grasping the essence of the playwright down at the center of his own soul."

Bingham, Robert. **"The Shakespeare Boom."** *The Reporter,* 17 November 1955, pp. 34–37.

Provides a general commentary on the recent Shakespeare revival on screen and stage and criticizes Welles's rearrangement of the play which gives him a monopoly of the screen as an actor and undermines film's effectiveness.

Cowie, Peter. **"The Study of Jealousy:** *Othello."* In his *A Ribbon of Dreams: The Cinema of Orson Welles,* pp. 116–27. New York: A.S. Barnes; London: Tantivy, 1973.

Offers solid cinematic analysis in defense of Welles's techniques. Well illustrated.

Crowther, Bosley. **Review.** *New York Times,* 13 September 1955, p. 27.

Welles has "wonderful skill at image-making but a blind spot where substance is concerned."

Dorsday, Michel. **"Othello, ou la solitude de notre temps."** *Cahiers du Cinema* (Paris) no. 16 (October 1952): 53–54.

Admires the psychological and profoundly human point of view of film.

Downing, Robert. *"Othello."* *Films in Review* 6 (August–September 1955): 341–42.

A "worthy attempt to bring Shakespeare to the screen"; film "is stamped with Orson Welles' amazing insight and gross negligence."

Goldstein, R. M. *"Othello."* *High Points* 37 (October 1955): 46–50.

"*Othello* is one of the most brilliantly imaginative experiments with Shakespeare ever filmed . . . ; it is Shakespeare spilling over into a flood of excitement."

Hamburger, Philip. "**The Moor.**" *The New Yorker,* 17 September 1955, p. 132.

Welles ruins the tale "by forgetting the story itself and concentrating on cinematic tricks."

Hatch, Robert. **Review.** *The Nation,* 1 October 1955, p. 290.

Objects to lines being cut and to how Welles tells the story.

Higham, Charles. *"Othello."* In his *The Films of Orson Welles,* pp. 135–44. Berkeley: University of California Press, 1970.

Provides comments on production problems and the vagaries of shooting in a film of "perfect unity, balance, and order, marred only slightly by the technical shortcomings of indifferent dubbing."

Jorgens, Jack J. "**Orson Welles'** *Othello***: A Baroque Translation.**" In *Focus on Orson Welles,* edited by Ronald Gottesman, pp. 146–56. Englewood Cliffs, N.J.: Prentice-Hall, 1976. Included in his *Shakespeare on Film,* pp. 175–90. Bloomington: Indiana University Press, 1977.

Argues that "the visual imagery compensates for the inevitable loss of complexity and dramatic voltage accompanying heavy alterations in the text."

Koval, Francis. "**Interview with Welles.**" *Sight and Sound* (London) 19 (December 1950): 314–16. Reprinted in *Film Makers on Film Making,* edited by Harry Geduld, pp. 257–64. Bloomington: Indiana University Press, 1967.

Includes Welles's comments on *Othello* (he only changed the character of Iago, making him more human) and *Macbeth* ("it is better Shakespeare than most stage productions" he has seen).

Kozelka, Paul. "**A Guide to the Screen Version of Shakespeare's** *Othello.*" *Educational Screen* 22 (October 1955): 31–40.

McBride, Joseph. *"Macbeth* **and** *Othello."* In his *Orson Welles,* pp. 106–22. London: Secker & Warburg; New York: Viking, 1972.

Discusses Welles's early love of Shakespeare and briefly comments on *Othello* as "self-absorbed and rhetorically diffuse."

MacLiammoir, Michael. "**Orson Welles.**" *Sight and Sound* (London) 24 (July-September 1954): 36–38.

MacLiammoir, Michael. **Put Money in Thy Purse: The Diary of the**

Film of *Othello.* London: Methuen, 1952.

An important discussion of Welles's film with a preface by the director. Excerpted in *Focus on Shakespearean Films,* edited by Charles W. Eckert, pp. 79–100. Englewood Cliffs, N.J.: Prentice-Hall, 1972. Reviewed by R. H. Ball, *Shakespeare Quarterly* 4 (1953): 479–81; and by E. H. Nash, *Films in Review* 4 (May 1953): 248.

Marie, Alain. **"L'Esthetique Tragique D'Othello."** *Etudes Cinematographiques* (Paris) 24–25 (1963): 90–99.

Contrasts *Othello* with *Citizen Kane,* the latter evoking the end of Titan, the former a funeral lament interspersed with cries of anger.

Noble, Peter. **"The *Othello* Saga."** In his *The Fabulous Orson Welles,* pp. 207–15. London: Hutchinson, 1956.

Brief account of the making of the film.

Phelps, Donald. **Review.** *Film Culture* 1 (Winter 1955): 32.

Praises natural setting and technique of investing each shot "with an impact and surprise which are greater than any relationship the shot bears to the dramatic content of the film."

Plotkin, Frederick. **"Othello and Welles: A Fantastic Marriage."** *Film Heritage* 4 (Summer 1969): 9–15.

Considers film "decadent"; "Certainly Welles . . . completely relinquishes the role of director as thinker for an interest in separate displays of technical virtuosity."

Robinson, David. *"Othello."* *Sight and Sound* 25 (Spring 1956): 196–97.

Regards the film as visually superb, though it's easy to fault the film in a dozen ways.

Review. *The Reporter* 13 (17 November 1955): 34–37.

Review. *Time,* 6 June 1955, p. 106.

"Despite the camera tricks, engulfing shadows, dizzying vistas of colonnades and architectural arabesques, the film moves forward with a pulse-quickening stir and bustle."

**"Welles's *Othello."* *Newsweek,* 23 May 1955, p. 120.

Finds it a dramatic success.

Whitebait, W. **"Big Brother."** *New Statesman and Nation,* 10 March 1956, pp. 210–12.

"For all its misdemeanors, Welles' version . . . is alive." Othello's conqueror is not Iago, "but that terror of a hostile world which has closed in on a simple hero invulnerable only on the battlefield."

Young, Vernon. **"The Brave American."** In his *On Film: Unpopular Essays on a Popular Art,* pp. 405–13. Chicago: Quadrangle Books, 1972.

Considers the film Welles's most personal achievement and critics are too conservative towards it. Argues there must be freedom in the movies to have creative cinema.

See also, in General section, Griffin, Skoller.

Othello *(1955). Directed by Sergei Yutkevich.*

Dent, A. *"Othello,* **Russian Film."** *Illustrated London News,* 13 July 1957, p. 82.

Drowne, Tatiana Balkoff. *"Othello."* *Films in Review* 11 (1960): 235.

"Dubbing is continuously disturbing."

Gillet, John. **"Between the Acts."** *Sight and Sound* (London) 25 (Spring 1956): 201–05.

Comments on the tightly edited text, unorthodox staging of key scenes, and mobile camera style.

"Holl." **Review.** *Variety,* 16 March 1960.

Visualization is a "meticulous and eyefilling spectacle."

Knight, Arthur. **Review.** *Saturday Review,* 14 May 1960, p. 29.

Calls film visually impressive but decries terrible dubbing.

Prouse, Derek. *"Othello."* *Sight and Sound* 26 (Summer 1956): 29–30. Reprinted in *Focus on Shakespearean Films,* edited by Charles W. Eckert, pp. 126–29. Englewood Cliffs, N.J.: Prentice-Hall, 1972.

Tragedy of "misplaced trust," "a total reconsideration of the subject from first to last in terms of cinema."

Robleto, Hernan. **"Otelo ha Vuelto."** *El Universal* (Mexico City) (April 1957): 3.

Finds the whole situation old-fashioned.

Rozental, Gennadi. **"Sergei Yutkevich, Film Director, Writer, Artist."** *USSR* no. 10 (1957): 50–53.

Sibirtsev, Gennadi. **"Her Debut is a Promise."** *USSR* (September 1956): 42–43.

On the appearance of Ivira Skobtevas.

Weiler, A. H. **Review.** *New York Times,* 16 May 1960, p. 39.

Praises visuals, acting, and voices of English actors but laments the dubbing is not synchronized to lip movements.

Yutkevich, S. *"Othello* **Vu Par Serge Yutkevitch."** *Cinema '56* (March–April 1956): 10–19.

Director comments on making his film.

See also, in General section, Johnson, Skoller.

Othello *(1965). Directed by Stuart Burge.*

Birstein, Ann. *"Othello.* **'a gorgeous blackness'."** *Vogue,* 1 March 1966, p. 95.

Olivier's Moor "is so powerful he could chew up the rest of the cast and spit it out."

Brown, Constance. **"Olivier's** *Othello."* *Film Quarterly* 19 (Summer 1966): 48–50.

As a recording of a stage performance, the film has a great deal to offer: brisk rhythm and variation of camera position sustain visual pace, but too many close shots mar Olivier's performance.

Coffey, Warren. **Review.** *Commentary* 41 (April 1966): 79–81.

As an actor Olivier appears simple-minded and vain and seems unable to get "very far intellectually" into the Shakespeare characters.

Crist, Judith. **"The Role or the Star?"** In her *The Private Eye, the Cowboy and the Very Naked Girl,* pp. 168–69. Chicago: Holt, Rinehart & Winston, 1968.

Lauds Olivier's portrayal of "a man who walks among strangers with super-sensitivities. . . . He is a taut man on an emotional tightrope."

Crowther, Bosley. **Review.** *New York Times,* 13 February 1966, sec. II, p. 1.

Reacts to Olivier's makeup.

Davies, Brenda. *"Othello."* *Sight and Sound* (London) 35 (Summer 1966): 149.

While mise-en-scene is theatrical, "the camera selects, and highlights in close-up, moments of emotional and narrative tension."

Fisher, James E. **"Olivier and the Realistic *Othello*."** *Literature/Film Quarterly* 1 (Fall 1973): 321–31.

While film fails to take advantage of the resources of the film medium, it is still a powerful "amplification" of the play.

Gill, Brendan. **"Black and White."** *The New Yorker,* 19 February 1966, p. 145.

Olivier's "perverse interpretation of Othello turns the production into a memorable catastrophe."

Gow, Gordon. *"Othello." Films and Filming* (London) 12 (May 1966): 6.

"Altogether, a fascinating muddle, from which can be derived an uncommonly privileged view of a great actor at work."

Hartung, Philip T. **Review.** *Commonweal,* 25 February 1966, pp. 614–15.

While costumes and sets are effective, "the total effect is often static and more theatrical than cinematic."

Jorgens, Jack J. **"Stuart Burge and John Dexter's *Othello*."** In his *Shakespeare on Film,* pp. 191–206. Bloomington: Indiana University Press, 1977.

Olivier's *Othello* is always larger than life and "reeks of the magnificence of the stage."

Kael, Pauline. **"Laurence Olivier as Othello."** In her *Kiss Kiss Bang Bang,* pp. 173–75. Boston: Little, Brown, 1968.

Praises greatness of Olivier's acting talents for almost making this "impossible play" work.

Kallct, Nathan. **"Olivier and the Moor."** *Holiday* 39 (April 1966): 143–44.

"It is neither a film version nor a re-creation, but a record, filmed almost cold off the stage."

Kenner, Hugh. **Review.** *National Review,* 22 March 1966, pp. 281–83.

Objects to Olivier's affecting Jamaican speech patterns and creating an Othello at odds with Shakespeare's text.

Kuhn, Weldon. *"Othello." Films in Review* 17 (January 1966): 52–53.

Calls it mediocre film which exemplifies non-cinema. Only Finlay's Iago is effective.

Miller, Don. **"Films on TV."** *Films in Review* 7 (April 1956): 179.

Nelson, Harland S. *"Othello."* *Film Heritage* 2 (Fall 1966): 18–22.

". . . images of Sambo and Mr. Bones have kept many viewers from seeing what Olivier has done. He has created a character who makes the pitch of Shakespeare's action believable. An Othello not far removed from savagery . . . his Othello is finally possessed."

"One Man's Moor." *Time,* 4 February 1966, pp. 103–04.

The film is too much of a one man show; it is "pitted less against Iago than against the Bard himself."

Review. *Newsweek,* 17 January 1966, p. 85.

Olivier has emancipated Othello from literary conventions by making him a dangerous fool.

"Robe." Review. *Variety,* 15 December 1965.

Olivier's is one of the great performances of all time.

Sarris, Andrew. *"Othello."* *Village Voice,* 17 February 1966. Reprinted in his *Confessions of a Cultist,* pp. 235–41. New York: Simon & Schuster, 1970.

Olivier shows Americans an unorthodox Othello when most people have never seen an orthodox one. Americans will get the wrong impression of the play from this film version.

Simon, John. *"Othello."* In his *Private Screenings,* pp. 210–14. New York: Macmillan, 1967. Reprinted in *Focus on Shakespearean Films,* edited by Charles W. Eckert, pp. 154–57. Englewood Cliffs, N.J.: Prentice-Hall, 1972.

Discusses problems of the stage production and of Olivier's interpretation of the Moor.

Tynan, Kenneth. **"Olivier: the Actor and the Moor."** In his *The Sound of Two Hands Clapping,* pp. 127–40. New York: Holt, Rinehart & Winston, 1975.

A penetrating look at Olivier with scene-by-scene notes kept during the rehearsal of the Old Vic Theatre production that was the basis for the film.

W. D. *"Othello."* *Monthly Film Bulletin* 33 (June 1966): 90.

"Burge has simply transported the stage production into a studio and filmed it straight." Olivier gives a "towering performance; but it is essentially a stage performance, and matches ill with the more restrained subtleties of Frank Finlay's Iago."

See also, in General section, Skoller.

Richard III *(1955). Directed by Laurence Olivier.*

Appleton, William. **Review.** *Films in Review* 7 (March 1956): 122–26.

Three short mixed reviews and a note on the music.

"At Home and Abroad with *Richard III.*" *Theatre Arts* 40 (March 1956): 22–24.

"Playbill" for TV premiere plus black and white photos.

Benson, Harold. **"Shakespeare in VistaVision."** *American Cinematographer* 37 (February 1956): 94–95, 119, 122.

Describes cinematographer Otto Heller's part in the film.

Brinkmann, Karl. **"Laurence Olivier's Film *Richard III.*"** *Shakespeare Jahrbuch* (Heidelberg) 92 (1956): 440–48.

Brinson, Peter. **"The Real Interpreter."** *Films and Filming* (London) 1 (April 1955): 4–5.

Predicts film will be a product of its time.

Brown, Constance. **"Olivier's *Richard III*: A Reevaluation."** *Film Quarterly* 20 (Summer 1967): 23–32. Reprinted in *Focus on Shakespearean Films,* edited by Charles W. Eckert, pp. 131–45. Englewood Cliffs, N.J.: Prentice-Hall, 1972.

A succinct appraisal of "an extraordinarily honest film."

Diether, Jack. **"*Richard III*: The Preservation of a Film."** *Quarterly of Film, Radio and Television* 11 (Spring 1957): 280–93.

The film's sound track provides not only a durable version of the uncut film but a means for studying the musical score as a vital and cooperative part of the artistic whole. The only record of the original version is RCA Victor LM-6126.

"The Dark History of a Wicked King: Olivier Makes a Brilliant Film Version of Shakespeare's *Richard III.*" *Life,* 20 February 1956, pp. 80–84.

Valuable for color photographs.

"Films on TV." *Films in Review* 7 (April 1956): 179.

Furse, Roger. **"Middle Ages through Modern Eyes."** *Films and Filming* (London) 1 (May 1955): 10–11.

Describes briefly the authentic fashions used in *Richard III*, and includes sketches of Furse's set designs.

Furse, Roger. **"A Wardrobe for Richard."** *Films and Filming* (London) 1 (April 1955): 8–9.

Comments on the 15th century fashions that inspired his costumes for the actresses.

Griffith, Alice Venezky. **"Shakespeare through the Camera's Eye, III."** *Shakespeare Quarterly* 7 (Spring 1956): 235–38.

Praises *Richard III*, but feels the "larger significance" was missed through cuts.

Hatch, Robert. **"Films."** *The Nation*, 10 March 1956, pp. 206–07.

This review also comments on how Shakespeare might be filmed.

Jorgens, Jack J. **"Laurence Olivier's *Richard III*."** *Literature/Film Quarterly* 4 (Spring 1976): 99–107. Reprinted in his *Shakespeare on Film*, pp. 136–47. Bloomington: Indiana University Press, 1977.

Olivier shows "how rituals, faced with Richardism, can no longer make the world cohere and have meaning."

Kozekla, Paul. **"A Guide to the Screen Version of Shakespeare's *Richard III*."** *Educational Screen* 22 (1956): 51–57.

Knight, Arthur. **"Sir Laurence and the Bard."** *Saturday Review*, 10 March 1956, pp. 26–28.

Offers brief description of film and comments on Henry Hewes's textual changes, the TV premiere, and the historical Richard.

Leyda, Jay. **"The Evil That Men Do . . ."** *Film Culture* 2 no. 1 (1956): 21–23.

"Some of the best film moments are not Shakespeare's contributions." Compares film to Welles's *Othello* and V. Stroyeva's *Boris Godunov*.

Life, 20 February 1956, pp. 80–84.

Provides color stills from the film.

Manvell, Roger. **"Laurence Olivier on Filming Shakespeare."** *Journal of the British Film Academy* n.s. (Autumn 1955): 2–5.

Brief comments with emphasis on *Richard III*.

Miller, Don. **"Films on TV."** *Films in Review* 7 (April 1956): 179–80.

Sees no objection to cuts made for film's U.S. premiere on TV watched by an estimated 20 million viewers.

"The New Pictures." *Time,* 12 March 1956, p. 112.

Praises Olivier's performance and his changes in the script.

Peck, Seymour. **"Sir Laurence Olivier Again Widens His Range."** *New York Times Magazine,* 26 February 1956, pp. 28–29.

Includes pictures and remarks on other Olivier films and stage productions.

Peck, Seymour. **"Now Olivier Acts a Shakespearean Villain."** *New York Times Magazine,* 30 January 1955, pp. 24–25.

A picture story with brief background notes on Olivier.

Phillips, James E. **"*Richard III*: Two Views. I. Some Glories and Some Discontents."** *Film Quarterly* 10 (1956): 399–407.

Praises superior acting in film but criticizes the cutting of some scenes, characters and dialogue. See also, in this section, Schein.

Prouse, Derek. **Review.** *Sight and Sound* (London) 25 (Winter 1955-56): 144–45.

"*Richard III* is not only a very worthy and remarkable achievement but a strong contender for the best Shakespearean film yet made."

Review. *Cue,* 18 November 1958, p. 45.

Review. *English* 11 (1956): 19–20.

Schein, Harry. **"*Richard III*: Two Views. II. A Magnificent Fiasco?"** *Film Quarterly* 10 (1956): 407–15.

Appreciates the acting but deplores editing of text and Olivier's interpretation. See also, in this section, Phillips.

Simko, Jan. **"A Few Notes Concerning the Film Version of *Richard III*."** *Zeitschrift fur Anglistik und Amerikanistik* (Leipzig) 6 (1958): 297–99.

Walker, Roy. **"Bottled Spider."** *Twentieth Century* 159 (January 1956): 58–68.

Attacks Alan Dent's adaptation and Olivier's interpretation.

Wenning, T. H. **"Sir Laurence Olivier: Triumph in Shakespeare's Great Year."** *Newsweek,* 19 March 1956, pp. 105–06.

Provides background about film, play, and historical Richard; cover has Olivier as Richard III.

See also, in General section, Camp, Durgnat, Gianetti, Kael.

Romeo and Juliet *(1936). Directed by George Cukor.*

"An Exhibit of the Source Material for the Filming of *Romeo and Juliet.*" *Library Journal* 61 (August 1936): 589–90.

Describes fourteen panels for an exhibit dealing with various phases of the film's production.

Aveline, Claude. **"Lettre de Londres."** *Revue Bleue: Politique et Littéraire* 74 (1936): 785–87.

Barnes, Howard. **Review.** *New York Herald-Tribune,* 21 August 1936.

"An engaging obeisance to the Bard" which carries visual imagery to extremes.

Barrymore, John. **"Three People in *Romeo and Juliet.*"** *Pictorial Review* 37 (September 1936): 4.

Provides three stills each of Howard, Shearer, and Barrymore asking reader to choose the best one.

"Boy Met Girl—Just 340 Years Ago." *Literary Digest,* 15 August 1936, p. 20.

Film "is Hollywood's best joust with Shakespeare to date."

Creelman, Eileen. **Review.** *New York Sun,* 21 August 1936.

A good picture but "falls short of being a great picture."

Cukor, George. **"Le Paradoxe du Comédien."** *Cahiers du Cinema* (Paris) no. 66 (1956): 68.

Includes comment on directing Norma Shearer.

Cunningham, James P. *"Romeo and Juliet."* *Commonweal,* 4 September 1936, p. 446.

Film is "no feeble Shakespeare imitation. . . . This is sensitive, delicate and as human as any of the great classics to reach the screen."

Elston, Laura. **Review.** *Canadian Magazine* 136 (September 1936): 28.

Brief catalogue of cast for this "great picture."

Erengis, George P. **"Cedric Gibbons."** *Films in Review* 16 (April 1965): 217–32.

Comments on art direction; Verona was "simplified, clarified, and intensified, and the reproduced . . . details were all correct in spirit."

Ferguson, Otis. **Review.** *New Republic,* 2 September 1936, p. 104.

The film is well done and will be widely accepted "as the framing of an old picture rather than the execution of a new one."

"Flin." **Review.** *Variety,* 23 August, 1936.

"A faithful and not too imaginative translation to the screen."

Gillet, John, and David Robinson. **"Conversation with George Cukor."** *Sight and Sound* (London) 33 (Autumn 1964): 188–93.

Comments on *Romeo and Juliet.*

Jacobs, Jack. **"Norma Shearer."** *Films in Review* 11 (August-September 1960): 398–99.

Gives background for her role in *Romeo and Juliet.*

Marks, John. **"Films of the Quarter."** *Sight and Sound* (London) 5 (Autumn 1936): 79.

Finds film "a real, solemn, slap-up costume piece of Shakespeare" which makes a fair beginning in filming Shakespeare.

Nugent, F. S. **"The *Romeo and Juliet* Film."** *New York Times,* 21 August 1936, p. 12.

"We reach the end of the film with this realization: the screen is a perfect medium for Shakespeare."

Review. *Literary Digest* 122 (15 August 1936): 20.

Review. *Scholastic,* 19 September 1936, p. 17.

"It is beautiful, it is authentic, it is moving, and when all is said and done, it is still Shakespeare."

"Romeo and Juliet." *Time,* 28 August 1936, pp. 30–32.

The extreme attention paid to detail and the spare no expense attitude help make this "probably the best [*Romeo and Juliet*] ever shown."

Rothwell, Kenneth S. **"Hollywood and Some Versions of *Romeo and Juliet*: Toward a 'Substantial Pageant'."** *Literature/Film Quarterly* 1 (Fall 1973): 343–51.

This film has been "the major Hollywood contribution to Shakespearean tragedy."

Shakespeare, William. *Romeo and Juliet.* **A Motion Picture Edition.** New York: Random House; London: Barker's, 1936.

Includes play (pp. 25–137) with a foreword by William Strunk, Jr. (pp. 21–24), and the scenario version (pp. 139–229). There are short appreciations by Norma Shearer on Juliet (pp. 233–35); by Leslie Howard on Romeo (pp. 239–40); by John Barrymore on Mercutio (pp. 243–44); by Cukor on directing (pp. 247–48); by Talbot Jennings on the script (pp. 251–52); by Cedric Gibbons on design of settings (pp. 255–57); by Adrian on costumes (pp. 261–63); by Oliver Messel on costumes (pp. 267–68); and Max Herzberg provides "A Preliminary Guide to the Study and Appreciation of the Screen Version of Shakespeare's *Romeo and Juliet* (pp. 269–90).

Stebbins, R. **Review.** *New Theatre* (September 1936): 21–22.

Wyatt, E.V.R. **"Shakespeare on the Screen."** *Catholic World* 144 (1936): 85–88.

The screen can be true to one important Elizabethan tradition: the rushing sequence of the story has no curtains to break the continuity. Those who love Shakespeare needn't fear this film version.

See also, in General section, Gianetti.

Romeo and Juliet *(1954). Directed by Renato Castellani.*

Charensol, G. *"Romeo et Juliette."* *Nouvelles Littéraires* (Paris), 2 December 1954, p. 10.

Crowther, Bosley. **Review.** *New York Times,* 22 December 1954, p. 28.

A "brilliant and exciting action film."

Fayard, Jean. **"L'Affaire Romeo."** *Revue de Paris* (January 1955), pp. 165–66.

Admires film for its rich mise-en-scene and cheerfulness.

Goodman, Walter. **Review.** *New Republic,* 10 January 1955, p. 20.

A "pictorially brilliant film"; Castellani's "best tool is the camera, his goal the direct visual image," yet, in part, the surroundings themselves defeat the young lovers.

Guernsey, Otis L. **Review.** *New York Herald-Tribune,* 22 December 1954.

Enthusiastic and lavish praise of film.

Hart, Henry. **"1954's Ten Best."** *Films in Review* 6 (March 1955): 1–7.

Considers this "one of the most beautiful color films made to date," with a decor integrated with cinematic means.

Hartung, Philip. **Review.** *Commonweal,* 10 December 1954, p. 289.

Praises use of technicolor and supporting cast, but criticizes neglect of Mercutio, overemphasis on Friar John, and slow pace of some scenes.

Hatch, Robert. **Review.** *The Nation,* 8 January 1955, p. 37.

Critical of "liberties taken with Shakespeare's timing and spatial relationships" which causes the film to lose contrasts, slows the dramatic action, and makes the climaxes fail.

Jorgens, Jack J. **"Teaching Manual,** *Romeo and Juliet."* Audio Brandon Films, 1978.

Part of the "Literature and Film" series, includes a critical interpretation, film outline, critic's round table, student questions, and a bibliography.

Jorgensen, Paul A. **"Castellani's** *Romeo and Juliet*: **Intention and Response."** *Film Quarterly* 10 (1955–56): 1–10. Reprinted in *Focus on Shakespearean Films,* edited by Charles W. Eckert, pp. 108–15. Englewood Cliffs, N.J.: Prentice-Hall, 1972.

Takes critics to task for recognizing only the film's scenic beauty.

Kass, Robert. **Review.** *The Catholic World* 180 (December 1954): 222.

Praises director for having "worked in all the physical grandeur of his natural setting . . . into a fast-moving completely cinematic *Romeo and Juliet."*

Knight, Arthur. **"Three Problems in Film Adaptation."** *Saturday Review,* 18 December 1954, pp. 26–28.

Castellani has "recast a triumph of the poetic theatre for a form that is in many ways its very antithesis."

Koval, Francis. **"Venice 1954."** *Films in Review* 5 (October 1954): 394–95.

Reports on how Castellani's film "elicited repeated bursts of spontaneous applause" at its premiere. Says the film "compares favorably" to *Henry V* "and should have a similar success all over the world."

Lambert, Gavin. **"Venice."** *Sight and Sound* (London) 24 (October–December 1954): 58.

Likes "sumptuous visual surface" but not the 'academic' approach.

Landsbergis, A. **Review.** *Film Culture* 1 (March–April 1955): 44–45.

A "visually splendid film," but "as film gains in speed and literal realism, it loses in complexity and character and plot."

Lewin, William. **"Guide to the Technicolor Screen Version of** *Romeo and Juliet*.**"** *Educational Screen* 21 (December 1954): 19–28.

Reviews the film with excerpts from Susan Shentall's (Juliet) rehearsal diary.

Littlefield, Joan. *"Romeo and Juliet."* *Films in Review* 5 (November 1954): 490–91.

Gives facts and details about production, location, and costume.

McCarten, John. **"Shakespeare in Italy."** *The New Yorker,* 1 January 1955, p. 46.

"While the picture is long on beauty, it is occasionally short on Shakespeare," and although it moves briskly, "speed is hardly of the essence in a drama like *Romeo and Juliet*."

Review. *Newsweek,* 20 December 1954, p. 83.

Though Castellani takes liberties with the play, it nevertheless "comes through more clearly and plausibly than it has in most cluttered stage versions."

Review. *Time,* 20 December 1954, pp. 48–49, 53.

"A fine film poem. Unfortunately, it is not Shakespeare's poem." Director ignores the rhythm of Shakespeare's scenes when he cuts from one frame to another.

"Romeo and Juliet." *The Reporter,* 24 February 1955, pp. 47–48.

The production is colorful and exciting but the director's editing will annoy those familiar with the play.

Siclier, Jacques. **"Le rossignol et l'alouette."** *Cahiers du Cinema* (Paris) no. 43 (January 1955): 44–47.

Film is an "excellent spectacle utilisait les moyens du cinema." Also comments on films by Olivier and Welles.

"Tragedy in Verona: New Film Version of *Romeo and Juliet*.**"** *Life,* 6 December 1954, pp. 133–34.

Good color photographs.

Venturi, Lauro. *"Romeo and Juliet."* *Films in Review* 5 (November 1954): 538–40.

This is a one-man film; director has given integrated unity to all parts.

Walker, Roy. **"In Fair Verona."** *The Twentieth Century* 156 (November 1954): 464–71. Reprinted in *Focus on Shakespearean Films,* edited by Charles W. Eckert, pp. 115–21. Englewood Cliffs, N.J.: Prentice-Hall, 1972.

Castellani lays his scenes in fair Verona to such effect that the town "is the indubitable star of the film."

See also, in General section, Griffin, Kael, Skoller.

Romeo and Juliet *(1968). Directed by Franco Zeffirelli.*

Cirillo, Albert R. **"The Art of Franco Zeffirelli and Shakespeare's** *Romeo and Juliet."* *Tri-Quarterly* 16 (Fall 1969): 69–93. Reprinted in *Film and Literature: Contrasts in Media,* edited by Fred H. Marcus, pp. 205–27. Scranton, Pa.: Chandler, 1971.

Zeffirelli "has recognized and used the difference between stage and film to make his *Romeo and Juliet* one of the most unified films ever made."

Cook, Page. *"Romeo and Juliet."* *Films in Review* 19 (October 1968): 513–14.

Regards the film as an "impressive cinemazation."

Cook, Page. **"The Sound Track."** *Films in Review* 19 (November 1968): 571–72.

Nino Rota's score is "cogent, eloquent, a major contribution to film music." See also *Films in Review* 20 (February 1969): 111, where Cook claims the score "has a sensuous ardor that goes well with Zeffirelli's lush visualization of Shakespeare's idea of tragedy in Renaissance Italy."

Delvin, Polly. **"I Know My Romeo and Juliet."** *Vogue,* 1 April 1968, p. 34.

Halio, J. L. **"Zeffirelli's** *Romeo and Juliet*: **The Camera** *versus* **the Text."** *Literature/Film Quarterly* 5 (Fall 1977): 322–25.

Discusses interplay between text and film.

Jorgens, Jack J. **"Franco Zeffirelli's** *Romeo and Juliet."* In his *Shakespeare on Film,* pp. 79–91. Bloomington: Indiana University Press, 1977.

For all its action, emotional power, and sense of theme and structure, the film transforms tragedy into a story of sentiment and pathos.

Kaufmann, Stanley. *"Romeo and Juliet."* In his *Figures of Light: Film Criticism and Comment,* pp. 112–14. New York: Harper and Row, 1971.

Suggests that films and Shakespeare are antagonists, and that lush settings and a patchy text are poor substitutes for the play.

Miller, Edwin. **Interview.** *Seventeen* 27 (January 1968): 82–83, 104–05.

An interview with Leonard Whiting and Olivia Hussey.

"A New Romeo and Juliet." *Look,* 17 October 1967, pp. 52–55, 58–59.

Picture story on Leonard Whiting and Olivia Hussey.

Rapf, M. **"Generation Gap in Verona."** *Life,* 6 September 1968, p. 10.

Praises use of real teenagers in the film because they give "a more convincing portrait of adolescents bursting with sexual hunger. . . ."

Rothwell, Kenneth S. **"Zeffirelli's *Romeo and Juliet*: Words into Picture and Music."** *Literature/Film Quarterly* 5 (Fall 1977): 326–31.

Throughout the film, "word, picture and music make a kind of cinematic conceit in which disparate elements combine to achieve a single effect."

See also, in General section, Dworkin, Gianetti.

The Taming of the Shrew *(1966). Directed by Franco Zeffirelli.*

Alpert, Hollis. **Review.** *The Saturday Review,* 18 March 1967, p. 40.

Birstein, Ann. **Review.** *Vogue,* 15 April 1967, p. 49.

Braddon, Russell. **"Richard Burton to Liz: 'I love thee not . . .'."** *Saturday Evening Post,* 3 December 1966, pp. 88–91.

Comerford, Adelaide. *"Shrew."* *Films in Review* 18 (April 1967): 238.

Complains of Zeffirelli's pro-Taylor bias, of incompetence of script writers having Kate "seem" to capitulate to Petruchio, of opening the film too busily, and of heavy handed direction throughout.

Cook, Page. **"The Sound Track."** *Films in Review* 18 (April 1967): 230–31.

Discusses Nino Rota's score as good functional film music: "lucid, balanced, charming and suited to the mise-en-scene."

Harrison, Carey. *"Shrew."* *Sight and Sound* (London) 36 (Spring 1967): 97–98. Reprinted in *Focus on Shakespearean Films,* edited by Charles W. Eckert, pp. 159–60. Englewood Cliffs, N.J.: Prentice-Hall, 1972.

"The poetry and flamboyance are not wholly missing, merely a little damp."

Jorgens, Jack J. **"Franco Zeffirelli's *Taming of the Shrew*."** In his

Shakespeare on Film, pp. 66–78. Bloomington: Indiana University Press, 1977.

A film version of the Saturnalian Revel, "the film is a beautiful idyll bathed in golden and rose-colored light."

Lane, John. **Review.** *Films and Filming* (London) 13 (October 1966): 50–52.

Marder, Louis. **"The Burton-Taylor *Taming of the Shrew."** Shakespeare Newsletter* 17 (September 1967): 33.

Review. *Time,* 3 June 1966, p. 58.

Sheed, Wilfrid. **Review.** *Esquire* 67 (June 1967): 42–43.

"This Time They're Taming the Shrew." *Look,* 4 October 1966, pp. 58–63.

Shakespeare on Television

"A Video 'Folio': BBC and the 36 Plays." *Shakespeare on Film Newsletter* 2 (April 1978): 1, 4.

Reports that WNET/13 (NYC) will present BBC Shakespeare plays for the American audience and plans to put the films to educational use.

Bunce, Alan. **"Chamberlain *Hamlet."** Christian Science Monitor,* 20 November 1970.

Carthew, Anthony. **"*Hamlet* Revisited; Elsinore Castle Gives the BBC an Authentic Setting for Tragedy."** *New York Times,* 13 October 1963.

Discusses the Plummer production on location in Denmark.

Chamberlain, Richard. **"Why Does an Actor Agree to Do Hamlet?"** *New York Times,* 15 November 1970, p. D21.

Compares his stage version to the forthcoming TV version; "our version is, avowedly and unashamedly romantic. . . ."

Coe, Fred. **"Televising Shakespeare."** *Theatre Arts* 35 (April 1951): 56, 96.

Studio One's *JC* and NBC Playhouse's *Othello* were "correctly transferred" from the stage to the TV studio because they attempt "to make a story with unfamiliar characters and unfamiliar settings understood."

Driberg, Tom. **"A Break for Shakespeare."** *New Statesman and Nation,* 10 March 1956, p. 210.

The ITV version of *Hamlet* is found wanting.

Gardner, Paul. **"The Bard's Play is the Thing."** *New York Times,* 15 November 1964.

Offers background on BBC production with director Plummer's comments on the character of Hamlet.

Gould, Jack. **"Chamberlain, Bouyed by English Cast, Portrays Hamlet on NBC."** *New York Times,* 18 November 1970, p. L94.

"Chamberlain's youthfulness and vigor stood him in excellent stead. In sensitivity and sincerity he had his triumphant moments."

Griffin, Alice. **"Shakespeare Through the Camera's Eye 1953–54."** *Shakespeare Quarterly* 6 (1955): 63–66.

Observes that TV productions of *Lear, R2,* and *Macbeth* are static and generally not well cast or convincingly acted. The camera is too busy roving during major speeches and "there is lacking an over-all artistic unity of spirit or style."

Guardamagna, Daniela. **"Shakespeare e la televisione italiana."** *Studi Inglesi* (Rome) 2 (1975): 465–504.

Hainfield, Harold. **"Studying Shakespeare from Television."** *School Activities* 30 (November 1958): 86, 87.

Hainfield, Harold. **"The Bard of Avon Makes Good on TV."** *Educational Screen* 22 (1956): 35.

Healy, John L. **"A Critical Study of Frank C. Baxter's 'Shakespeare on TV'."** Ph.D. dissertation, University of Southern California, 1965. *Dissertation Abstracts* 26 (1965): 2213.

Analyzes a successful TV series that presented five lectures on *Hamlet.*

Hechinger, Fred. **"Why Shylock Should Not Be Censored."** *New York Times,* 31 March 1974, sec. II, pp. 23, 47.

Response to Jewish pressure groups protesting Olivier's TV production, suggesting "the issue ought to be decided on the grounds of rational analysis rather than the reflex action of programmed emotions."

"*Julius Caesar* Begins TV Series." *Shakespeare on Film Newsletter* 3 (December 1978): 1, 6.

Announces BBC-TV/Time Life Series and various pedagogical and non-print resources available for classroom use.

Jones, Claude E. **"The Imperial Theme—*Macbeth* on Television."** *Quarterly of Film, Radio and Television* 9 (1954–55): 292–98.

Considers M. Evans's *Macbeth* (28 November 1954, "Hall of Fame" series) in terms of principal cuts, stagecraft, and technical aspects of production.

Jones, Edward T. **"Another Noting of the Papp/Antoon *Much Ado.*"** *Shakespeare on Film Newsletter* 3 (December 1978): 5.

This "determinedly American *Much Ado About Nothing*, . . . preserved the timeless world of the text."

Kiley, Frederick S. **"Teaching Guide for *The Tempest.*"** *English Journal* 49 (February 1960): 131–33.

An overview of the play with study questions on John Friend's adaptation with Maurice Evans and Richard Burton.

Kiley, Frederick S. **"Teaching Guide for *Twelfth Night.*"** *English Journal* 46 (December 1957): 582–85.

William Nichol's adaptation for NBC with Maurice Evans "provides a rich field for critical insight and comparison."

Mackin, Thomas. **"Shakespeare as TV Critic."** *Clearing House* 43 (November 1968): 188–89.

Malone, Henry B. **"Half of Hamlet Better Than None."** *English Journal* 48 (February 1959): 94–96.

Provides ten questions for students to answer after viewing TV *Hamlet.*

Marder, Louis. **"An Age of Kings."** *English Journal* 50 (November 1961): 566–68.

Discusses series of fifteen TV programs based on Shakespeare's histories directed by Michael Hayes and produced by Peter Dews for the BBC.

Marill, Alvin H. **"Films on TV."** *Films in Review* 18 (1977): 295–97.

Mentions Olivier's *Merchant of Venice* briefly.

Pierson, Frank R. **"Hamlet and Ben Hecht."** *New Republic,* 20 April 1959, pp. 22–23.

Ralph Nelson cuts the play for the Dupont TV Show of the Month so that melodrama and action are emphasized but "Nelson's accepting suspense for drama, a poor exchange. And his cuts left the residue of action meaningless."

"Russia's TV Viewers See *Romeo.*" Los Angeles *Times,* 23 November 1955, pt. 1, p. 20.

The first soviet TV presentation of a full-length English play in English is Brook's production of *Romeo and Juliet.*

Rosenberg, Marvin. **"Shakespeare on TV: An Optimistic Survey."** *Film Quarterly* 9 no. 2 (1953): 166–74.

Shakespeare can fit the television medium if the plays: are judiciously cut; preserve character, story and meaning; and are acted in nondistracting backgrounds by actors with a knowledge of Shakespeare's language and music and with an ability to communicate these to the audience.

Saville, Philip. **"Record of a Television Production."** *Journal of the Society of Film and Television Arts* 37 (Autumn 1969): 8–11.

Describes how his three hour BBC-TV *Hamlet* was made at Kronberg in eight days and five nights.

Schreiber, Flora Rheta. **"Television's *Hamlet.*"** *Film Quarterly* 8 (Winter 1953): 150–57.

This production (with Maurice Evans) "showed that television . . . has an aesthetic all its own." Praises use of close ups and laments that production was truncated.

"Shakespeare and the People: Elizabethan Drama on Video." *Shakespeare on Film Newsletter* 1 (April 1977): 4, 7.

Discusses various TV productions.

Shanley, John P. **"Tailored *Hamlet.*"** *New York Times,* 22 February 1959.

"Du Pont Show of the Month" featuring Old Vic Company uses technical innovations to cover textual cuts.

Shayon, Robert Lewis. **"A Hit at Elsinore."** *Saturday Review,* 12 December 1964, p. 41.

Claims that Saville's production "succeeded spectacularly."

S., R.L. **"Wm. Shakespeare, Esq. 'The undiscover'd country . . .'."** *Saturday Review,* 16 May 1953, p. 33.

Finds a few particulars praiseworthy in Evan's TV *Hamlet.*

Wadsworth, Frank W. **"'Sound and Fury'—*King Lear* on Television."** *Film Quarterly* 8 (Winter 1953): 254–68.

Finds the Omnibus production directed by Peter Brook disappointing because of the drastic cutting and Orson Welles's portrayal of Lear as a pathetic hero.

Weber, Verne, and Bornstein, Ron. **"Staging Shakespeare on TV."** *National Association of Educational Broadcasters Journal* 21 (November-December 1962): 41–43.

Reports on group involvement in University of Michigan's educational television production of a fifteen-part series of half hour Shakespeare programs.

Part Three

Title Abbreviations

Ado: Much Ado About Nothing
Ant: Antony and Cleopatra
AWW: All's Well That Ends Well
AYL: As You Like It
Cor: Coriolanus
Cym: Cymbeline
Err: Comedy of Errors
Hamlet: Hamlet
1H4: 1 Henry IV
2H4: 2 Henry IV
H5: Henry V
1-3H6: 1-3 Henry VI
H8: Henry VIII
JC: Julius Caesar
John: King John
LLL: Love's Labor's Lost
Lear: King Lear
Macbeth: Macbeth

MM: Measure for Measure
MND: Midsummer Night's Dream
MV: Merchant of Venice
Othello: Othello
Per: Pericles
R2: Richard II
R3: Richard III
Rom: Romeo and Juliet
Shr: Taming of the Shrew
Temp: The Tempest
TGV: Two Gentlemen of Verona
Tim: Timon of Athens
Tit: Titus Andronicus
TN: Twelfth Night
TNK: Two Noble Kinsmen
Tro: Troilus and Cressida
Wiv: Merry Wives of Windsor
WT: Winter's Tale

Guide to Media for
Teaching Shakespeare

Audio Visual Materials

Shakespeare's Life and Times: Filmstrips

The Country Boy from Stratford. Producer: Media Systems Consultants, 1976. Distributor: PERF.

Elizabeth: The Queen Who Shaped an Age. (J,C) two filmstrips approx. 150 fr. ea., col., with cassettes. 1975. Distributor: LCA.
Spans her fifty year reign.

Elizabethan Age. Two parts. (J,H) Distributor: EAV.
"Reign of Elizabeth." "Elizabethan Everyday Life."
Covers political, social, and everyday life of Elizabethan England.

The Elizabethan Era. Producer: SCHLOAT. Distributor: PHM.

Introduction to Shakespeare. Producer-Distributor: EGH, 1961.

Life and Times of William Shakespeare. (H,C) 37 fr. Producer-Distributor: EGH. Shakespeare, Mirror of Man Series.

Life in Elizabethan Times—A Series. Four parts. (J,H) Producer: Wm. Gottlieb, 1958. Distributor: MGH.
"England During the Reign of Queen Elizabeth," 40 fr. "Life in Elizabethan London," 44 fr. "Life of William Shakespeare," 47 fr. "Theater and the Players," 42 fr.
Presents a picture of Shakespeare's England.

Life of Shakespeare. (J,H) 1965. Distributor: EAV.

The Multimedia Shakespeare—A Series. (J,H) col. Kit: 1 book, 8 filmstrips, 24 slides, 4 wall displays. Producer: TERF, 1971. Distributor: CU.
"Shakespeare's Living Words," 45 fr. "Shakespeare, the Man," 51 fr. "Shakespearean Playhouse: The Globe," 61 fr. "Shakespeare's Unfor-

214 Guide to Media for Teaching Shakespeare

gettable People," 50 fr. "Shakespeare, Master of Comedy," 40 fr. "Shakespeare, Master of Tragedy," 51 fr. "Shakespeare as Historian and Poet," 53 fr. "Shakespeare's World Today," 84 fr.

Reviewed by J. S. Windham in *Booklist*, 1 February 1975, p. 589; and by B. H. Herbert in *Simul Games* 5 (March 1974): 105.

The Renaissance. (J,H) 47 fr., b/w. Producer: HEP, 1968. Distributor: DUFOUR. British and European History Series.

Discusses all aspects of the Renaissance in Europe.

Renaissance and Reformation and the Neoclassic Period. (J,H) Distributor: CU. A Survey of English Literature Series.

Shakespeare. (J,H) col., with record/script. Producer-Distributor: FSH. The Great Writers Series.

Describes his life, times, and works.

Shakespeare. (J,H) col. Distributor: HEP. The Pictorial Biographies Series.

Uses contemporary prints and episodes from historical references.

Shakespeare—His Life. (J,H) 52 fr., col., sd. Producer: AV Media, 1974. Distributor: CORF. The Shakespeare Series.

Examines the influence of Shakespeare's environment on his work; uses a cartoon format. Reviewed by B. Montgomery in *Previews*, 3 November 1975, p. 28.

Shakespeare—A Series. Four parts. (J,H) col., with record/script. Distributor: EAV, FSH.

"Shakespeare: His Life," 32 fr. A pictorial biography. "Shakespeare: His Times," 29 fr. Describes the Elizabethan environment and theater. "Shakespeare: His Works," 31 fr. Emphasizes human interest background and major plot lines. "Shakespeare: His Style," 29 fr. Discusses imagery, word play, and blank verse.

Reviewed in *English Journal* 60 (March 1971): 419.

Shakespeare, The Man. (J,H) 51 fr., with record/cassette. Distributor: CU.

Shakespeare, The Man. (J,H) col. 1971. Distributor: TERF. Shakespeare—A Series.

Shakespeare's Living Words. (J,H) 45 fr., with record/cassette. Distributor: CU.

Shakespeare's London. (J,H) 42 fr., sd. 1962. Distributor: EAV, LA.

Uses period prints, paintings, and woodcuts of London. One side of record/cassette is correlated with filmstrip; other side presents collection of songs from Shakespeare's plays. Reviewed in *Visual Education* (April 1975): 42.

Shakespeare's People—A Series. Five parts. (H,C) 1972. Distributor: OLESEN.

"Elizabethan Adventure and Refinement," 23 fr. "Elizabethan Daily Dress," 31 fr. "Elizabethan Government," 33 fr. "Provincial Life in Elizabethan England," 29 fr. "Vital Life of England," 45 fr.

Examines the social and political atmosphere and explains the setting of Shakespeare's plays.

Shakespeare's Stratford. (J,H) 36 fr., col., with script. 1970. Distributor: PERF.

Includes exterior and interior views of Shakespeare's birthplace.

Shakespeare's Stratford. (H,C) 20 fr., col., with captions/script. Producer: George H. Russell, 1970. Distributor: EFS. The England Slidestrips Series.

Shows buildings and important sites during Shakespeare's time.

Shakespeare's Stratford. 76 fr., col., with record. Producer: Literary Backgrounds, 1957. Distributor: OPRINT.

Presents Morris dancers, the markets, the Mop Fair, a birthday celebration, and scenes from *King Lear.*

Shakespeare's Writing Lifetime, 1585–1610. 36 fr., col. Producer: Visual Publications, 1967. Distributor: OPRINT. The Looking into History Series No. 10.

Illustrates the English social scene. Reviewed by F. A. Youngs in *History Teacher* 7 (May 1974): 386.

Time, Life and Works of Shakespeare. (J,H) col., with record/cassette. Distributor: EAV, LA.

Uses paintings, prints, and woodcuts of the period. Record/cassette also presents twenty-two Shakespeare sonnets.

William Shakespeare. (J,H) Distributor: EAV.

Traces his life, highlighting events that contributed to his development.

William Shakespeare: His Life and Times. Two parts. (J,H,C) 56/54 fr., col., with audio tape. 1969. Distributor: PATE. The Great Writers of the British Isles Set 1 Series.

Part I: uses photographs of Stratford, models, maps, and portraits of Elizabethan London. Part II: discusses Elizabethan theater, its construction, and several Shakespearean characters. Reviewed in *History Teacher* 7 (May 1974): 386.

Shakespeare's Life and Times: Films

Elizabeth: The Queen Who Shaped an Age. (J,C) 27 min., col. Producer: LCA, 1970. Distributor: BU, CAFC, FLU, KENT, LCA, IU, OKSU, SCU, SYRCU, UME, UMICH, UMINN, UMO, UNEB, UWLA-CROSSE. The Western Civilization Series.

Explores the Queen's character and her role in leading England to a position of world power.

Elizabethan England. (J,H) 10 min., col. Producer: GEF, 1956. Distributor: UILL, UWASH.

Shows everyday scenes as an apprentice rides to Dover to deliver his merchant master's letter.

England of Elizabeth. (H,C) 26 min., col. Producer: British Transport Films/IFB, 1960. Distributor: BAVI, FLU, IFB, UCOL.

Moments in history of the period (e.g., the Reformation, printing press, sea voyages, Armada) and scenes from Stratford and environs.

English History: Tudor Period. (J,H) 11 min., b/w. Producer: CORF, 1954. Distributor: BAVI, CORF, FLU, UMISS.

The growth of the national state under Henry VII and Henry VIII, concluding with England as a world power under Elizabeth.

English Literature: The Elizabethan Period. (J,H) 12.5 min., col. and b/w. Producer: CORF, 1958. Distributor: BAVI, BU, BYU, CAFC, CORF, FLU, IU, KENT, OKSU, SCU, SYRCU, UARIZ, UCOL, UILL, UIOWA, UMINN, UMO, UNEB, UTAH, UTENN, UWASH.

In a London theater people represent various social classes. Douglas Bush presents excerpts from Elizabethan works. *Comment:* Informative and factually valid, although fictional setting, people enroute to the Globe, is somewhat contrived.

Sir Francis Drake: The Rise of English Sea Power. (J,H) 30 min., b/w. Producer: EBEC, 1957. Distributor: BAVI, EBEC, FLU, UCOL.

Recreates episodes in Drake's life.

Sir Francis Drake's Life and Voyages. (J,H) 13 min., b/w. Producer:

CORF, 1956. Distributor: BAVI, CORF.

Depicts his career as sea captain, navigator, and explorer.

Hamlet: Age of Elizabeth. (H,C) 31 min., col. Producer: EBEC, 1959. Distributor: BU, BYU, EBEC, FLU, IOWA, ISU, KENT, MSU, NILL, OKSU, PSU, SCU, SILU, SUCB, SYRCU, UARIZ, UCEMC, UCOL, UCONN, UILL, UMICH, UMINN, UNC, UNEB, UTAH, UWYO, UWLACROSS, WSU. The Humanities Series.

Maynard Mack introduces Elizabethan life and time with brief scenes from three plays. *Comment:* An intelligent and useful introduction, but not without its faults.

The Life of William Shakespeare. (H,C) 28.5 min., b/w. Producer: WEBC, 1964. Distributor: ASF, AUDB, MACMIL. The World of William Shakespeare Series.

Frank Baxter presents Shakespeare's biography from historic evidence. *Comment:* A static film lecture; uses graphics poorly.

Master Will Shakespeare. (J,H) 11 min., b/w. Producer: Public Media, Inc., 1936. Distributor: SYRCU, UCOL, USC. The Miniature Series.

Presents biography and brief scenes from *Romeo and Juliet.*

The Printing of the Plays. (H,C) 28.5 min., b/w. Producer: WEBC. Distributor: ASF, MACMIL. The World of William Shakespeare Series.

Using four original Shakespeare folios, Frank Baxter and librarian Richard Dillon demonstrate how Shakespeare's works were printed.

Shakespeare. (H,C) 30 min. Distributor: LCA. Great Writing through the Ages Series.

Reviewed in *Education and Industrial Television* 5 (July 1974): 10.

Shakespeare of Stratford and London. (H,C) 32 min., col. 1978. Distributor: KAROL, NGES. The World of Shakespeare Series.

Beautifully photographed and effective use of color and location to capture the world of Shakespeare. Also available in video-cassette.

Shakespeare: Soul of an Age. Two parts. (J,C) 54 min., col. Producer: MGH, 1963. Distributor: BU, BYU, CAFC, FLU, KENT, MGH, MSU, OKSU, PSU, SILU, SYRCU, UCOL, UMICH, USC.

In the first part maps and scenes of English towns point out landmarks in Shakespeare's life. Michael Redgrave recites key speeches. Second part deals with the history plays. *Comment:* References to "today" date film, although it uses interesting technique of pairing on-location shots of sites with plays.

Shakespeare's England Today. (J,H,C) 16 min., b/w. Producer: EASTIN, 1952. Distributor: BAVI, EASTIN, PSU.

Includes scenes of London, Stratford, Welford, Henley-in-Arden, and Shottery to illustrate the influence of these areas on Shakespeare's life and works.

Shakespeare's Stratford. (H,C) 29 min., b/w. Producer: WEBC. Distributor: ASF, AUBD, MACMIL, UMINN. The World of William Shakespeare Series.

Frank Baxter recreates the atmosphere of Stratford-on-Avon.

Shakespeare's World and Shakespeare's London. (H,C) 28.5 min., b/w. Producer: WEBC, 1964. Distributor: ASF, AUBD, MACMIL, WSU. The World of William Shakespeare Series.

Frank Baxter recreates the climate of Elizabethan England by showing old engravings and filmclips of London landmarks.

The Sonnets: Shakespeare's Moods of Love. (H,C) 21 min., col. Producer: EMI, Ltd., 1972. Distributor: BU, KENT, LCA, SCU, SYRCU, UME, UMINN.

Three members of the Royal Shakespeare Co. depict silently words spoken offscreen as dramatic counterpoint. Reviewed in *Landers* 18 (September 1973): 22.

Stratford Adventure. (H,C) 40 min., b/w. Producer: NFBC, 1953. Distributor: IU.

Reviews the origin of Shakespeare's Garden and Theater in Stratford, Canada.

The Stratford Shakespeare Knew. (J,C) 17 min., col. 1971. Distributor: PERF.

A photographic study.

Will Shakespeare—Gent. Producer: BBC-TV, 1967. Distributor: TIMLIF.

William. (H,C) Producer: ABC-TV. After School Series.

Introduces Shakespeare's works. Reviewed in *Sneak Preview* 2 (January 1974): 8.

William Shakespeare. (J,H,C) 25 min., col. Producer: EBEC, 1955. Distributor: BAVI, BU, CAFC, EBEC, FLU, IOWA, IU, KENT, MSU, OKSU, PSU, SILU, SUCB, SYRCU, UCOL, UCONN, UIOWA, UKANS, UMICH, UMISS, USC, UTAH, UWYO.

Life from boyhood through years as actor and playwright.

William Shakespeare: Background for His Works. (H,C) 13.5 min., b/w. Producer: CORF, 1951. Distributor: BU, CAFC, CORF, IU, FLU, KENT, OKSU, SILU, SUCB, SYRCU, UCOL, UCONN, UIOWA, UKANS, UMICH, UMO, UTAH.

Shows places of Shakespeare's time and brief episodes from five plays. *Comment:* Script is both condescending and dull.

Shakespeare's Life and Times: Audio-cassette Tapes

The Autobiography of Shakespeare/A Poet in Italy. (H,C) Distributor: JNP.

G. Highet lectures on Shakespeare as a young man, as revealed through the sonnets, and on the Italian settings of several plays.

Elizabethan Age—A Series. (H,C) Distributor: VALINT.

Records the literature of the Elizabethan Age, focusing on the works of Shakespeare. Includes *AYL, Macbeth, JC, MV, Rom,* selected sonnets, and soliloquies from *Hamlet, Othello,* and *Lear,* as well as songs from Shakespeare.

Elizabethan England. (H,C) 60 min. Distributor: BFA. The Tudors and the Stuarts Series.

Features Joel Hurstfield and A. G. R. Smith.

Elizabethan England—A Series. Nine parts. (H) 15 min. ea. Distributor: DOUBCO.

"Diplomatic Revolution of the 16th Century." "Elizabethan Background of American Civilization." "The Elizabethan Playhouse." "English Dress in the Age of Shakespeare." "English Sea Power in the Tudor Period." "Life of William Shakespeare." "Masters of Elizabethan Literature." "Music: An Integral Part of Elizabethan Life." "Sports, Pastimes, and Amusements."

Discusses the life, times, and literature of an era that represents one of the important backdrops for understanding the American tradition.

A Fellow of Infinite Jest: Shakespeare's Humor. (H,C) 15 min. 1966. Distributor: NCAT. Meet Mr. Shakespeare Series.

His Infinite Variety: A Shakespearean Anthology. 4 tapes, 30 min. ea. Margaret Webster lectures. Reviewed in *Booklist,* 1 November 1975, p. 395.

The Historical Shakespeare. (H,C) 59 min. Distributor: CCASS.

A. L. Rowse is interviewed. Reviewed by J. L. Limbacher in *Previews* 2 (February 1974): 49.

Interviews with Playwrights, Pt. 1: Shakespeare. (J,H) Distributor: CONDS.

Discusses some tragedies and sonnets, Shakespeare's times, and his money motivations.

Introduction to Shakespeare. (H,C) 25 min. 1961. Distributor: NCAT. The Shakespeare at Work Series.

Life in Shakespeare's London. (J,H,C) 30 min. Distributor: SPA. The Shakespeare Library Series.

Lines from Shakespeare for His 400th Birthday. (J) 15 min. Distributor: UMINN. The Your Health and You Series.

Political Ideas/Dramatic Qualities. (C) Distributor: AL.

Lectures by A. R. Humphreys and R. Warren.

Seventeenth Century Literature. (H,C) 60 min. Distributor: BFA. The Approach to Literary Criticism Series.

Lectures by Frank Kermode and A. J. Smith.

Shakespeare. (J,H) Distributor: LISTEN. The World Writers Series.

Shakespeare in the Global Village. (C) 30 min. Distributor: CBCLS.

Comments on the aims of the first world Shakespeare Congress and describes Shakespeare's continued popularity around the world.

Shakespeare or Not, That Is the Question. (J,H) 15 min. 1961. Distributor: NCAT. The Why Is a Writer Series.

Shakespeare, the Man/Shakespeare's Unforgettable People. (J,H) Distributor: CU.

Shakespearean Atmosphere, Pt. 1. (H,C) 30 min. Distributor: UMICH. The Shakespeare at Work Series.

Illustrations from several plays to discuss atmosphere, weather, and horror in Shakespeare.

Shakespearean Atmosphere, Pt. 2. (H,C) 30 min. Distributor: UMICH. The Shakespeare at Work Series.

G. B. Harrison discusses how Shakespearean techniques create dramatic effects with illustrations from *Macbeth.*

Shakespearean Comedy. (H) 29 min. 1961. Distributor: NCAT. The Shakespeare at Work Series.

Uses dramatized excerpts to demonstrate capacity for creating comic episodes.

Shakespearean Diction and Speech. (H) 28 min. 1961. Distributor: NCAT. The Shakespeare at Work Series.

Discusses Shakespeare's techniques for providing the best kind of speech for every occasion.

Shakespeare's Living Words/Shakespeare as Historian and Poet. (J,H) Distributor: CU.

Shakespeare's Many Facets: A Series. Four parts. (H,C) 30 min. ea. 1961. Distributor: NCAT.

"Shakespeare and Religion." "A Shakespeare Gallery, Pt. 1: The Common People." "A Shakespeare Gallery, Pt. 2: The Royal Lines." "Shakespeare's Music."

Discusses the life and plays of Shakespeare.

Shakespeare's Rhetoric. (C) 24 min. Distributor: JNP, LA, LISTEN.

G. Wilson Knight comments on points of structure in some of Shakespeare's long speeches.

This Was A Man. Five parts. 25–31 min. ea. Distributor: PTL.

What a Piece of Work Is Man: Shakespeare's Knowledge of Human Nature. (H) 15 min. 1961. Distributor: NCAT. The Meet Mr. Shakespeare Series.

What Fools These Mortals Be. (H) 15 min. Distributor: NCAT. The Meet Mr. Shakespeare Series.

When Good Queen Bess Ruled England's State: The Elizabethan World. (H) 15 min. 1961. Distributor: NCAT. The Meet Mr. Shakespeare Series.

William Shakespeare. (H) 30 min. Distributor: CU. Masters of Literature Series.

William Shakespeare. (H) 40 min. Distributor: JNP. The History Makers Series.

William Shakespeare. (H) 15 min. 1961. Producer: IU. Distributor: NCAT. The Portraits for Today, 2 Series.

William Shakespeare (1564–1616). (C) 30 min. Producer: Ivan Berg Assoc. Distributor: JNP, LA.

Relates Shakespeare's life and times to the Elizabethan theater.

William Shakespeare (1564–1616). (H,C) Producer: IU. Distributor: NCAT. The Portraits for Today, 1 Series.

Your Mr. Shakespeare. (C) 23 min. Distributor: JNP, LA, LISTEN.

Margaret Webster discusses Shakespeare's theater and various approaches to him.

Shakespeare's Life and Times: Transparencies

Shakespeare and Character: A Series. (H,C) 1966. Distributor: MMAMC.

Shakespeare and Imagery: A Series. (H,C) 1966. Distributor: MMAMC.

Shakespeare: Life, Times, and Theater: A Series. (H,C) Distributor: ERS, TECN.

Uses maps, charts, facsimiles, diagrams, and Elizabethan prints to study the evolution of the theater, Shakespeare's life, historical and literary events of the period, and Shakespeare's language and sources for his plays.

Stratford-on-Avon Church, Shakespeare's Burial Place. (H,C) 1966. Distributor: MMAMC. The Art of Shakespeare Series.

William Shakespeare. (H,C) 8 in. x 10 in. 1966. Distributor: MMAMC. The Art of Shakespeare Series.

Shakespeare's Theater: Filmstrips

Development of English Drama. (H) col., record/cassette/script. Distributor: EAV. The Audio Visual History of English Literature Series.

Drama from Shakespeare to the Restoration.

Early English Drama: The Roots of Shakespeare's Theater—A Series. Four parts. (J,H) with records. 1967. Distributor: EGH.

"Development of the Theaters," 37 fr. "Marlow Leads the Way," 31 fr.

"Medieval Drama," 35 fr. "Pre-Shakespeare Dramatists," 29 fr.

The Elizabethan Theater. (H) col. Distributor: EAV.

Uses paintings, documents, prints, and books.

Shakespeare: His Theater. (J,H) 55 fr., col., record/cassette. 1974. Distributor: CORF. The Shakespeare Series.

Shows development of theater, use of stage areas, and differences from the modern stage.

Shakespeare: Mirror of Man. (J,H) col., sd. Distributor: EGH.

Reviewed in *Booklist,* 15 February 1970, p. 724.

Shakespearean Playhouse: The Globe. (J,H) 61 fr., sd. Distributor: CU.

Shakespearean Production in England: General, 1700–1800. Producer: Common Ground, London, 1948. Distributor: CARMAN.

Shakespearean Stage Production. (H) 40 fr., col., sd. 1966. Distributor: EAV.

Explains how a play was staged in the Globe. Reviewed by F. A. Youngs in *History Teacher* 7 (May 1974): 386.

Shakespeare's Playhouse: The Globe. (J,H) col. 1971. Distributor: TERF. Shakespeare: A Series.

Shakespeare's Theatre. (J,H) 49 fr., col., sd. 1963. Distributor: EAV.

Uses contemporary prints, paintings, maps, and woodcuts.

Shakespeare's Theater. (J,H) 43 fr., b/w. Producer: William Lewis, 1949. Distributor: OPRINT.

Records how a class built a model of the Globe.

Shakespeare's Theater: A Series. Four parts. (J,H) col. 1961. Distributor: EBEC.

"A Day at the Globe Theater," 41 fr. "The Globe Theater: Its Design," 49 fr. "The Playhouse Comes to London," 42 fr. "Prologue of the Globe Theater," 46 fr.

Combines paintings by C. Walter Hodges and photographs of model of the Globe to show the development of Shakespeare's theater. Reviewed in *Visual Education* (August/September 1971): 48.

Shakespeare's Theater and His Audience. (H,C) 33 fr. Distributor: EGH. The Shakespeare, Mirror of Man Series.

Theater in Shakespeare's England: A Series. Four parts. (H) col., sd. 1974. Distributor: EBEC, EAV.

"Origins of English Drama," 55 fr. Explains how early dramatic forms are the basis for the growth and development of Elizabethan drama. "Theater in Elizabethan London," 56 fr. Focuses on the transition from religious morality plays to secular dramatic forms. "The Globe: A Day at Shakespeare's Theater," 53 fr. Shows how playgoers arrive at the Globe and preparations for the day's performance. "The Globe: Design and Construction," 53 fr. Examines the Globe as built from the salvaged timber of James Burbage's Theatre and operated by a group of actors.

Theatrical Costume, Pt. 2. (H,C) Producer: Common Ground, London, 1949. Distributor: CARMAN.

Understanding Shakespeare—His Stagecraft; His Sources. 2 filmstrips, col., sd. Producer: GEF.

Reviewed in *Visual Education* (February 1974): 45.

Shakespeare's Theater: Films

A Creative Rehearsal. (H,C) 15 min., col. Distributor: HRAW. The Art of Shakespeare in *Macbeth* Series.

A rehearsal of *Macbeth* allows a look at how the director and actors come to understand what Shakespeare intended.

How to Read a Shakespeare Play. (H,C) 28.5 min., b/w. Producer: WEBC, 1964. Distributor: ASF, BAVI, MACMIL. The Fair Adventure Series.

Frank Baxter outlines an approach to understanding a Shakespearean play.

A Sense of the Other. (C) 33 min., col. Distributor: NU.

Shows Wallace Bacon conducting a class at Northwestern University on interpreting Shakespeare. See *Shakespeare Newsletter* 28 (February 1978): 5.

Shakespeare and His Stage: Approaches to *Hamlet*. (H,C) 45 min., col. 1975. Distributor: FOTH.

Recreates Shakespeare's theater by staging scenes from *Hamlet* in an Elizabethan courtyard. Director Daniel Seltzer helps a young actor (Stephen Tate) realize Hamlet in himself; includes excerpts from performances by Olivier, Gielgud, Williamson, and Barrymore, and views of landmarks in London, Stratford, and Warwick. Reviewed by M. Z.

Weigler in *Booklist,* 1 December 1975, p. 520; in *Landers* 20 (November/ December 1975): 86; and in *Media and Methods* 12 (December 1975): 73. *Comment:* Film succeeds in getting audience to know Hamlet along with the actor.

Shakespeare: A Mirror to Man. (J,H,C) col. Producer: John Secondari/ Rank/LCA, 1971. Distributor: BU, CAFC, FLU, IU, KENT, LCA, OKSU, SCU, SYRCU, UILL, UME, UMICH, UMINN, USC, UTAH, UWLACROSSE, WSU. The Western Civilization—Majesty and Madness Series.

Background on Elizabethan theater. Reviewed in *Oregon AV* 27 (December 1973): 7; in *Visual Education* (April 1974): 35; in *AV Journal* 7 (September 1972): 45; in *Booklist,* 15 February 1970, p. 724 and 1 July 1971, p. 900; in *Landers* 16 (September 1971): 15; and in *EFLA* 71-7669. *Comment:* Attempts to cover too much material; "a talky film, much like a lecture."

Shakespeare Primer. (H,C) 28 min., col. Distributor: BU, SUCB, SYRCU, UILL, UKANS, UME, UMICH, UMINN.

Hans Conreid recites excerpts from *R3, Rom, Hamlet, Lear, AYL,* and *MV.* Reviewed in *Illinois Education* 59 (April 1971): 187.

Shakespeare Special. 7 min., b/w. Distributor: AAR.

Shows the Canadian national train that brings Canadian high school students to the Stratford Shakespeare Festival.

Shakespeare's Mirror. (H,C) 15 min., b/w. Producer-Distributor: OSU.

Follows teacher/actors' rehearsals and post-performance discussions on segments from Shakespeare. Poor technical and editing work. Reviewed in *EFLA* 71-7498.

Shakespeare's Theater. (H,C) 13 min., col., sd. 1960. Distributor: ISU, IU, PSU, SYRCU, UCEMC, UCONN, UIOWA, UKANS, UMICH, UMINN, UWASH.

Excerpt from opening scene of Olivier's *Henry V* (1944) that shows a 'live' performance at the Globe. Reviews key scenes with drawings and animated maps.

Shakespeare's Theater. (H) 29 min., b/w. Producer: WEBC. Distributor: ASF, MACMIL, UIOWA. The Fair Adventure Series. The World of William Shakespeare Series.

Pictures and a miniature model of the Globe theater show evolution of areas of Elizabethan theater.

Shakespeare's Theater: The Globe Playhouse. (H,C) 18 min., b/w. 1953. Distributor: BAVI, BU, BSU, BYU, CAFC, FLU, IU, MSU, NILL, PSU, SILU, SUCB, SYRCU, UARIZ, UCEMC, UCOL, UCONN, UIOWA, UMICH, UMINN, UTAH, UTEX, UWASH, WSU.

Uses a reconstruction of the Globe (based on J. C. Adams's conjectures) to demonstrate the use of staging area in Elizabethan times. Written and directed by William and Mildred Jordon. Reviewed by F. A. Youngs in *History Teacher* 7 (May 1974): 387.

The Staging of Shakespeare. (H,C) 55 min., col. Distributor: Case Western Reserve University.

Directed by Robert Ornstein, attempts to show how important stage techniques are in bringing text to life. See *Shakespeare Newsletter* 28 (February 1978): 5. *Comment:* Presentation flawed by amateurish acting, directing, and production.

Stratford Adventure. (H,C) 40 min., b/w. Distributor: IU.

Emergence of Shakespeare Theater in Stratford, Ontario, Canada.

The Theater in Shakespeare's Time. (J,H,C) 14 min., col. 1973. Distributor: BFA, BAVI, BU, FLU, IOWA, IU, KENT, NILL, OSU, SCU, SILU, SYRCU, UCEMC, UCOL, UME, USC, UWLACROSSE, UWYO.

Re-enactments of Elizabethan theatrical events with focus on traditions and characteristics of the stage. Reviewed by R. Watts in *Previews* 2 (January 1974): 48.

Understanding Shakespeare: His Sources. (J,H,C) 20 min., col., b/w. Producer: CORF, 1971. Distributor: BAVI, BU, CORF, IU, KENT, MFR, MSU, SYRCU, UME.

Excerpts from *JC, H5, MND,* and *Hamlet* show how Shakespeare enhanced his sources. *Comment:* Rather pedantic approach with poor acting clips.

Understanding Shakespeare: His Stagecraft. (J,H,C) 23.5 min., col., b/w. Producer: CORF, 1971. Distributor: BAVI, BU, CORF, IU, KENT, MFR, MSU, SYRCU, UCONN, UILL, UKANS, UME.

How the Elizabethan theater affected the way plays were written. Reviewed in *Visual Education* (February 1974): 45. *Comment:* Shows clearly the simplicity of pre-Shakespearean drama and explains the parts of the stage, their use, and theatrical conventions.

Will Shakespeare, Gent. (H,C) 50 min., b/w. Producer: BBC-TV, 1967. Distributor: IU.

Documentary evidence and conjectures about the riddle of Shakespeare. Visits Stratford-on-Avon and London.

William Shakespeare: Background for His Works. (J,H,C) 14 min., col., b/w. Producer: CORF, 1951. Distributor: CORF, IU.

Shows the places of Shakespeare's times and the elements of English life with brief episodes from plays.

Shakespeare's Theater: Audio-cassette Tapes

Elizabethan Playhouse: Cultural Center for London. (H) 15 min. Distributor: DOUBCO. The Elizabethan England Series.

Discusses the English dramatic tradition and the birth of the formal theater.

Elizabeth's Theatre. (H) 45 min. Producer: UIOWA, 1961. Distributor: NCAT. The Modern Theater Series.

Hamlet on the Stage. (H,C) 21 min. Distributor: JNP, LISTEN.

T. M. Parrott discusses portrayals of Hamlet by actors from Edwin Booth to Maurice Evans.

Producing Shakespeare. (C) 40 min. Distributor: JNP.

Jonathan Miller discusses problems of a modern producer.

The Secret of Shakespeare. (H,C) Distributor: JNP, LISTEN.

C. B. Purdhom analyzes nine Shakespearean plays to distinguish great drama from entertainment.

Shakespeare and the Audience. (C) 60 min. Distributor: CBCLS.

Discusses audience response to drama and examines the scholar's role in the theater world.

Shakespeare and the Director. (C) 60 min. Distributor: CBCLS.

An interview with director Peter Brook about his work on stage and screen; discusses his production of *Midsummer Night's Dream.*

Shakespeare and the Fundamental Law of Drama. (C) 30 min. Distributor: JNP, LA, LISTEN.

C. B. Purdhom attempts to find the quality that makes Shakespeare the supreme dramatist.

Shakespeare in Canada. (C) 30 min. Distributor: CBCLS.

Discusses production styles, the speaking style, and other topics concerning the Stratford (Ontario) Theater.

The Shakespearean Heritage. (C) 28 min. Distributor: CCASS.

Peter Brook discusses the similarities between Shakespeare's *King Lear* and Peter Weiss's *Marat/Sade,* and the functions of the Royal Shakespeare Theater of England.

Shakespeare's Theater/Shakespeare's Audience. (H) 30 min. Distributor: CU. Shakespeare's Living Library Series.

Shakespeare's Theater: Transparencies

Introduction to the Elizabethan Theater. Two color transparencies. Distributor: LA.

Globe theater: theater in Shakespeare's time and the theater today.

Shakespeare's Plays: Filmstrips

As You Like It: **Shakespeare.** (J) 26 fr., b/w, sd. Distributor: UEVA.

Uses actual cast photographs.

Filmstrips of the Plays: A Series. Seventeen parts. (H,C) Distributor: EAV.

"As You Like It." "Hamlet." "Henry IV, Part 1." "Henry IV, Part 2." "Henry V." "Julius Caesar." "Macbeth." "Measure for Measure." "Merchant of Venice." "Merry Wives of Windsor." "Midsummer Night's Dream." "Much Ado about Nothing." "Richard II." "Romeo and Juliet." "Tempest." "Twelfth Night." "Winter's Tale."

Reproduces Shakespeare productions, many done by the Old Vic Company.

Genius of Shakespeare I: A Series. Four parts. (J) sd. 1969. Distributor: EAV, LA.

"Hamlet, Part 1," 36 fr. *"Hamlet,* Part 2," 36 fr. *"Romeo and Juliet, Part 1,"* 42 fr. *"Romeo and Juliet,* Part 2," 61 fr.

Illustrates *Hamlet* and *Rom* with old etchings, drawings, and engravings. Reviewed by L. Crowe in *School Library Journal* 95 (October 1970): 115.

Hamlet. (J,H) 44 fr., col., sd. Producer: Popular Science AV, 1969. Distributor: DGC.

Examines the nature of justice, the futility of revenge, and analyzes psychological patterns.

Hamlet. (C) 39 fr., with script. 1963. Distributor: EAV.

Illustrates play's high points by using scenes from actual production.

Hamlet: Prince of Denmark. (J,H,C) 58 fr., col. 1968. Distributor: TENMUS.

Explores the play as seen through the eyes of a contemporary director.

Hamlet: Shakespeare. (J,H) 40 fr., b/w., sd. Distributor: UEVA.

Reveals the great moments of the play, through the opening illustration of the Swan Theatre where *Hamlet* was first presented.

Henry V: Shakespeare. (J,H) 24 fr., b/w., sd. Distributor: UEVA.

Depicts presentation in the Globe.

Histories of William Shakespeare. (H,C) 1969. Distributor: EGH.

Julius Caesar. (J,H,C) 649 fr., col., sd. 1970. Distributor: LA, SCHLOAT. The Great Plays of the Stage Series.

Illustrates the play as presented by Roundabout Repertory Company in association with Drury Lane Productions.

Julius Caesar. (H) 44 fr., col., sd. Producer: Popular Science AV, 1968. Distributor: DGC. The Secondary Literature Series.

Play's themes applied to contemporary problems (e.g., directions of national power, the nature of friendship).

Julius Caesar. Producer: EALING, 1971. Distributor: FI.

Julius Caesar by William Shakespeare. (J,H,C) 38 fr., col., sd. 1964. Distributor: EAV.

Highlights scenes using photographs of production.

Julius Caesar, Politician and Dictator. (J,H) approx. 53 fr. Distributor: EBEC. Ancient Rome Series.

Julius Caesar: Shakespeare. (J) 38 fr., b/w., sd. Distributor: UEVA.

Highlights the play as it was first presented at the Swan Theater.

King Lear. (J,C) 75 fr., col., sd. 1970. Distributor: LA, SCHLOAT. The Great Plays of the Stage Series.

Focuses on themes of sanity vs. madness, authority vs. obedience, and devotion vs. ingratitude.

King Lear. (J,H) col., with script. 1968. Distributor: TENMUS.

Explores the play as seen through the eyes of a contemporary director.

Lyrics from the Plays of William Shakespeare. (J,H) 55 fr., col., sd. Distributor: CU.

Costumed actors on pageant wagon invite youngsters to journey back in time.

Macbeth. (H,C) col. 1978. Distributor: Stratford Festival Theatre, Stratford, Ontario, N5A 4M9, Canada.

Kit contains 3 color filmstrips and matching sound cassettes, 2 large wall posters, a packet of material on witchcraft for classroom display, *A Guide to the Play,* and 2 copies of a Teacher's Resource Booklet. Filmstrips entitled: "Unruly Chaos," which discusses plot and themes; "Shapes of Horror," which discusses superstitions and witchcraft; and "The Night Shriekers," which is a study of Macbeth and Lady Macbeth. Based on Festival performance.

Macbeth. (H) 46 fr., col., sd. Producer: Popular Science AV, 1967. Distributor: DGC. The Secondary Literature Series.

Discusses Shakespeare's historical sources, his play's plots, themes, and character development.

Macbeth. (J,H) 47 fr., col, with script. 1968. Distributor: TENMUS.

Explores the play as seen through the eyes of a contemporary director.

Macbeth **by William Shakespeare.** (H) 36 fr., col., with script. 1964. Distributor: EAV.

Shows major scenes.

Measure for Measure. (J,H) 46 fr., col., with script. 1968. Distributor: TENMUS.

Play as seen by a contemporary director.

A Midsummer Night's Dream. Col. Distributor: EDUPRO.

The play as performed by the Royal Shakespeare Theatre Company under Peter Hall.

A Midsummer Night's Dream. (J,H) 37 fr., col., captions. Distributor: UEVA.

Photographs from Max Reinhardt's 1935 motion picture.

Midsummer Night's Dream, **by William Shakespeare.** (H) 41 fr., col., with script. 1965. Distributor: EAV.

Shows major scenes.

Romeo and Juliet. Two parts. (J,H,C) 162/193 fr., col., sd. Producer: FI, 1975. Distributor: EALING.

Condenses Zeffirelli's film version. Reviewed by E. Mandell in *Booklist,* 1 September 1976, p. 48; and by K. J. Scudder in *Media and Methods* 12 (April 1976): 54.

Romeo and Juliet. (J,H) col., captions. Producer: Brunswick Prod., 1968. Distributor: ERS.

Drawings present Shakespeare's play.

Romeo and Juliet. (J.H) 57 fr., col., with script. 1968. Distributor: TENMUS.

The play as seen by a contemporary director.

Romeo and Juliet. (J,H,C) 72 fr., col., captions. 1970. Distributor: EAV. The Shakespeare's Plays Series.

Photographs from an original production are combined with notes to give a full synopsis of the play.

Romeo and Juliet. (J,H) 44 fr., col. Producer: Popular Science AV, 1968. Distributor: DGC.

Themes of the play are applied to the contemporary scene.

Romeo and Juliet: **Tchaikovsky.** (J,H) 81 fr., b/w., sd. 1970. Distributor: EAV. The Music Appreciation Series.

Presents scenes from Zeffirelli's motion picture to illustrate Tchaikovsky's musical version of the play.

Selected Shakespeare Tragedies, Plots and Analyses: A Series. Six parts. (J,H) sd. 1965. Distributor: SVE.

"*Hamlet*: Analysis and Interpretation," 51 fr. "*Hamlet*: The Plot," 50 fr. "*Julius Caesar*: Analysis and Interpretation," 50 fr. "*Julius Caesar*: The Plot," 52 fr. "*Macbeth*: Analysis and Interpretation," 41 fr. "*Macbeth*: The Plot," 49 fr.

Three tragedies are examined for character development, story structure, and use of supernatural elements. Narration and dialogue by Maurice Copeland.

Shakespeare: A Series. Eight parts. (J,H) 8 filmstrips, 4 records, or 8 cassettes, 16 min. ea.; or 2 carousels with 80 slides ea., guide. 1974. Distributor: CORF.

"Shakespeare: His Comedies," 47 fr. Shakespeare's influence on the form of comedy. "Shakespeare: His Historical Plays," 57 fr. The historical period Shakespeare wrote about and his major source material. "Shakespeare: His Life." (See Shakespeare's Life and Times: Filmstrips.) "Shakespeare: His Poems," 57 fr. Poetry in the context of his plays, sources of the narrative poems, and the form and content of the sonnets. "Shakespeare: His Theater." (See Shakespeare's Theater: Filmstrips.) "Shakespeare: His Tragedies," 47 fr. The effect of the Renaissance on Shakespeare and his times. "*Macbeth,* Part 1," 57 fr. Use of character, situation, language, imagery, and symbolism. "*Macbeth,* Part 2," 55 fr. Concerns the second half of the play.

Introduces Shakespeare, the Elizabethan environment, and *Macbeth.* Reviewed by J. Bolt in *Booklist,* 5 December 1975, p. 590; by M. Watts in *Previews* 4 (November 1975): 34; and by B. Montgomery in *Previews* 4 (November 1975): 28.

Shakespeare: A Series. Eight parts. (J,H) 1949. Distributor: MGH.

"*As You Like It,*" 50 fr. "*Hamlet,*" 62 fr. "*Henry V,*" 42 fr. "Introduction to William Shakespeare," 40 fr. "*Macbeth,*" 45 fr. "*Midsummer Night's Dream,*" 53 fr. "*Romeo and Juliet,*" 62 fr. "Shakespeare's Theater," 43 fr.

Adapted from motion pictures; introduces life, times, and plays.

Shakespeare: A Series. Eight parts. (J,H) 1971. Distributor: TERF.

"Shakespeare as Historian and Poet.""Shakespeare, Master of Comedy." "Shakespeare, Master of Tragedy." "The Man Shakespeare." "Shakespeare's Living Words." "Shakespeare's Unforgettable People." "Shakespeare's World Today." "Shakespearean Playhouse: The Globe."

Designed to motivate students toward an enjoyable reading of Shakespeare's plays.

Shakespeare, Mirror of Man: A Series. Six parts. (H,C) 1969. Distributor: EGH.

"Comedies of Shakespeare," Vol. 1, 47 fr.; Vol. 2, 50 fr.; Vol. 3, 48 fr. "Histories of William Shakespeare," 51 fr. "Life and Times of William Shakespeare," 37 fr. "Poetry of William Shakespeare," 32 fr. "Shakespeare's Theater and His Audience," 33 fr. "Tragedies of William Shakespeare," Parts 1, 2, 3, 50 fr.

Shakespearean Production in England: *Hamlet,* **1709–1948.** (H,C) Producer: Common Ground, London, 1948. Distributor: CARMAN.

Made by M. St. Clare Bryn.

Shakespeare's *Julius Caesar.* (J,H,C) 38 fr., b/w. 1962. Distributor: UEVA.

Contains photographs from various productions.

Shakespeare's *The Merchant of Venice.* (H,C) 52 fr., b/w. 1962. Distributor: UEVA.

Presents scenes, costumes of principal characters, and portraits of actors who have played Shylock.

Simply Shakespeare: A Series. Five parts. (J,H) 1970. Distributor: PHM.

"*As You Like It,*" 90 fr. "*Midsummer Night's Dream,*" 90 fr. "*Romeo and Juliet,*" 90 fr. "*Tempest,*" 93 fr. "*Twelfth Night,*" 90 fr.

Stories from Shakespeare: A Series. Six parts. (J,H) approx. 49 fr. ea. 1954. Distributor: EBEC.

"*As You Like It.*" "*Hamlet.*" "*Henry V.*" "*Julius Caesar.*" "*Macbeth.*" "*Midsummer Night's Dream.*"

Taming of the Shrew. (J,H) 80 fr., b/w. Producer: Brunswick Prod., 1971. Distributor: ERS.

An adaptation of the play.

Tempest. Four parts. (H,C) 21 min. ea., b/w. Distributor: ASF. The Fair Adventure Series.

Frank Baxter discusses background and explains important passages.

Twelfth Night. (J,C) 72 fr., b/w., with script. 1970. Distributor: EAV. The Shakespeare's Plays Series.

Photographs from the Oxford and Cambridge Shakespeare Company production, directed by Jonathan Miller.

Shakespeare's Plays: Films

Ages of Man. Four parts. (H,C) b/w. Producer: CBS-TV, 1965. Distributor: KENT, PSU, SYRCU, UCOL, USC, UTAH.

"Youth," 29 min. "Adulthood," 29 min. "Maturity," 26 min. "Death," 27 min.

Excerpts from the plays and sonnets read by Sir John Gielgud.

Antony and Cleopatra. (H,C) 15 min., b/w. Producer: Charles Deane, 1957. Distributor: BYU, FLU, IU, MSU, OKSU, UCOL, UCONN, UILL, UMINN, UTENN.

The Old Vic Repertory Company presents the quarrel between Caesar and Antony (III. xiii).

Antony and Cleopatra. (H,C) 34 min., b/w. 1952. Distributor: BYU, IU, MSU, OKSU, UCOL, UMISS, UTAH, UTENN, UTEX.

Performed by British repertory company.

Character. 21 min., col. 1965. Distributor: SVE.

Examines Shakespeare's skill in developing character.

Explorations in Shakespeare: A Series. Eleven parts. (J,H,C) 23 min. ea., col. Producer: NBC-TV, 1969. Distributor: FI, SYRCU, UCONN, UNEB.

"*Antony and Cleopatra*: The World Well Lost." Examines the conflict between Antony's roles, his duty as a statesman and his obligation as Cleopatra's lover. "*As You Like It*: Doing Your Own Thing." Presents the superficiality of relationships and the romanticism of 'dropping out' of society. (Additional distributor: UARIZ.) "*Coriolanus*: The People's Choice." Examines the relationship between the politician and his electorate, and how a politician, in order to be successful, must be an actor, even at the cost of his own self-respect. "The Trouble with Hamlet." Explores Hamlet's despair and existentialist's dilemma. (Additional distributor: UARIZ.) "*Henry IV, Part 1*: The Making of the Ideal King." Demonstrates the transformation of Prince Henry from libertine to responsible leader, focusing on his development as the ideal king. (Additional distributor: UARIZ.) "*King Lear*: Who Is It Can Tell Me Who I Am." Explores the world of folly, madness, despair, and Lear's growth in self-knowledge. Reviewed by R. M. Williams in *Previews* 1 (March 1974): 15. "*Macbeth*: Nothing Is But What Is Not." Macbeth described as a man who lives in a fantasy world. "*Othello*: An Anatomy of a Marriage." Emphasizes poisonous nature of jealousy and its consequences. "*Richard II*: How to Kill the King." The precarious position of the mighty and how rebellion and assassination are constant threats to statesmen. Reviewed by R. M. Williams in *Previews* 1 (March 1974): 16. (Additional distributor: UARIZ.) "*Romeo and Juliet*: The Words of Love." Stresses the social barriers love has to overcome. "*The Tempest*: O Brave New World." On the struggle to control and prevent evil from controlling one's life. "*Troilus and Cressida*: War, War, Glorious War." Presents a black comedy, where no value survives. Reviewed in *Education and Industrial Television* 6 (November 1974): 47.

Hamlet. (H,C) 20 min., col. 1958. Distributor: BAYLU.

Presents major scenes of an unorthodox staging. Made by Gene McKinney.

Hamlet. 152 min., b/w. Producer: LCA, 1948. Distributor: UARIZ.

Slightly cut version of Olivier's film version.

Hamlet: **Act III, Scene I.** (J,H,C) 8 min., col. 1970. Distributor: BAVI, BFA, OKSU, UILL, UWLACROSSE. The Great Scenes from Shakespeare Series.

Shows Shakespeare's understanding of man as an individual and as a member of society. Actors perform on stage patterned after an Elizabethan theater.

Hamlet: **The Readiness is All.** (H,C) 30 min., b/w. Producer: OPU. Distributor: ASF, OPU.

Analyzes Hamlet's state of mind as he faces death and asks what kind of hero he is.

Hamlet: **A Series.** Four parts. (H,C) 30 min. ea., col. Producer: EBEC, 1959. Distributor: BAVI, BSU, BU, CAFC, EBEC, ISU, IU, KENT, MSU, NILL, OKSU, PSU, SCU, SILU, SUCB, SYRCU, UARIZ, UCEMC, UCOL, UCONN, UILL, UIOWA, UME, UMICH, UMINN, UMO, UNC, UNEB, USC, UTAH, UWYO, UWLACROSSE, WSU.

"*Hamlet* (I): Age of Elizabeth." (See Shakespeare's Life and Times: Films.) "*Hamlet* (II): What Happens in Hamlet." Discusses the play as a ghost story, a detective story, and a revenge story. "*Hamlet* (III): The Poisoned Kingdom." Discusses the poisonings in the play and their meaning through the eyes of the Elizabethan audience. "*Hamlet* (IV): The Readiness Is All." Presents play as dealing with the problems of a young man growing up.

Hamlet: **Studies in Interpretation.** (H,C) 30 min., b/w. Producer: OPU. Distributor: ASF, OPU.

Two scenes show how an academic interpretation comes to life in performance.

Enter Hamlet. (H,C) 4 min., col. Producer: School of Visual Arts, 1965. Distributor: IU, PYF, UCEMC, USC.

Pop-art visual puns mock each word of Hamlet's "To be or not to be." By Fred Mogubgub. Voice of Maurice Evans.

Hamlet Screen Tests. (H,C) 5 min., col. Producer: Glenn Photo Supply, 1933. Distributor: EMGEE, MOMA.

Two test shots of John Barrymore. Reviewed in *Filmmakers* 7 (October 1974): 46.

Hamlet's Castle. (H,C) 6 min., col. 1956. Distributor: UCOL.

Camera captures Kronberg Castle, Denmark.

1 Henry IV: **II. iv., V. iv.** (H,C) 16 min., col. 1970. Distributor: BFA, OKSU, SYRCU, UILL, UIOWA, UWLACROSSE. The Great Scenes from Shakespeare Series.

Performed in authentic costumes on an Elizabethan-style stage.

2 Henry IV: **V. v.** (H,C) 7.5 min., col. 1970. Distributor: BFA, OKSU, SYRCU, UILL, UWLACROSSE. The Great Scenes from Shakespeare Series.

Performed in authentic costumes. Reviewed in *Sightlines* 5 (November/December 1971): 26; and in *Readings* 15 (May 1972): 641.

Henry V. Three parts. (H,C) 28.5 min., b/w. Producer: WEBC, 1964. Distributor: ASF, MACMIL.

Frank Baxter discusses background and key passages.

Julius Caesar. (J,H) 33 min., col. 1952. Distributor: BU, CAFC, FLU, KENT, OKSU, SILU, SYRCU, UILL, UIOWA, UKANS, UME, UMICH, UMINN, UNEB, UTAH, UWYO.

Condensed play stars Robert Speaight (Caesar) and Cecil Trouncer (Brutus).

Julius Caesar. (H,C) 19 min., b/w. Producer: British Information Service, 1946. Distributor: BAVI, BU, BUD, CAFC, FLU, IOWA, ISU, IU, OKSU, SCU, SILU, SUCB, UCONN, UILL, UIOWA, UKANS, UME, UMICH, UMINN, UNC, UNEB, UTAH, UTENN, UTEX, WSU.

Leo Genn and Felix Aylmer perform the Forum scene (III. ii.).

Julius Caesar. (H,C) Producer: BBC-TV, 1969. Distributor: TIMLIF.

Julius Caesar: **Act I, Scene II.** (H,C) 7 min., col. 1971. Distributor: BFA, OKSU, SYRCU, UILL, UWLACROSSE. The Great Scenes from Shakespeare Series.

Shakespeare's understanding of man as an individual and as a member of society. Actors perform in authentic costumes on stage patterned after Elizabethan theaters.

Julius Caesar **(Forum Scene).** (H,C) 23 min., b/w. 1961. Distributor: BAVI, BU, IFB, SYRCU, UNCONN.

Presents an excerpt (III. ii.) from the feature film starring Charleton Heston.

Assassination of Julius Caesar. (J,H,C) 27 min., b/w. Producer: MGH, 1955. Distributor: BAVI, BU, CAFC, IOWA, IU, KENT, NILL, PSU, SILU, SYRCU, UCOL, UILL, UIOWA, UKANS, UMICH, UMINN, UNC, UTAH, UTENN, UTEX, WSU. The "You Are There" Series.

Dramatizes events on 15 March 44 B.C.

Four Views of Caesar. (H,C) 23 min., b/w. Producer: CBS-TV, 1964. Distributor: BAVI, BFA, BU, CAFC, IU, KENT, PSU, SCU, SYRCU, UIOWA, UMINN, UMO, UNEB.

Caesar as he saw himself and as seen by Plutarch, Shakespeare, and Shaw.

Julius Caesar: Rise of the Roman Empire. (J,H) 22 min., col., b/w. Producer: EBEC, 1964. Distributor: BAVI, BU, BYU, CAFC, EBEC, FLU, IOWA, IU, KENT, NILL, PSU, SCU, SYRCU, UARIZ, UCEMC, UCONN, UILL, UIOWA, UKANS, UME, UMICH, UMO, UNEB, UTAH, UWLACROSSE, UWYO.

Dramatizes Caesar's rise to power and what enabled him to transform a city-republic into a world empire.

Marc Antony of Rome. (H,C) 20 min., b/w. 1948. Distributor: BAVI, IU, SYRCU, UCEMC, UCONN, UILL, UME, UMICH, UMO, UTEX, UWYO.

Cuts original screen play of *Cleopatra* to retain details of period.

Shaw Versus Shakespeare: A Series. (H,C) 33–35 min. ea., col. Producer: EBEC, 1970. Distributor: BU, BSU, BYU, CAFC, EBEC, FLU, IOWA, IU, KENT, NILL, PSU, SILU, SYRCU, UARIZ, UCEMC, UCOL, UCONN, UMICH, UMINN, UMO, UNEB, USC, UWLACROSSE.

"The Character of Caesar." Compares the characterization of Julius Caesar by Shakespeare and Shaw. "The Tragedy of Julius Caesar." Compares the treatment of Caesar's death by Shakespeare and Shaw. "Caesar and Cleopatra." Compares the works of Shakespeare and Shaw as they deal with problems of the progress of the human species.

The Spirit of Rome. (J,H) 29 min., col. Producer: EBEC, 1964, Distributor: BU, BYU, CAFC, EBEC, FLU, IU, KENT, OKSU, PSU, SILU, SUCB, SYRCU, UCEMC, UCOL, UCONN, UMICH, UWYO. The Humanities Series.

Uses scenes from *Julius Caesar* and Shaw's *Caesar and Cleopatra* to recreate grandeur of Rome.

King Lear. Five parts. (H,C) 28.5 min., b/w. Producer: WEBC, 1964.

Distributor: ASF, MACMIL. The Fair Adventure Series.

Frank Baxter presents background and explains important passages.

King Lear. (H,C) 15 min., b/w. Producer: MACMIL, 1954. Distributor: ASF, MACMIL, SYRCU. The On Stage Series.

Monty Woolley performs scene in which Lear is rejected by two of his daughters.

King Lear: **The Fool.** (H,C) 30 min., b/w. Producer: OPU. Distributor: ASF, OPU.

Analyzes the Fool's part in play's action and poetry, and includes scenes performed in a reconstruction of the Globe.

Kings and Queens. (H,C) 28 min., b/w. Distributor: MACMIL. The Fair Adventure Series.

Frank Baxter provides background.

All the World's A Stage. (H,C) 10 min., b/w. Distributor: MACMIL, USC.

Wiener Burgtheater's Raoul Aslan depicts scenes including one from *King Lear.* German language.

World's a Stage: *King Lear.* (H,C) 13 min., b/w. 1935. Distributor: WASU.

The Old Vic Repertory Company performs excerpts from I. iv. and III. ii.

Macbeth. (H,C) 17 min., b/w. Producer: MGH, 1947. Distributor: BAVI, BU, FLU, IU, PURDUE, SCU, SILU, SUCB, UCOL, UCONN, UILL, UIOWA, UKANS, UME, UMICH, UMINN, UMISS, UNC, USC, UTAH, UTENN, UTEX, WSU.

English cast led by C. Nesbit and W. Laeson present the murder scene (II. ii.) and the sleep walking scene (V. i.).

Macbeth. Five parts. (H,C) 28.5 min., b/w. Producer: WEBC, 1964. Distributor: ASF, MACMIL. The Fair Adventure Series.

Frank Baxter presents background and discusses important passages.

Macbeth. Three parts. (J,H,C) 28–33 min. ea., col. Producer: EBEC, 1964. Distributor: BAVI, BU, BYU, CAFC, EBEC, FLU, IOWA, IU, KENT, NILL, OKSU, PSU, SCU, SILU, SUCB, UARIZ, UCEMC, UCOL, UILL, UIOWA, UME, UMICH, UMINN, UMO, UNEB, USC, USFL, USU, UTAH, UWYO, WSU.

"*Macbeth,* Part I: Politics of Power." Considers relationships between the leading characters. "*Macbeth,* Part II: Themes of Macbeth." Analyzes the play as a paradox. "*Macbeth,* Part III: The Secret'st Man." Focuses on the tortured mental states of Macbeth and his wife.

Macbeth, Act I, Scene VII. (H,C) 8 min., col. 1970. Distributor: BFA, OKSU, SYRCU, UILL, UWLACROSSE. The Great Scenes from Shakespeare Series.

Focuses on atmosphere and theme of the play.

Art of Shakespeare in *Macbeth*: A Series. Five parts. (H,C) col. Producer: King Screens, 1967. Distributor: HRAW, SYRCU.

"Character," 21 min. "A Creative Rehearsal," 15 min. "Imagery," 17 min. "Patterns of Sound," 13 min. "Tragedy," 15 min.

The Drama and Language of *Macbeth*. Five parts. (H,C) 12–20 min. ea., col. 1966. Distributor: NILL, SYRCU, UMINN, UWASH. The Artistry of Shakespeare Series.

"Part I: Sound." Focuses on four language patterns: word repetition, alliteration, rhyme, and antithesis. "Part II: Imagery." Shows how usual images function in three ways as integral parts of the action. "Part III: Character." Examines relationships of Macbeth and his wife, and Macbeth and Banquo. (Additional distributor: SILU.) "Part IV: Turning Points." How the structure of a play reveals itself through turning points in the plot. "Part V: Sense of Tragedy." How intense feelings of pity and fear for Macbeth are progressively provoked.

Power and Corruption. (H,C) 34 min., col. Producer: Columbia/LCA, 1973. Distributor: BAVI, BU, BUD, CAFC, KENT, LCA, MSP, NILL, ROA, QUAD, SCU, SILU, UARIZ, UIOWA, UME, UMICH, UNEB, USC, UWLACROSSE, WCF. The Great Themes of Literature Series.

Key scenes from Roman Polanski's *Macbeth* as the story of an ambitious quest for power that leads to corruption, with a commentary by Orson Welles. Reviewed in *Landers* 19 (December 1974): 12; by G. F. Heizze in *School Teachers* (November/December 1974): 32; and in *Audio Visual* 3 (October 1974): 42.

The Merchant of Venice, **Act I, Scene III; Act IV, Scene I.** (J,H,C) 26 min., col. 1971. Distributor: BFA, UIOWA, OKSU, SYRCU, UILL, UWLACROSSE.

Mid-summer Night's Dream. (J) 26 min., col. Distributor: BU, MACMIL.

Mr. Magoo as Puck; Greek mythological heroes introduce play.

Midsummer Night's Dream. (H,C) 15 min., col., b/w. Producer: CORF, 1954. Distributor: BAVI, BYU, CAFC, FLU, KENT, PSU, SCU, SYRCU, UCOL, UILL, UKANS, UMICH, UNC, UNEB.

Introduces play by stressing differences in language, customs, and manners between 16th century and today.

Midsummer Night's Dream. **V. I. Pyramus and Thisbe.** (H,C) 13 min., b/w. Producer: UEVA, 1957. Distributor: UILL.

Performed by the Old Vic Repertory Company.

Midsummer Night's Dream: **Acts I, II, III (Lover's Scene).** (H,C) 13 min., b/w. Producer: UEVA, 1957. Distributor: UILL.

Performed by the Old Vic Repertory Company.

Much Ado About Nothing. (H,C) 180 min. Producer: CBS-TV.

Reviewed in *Sneak Preview* 2 (January 1974): 8; 2 (February 1974): 8.

Othello. (H,C) 44 min., b/w. Producer: EASTIN, 1947. Distributor: BAVI, BU, IU, NILL, UCOL, UCONN, UIOWA, UKANS, UTENN.

A condensed version with John Slater, Sebastian Cabot, Lavanna Shaw. *Comment:* Not worth the effort.

Othello. Five parts. (H,C) 28.5 min., b/w. Producer: WEBC, 1964. Distributor: ASF, MACMIL. The Fair Adventure Series.

Frank Baxter presents background and discusses important passages.

The Poet's Eye: Shakespeare's Imagery. (H,C) 16 min., col. Producer: Central Office of Information, 1964. Distributor: FOTH, UARIZ, USC.

Robert Stephens narrates introduction to Shakespeare's language and poetry; includes a scene from Olivier's *Henry V.* Reviewed by A. N. Garwood in *Previews* 5 (December 1976): 5; in *Landers* 20 (May 1976): 238; and in *Media and Methods* 12 (March 1976): 64.

Richard II. Four parts. (H,C) 28.5 min. Producer: WEBC. Distributor: ASF, MACMIL. The Fair Adventure Series.

Narrated by Frank Baxter.

Richard II: **How to Kill the King.** (H,C) 23 min., col. Producer: NBC Educational Enterprises, 1969. Distributor: SYRCU, UARIZ, UCONN, UNEB.

Includes Bolingbroke's exile, Henry's return, Richard's imprisonment and death. Reviewed by R. M. Williams 1 (March 1974): 16.

Richard III. (H,C) 28 min., b/w. Producer: WEBC, 1964. Distributor: ASF, MACMIL. The Fair Adventure Series.

Frank Baxter discusses background and passages.

Glouster's Soliloquy. (H,C) b/w. Distributor: EMGEE.

John Barrymore delivers Richard III's speech in which he declares how much he wants to be king.

Romeo and Juliet. Five parts. (H,C) 28.5 min., b/w. Producer: WEBC, 1964. Distributor: ASF, MACMIL. The Fair Adventure Series.

Frank Baxter discusses background and key passages.

Romeo and Juliet. (H,C) 40 min., b/w. Producer: Public Media, Inc., 1936. Distributor: ASF, BAVI, IU, MSU, SILU, SYRCU, UCEMC, UCOL, UMICH, USC. Classics in Literature Series.

Sequences from MGM film show John Barrymore, Leslie Howard, and Norma Shearer, in the feud between the two families, the ballroom scene, Friar Lawrence's cell, the duel scene, the death scene, and others.

Romeo and Juliet. **II. ii.** 10 min., col. 1970. Distributor: SYRCU, UILL, UWLACROSSE.

The balcony scene.

Romeo and Juliet, **Part I, II, III.** (H,C) 105 min., b/w. 1966. Distributor: BAVI, MGH, UARIZ.

A full-length version produced by the youthful cast of the Royal Academy of Dramatic Art in London on a facsimile of an Elizabethan stage.

Romeo and Juliet **in Kansas City.** (H,C) 27 min., col. Producer: PYF, 1975. Distributor: BU, KENT, PYF, UILL, UMINN.

Tchaikovsky's "Overture" played for young adult audiences. Directed by Allan Miller. Reviewed in *Landers* 20 (March/April 1976): 197; and by D. Weighart in *Previews* 5 (September 1976): 18.

Shakespeare on TV. (H,C) 50 min., b/w. Producer: CBS-TV. Distributor: UKANS.

A Frank Baxter series; includes excerpts from *Romeo and Juliet.*

Shakespeare Series. Eleven parts. (H,C) col. Distributor: BU, IFB, SYRCU.

"Antony and Cleopatra," 11 min. Excerpts from II. ii. and V. ii. *"Hamlet,"* 10 min. Excerpts from I. iv. and V. i. Reviewed in *Landers* 19

(September 1974): 9. "*Henry IV* (Part 2)," 5.5 min. Excerpt from II. ii. (Additional distributor: UCONN, OKSU.) "*Julius Caesar*," 14 min. Excerpts from II. ii. and IV. iii. "*Macbeth*," 11 min. Excerpts from I. i., I. iii., IV. i., and II. i. Reviewed in *Landers* 19 (September 1974): 12. "*Much Ado about Nothing*," 11.5 min. Excerpts from IV. i. and V. ii. (Additional distributor: UCONN.) "*Othello*," 9.5 min. Excerpts from II. i. and V. ii. "*Richard III*," 11.5 min. Excerpts from I. i. and I. ii. (Additional distributor: UCONN.) Reviewed in *Landers* 19 (September 1974): 15. "*Romeo and Juliet*," 8 min. Excerpts from Prologue and V. ii. "*Taming of the Shrew*," 13 min. Excerpts from I. ii. and III. i. (Additional distributor: UCONN.) "*Tempest*," 13.5 min. Excerpts from I. ii. and III. i. (Additional distributor: UCONN.)

Shakespeare: A Series. Six parts. (J,H,C) col. Distributor: BFA.

"*As You Like It*—An Introduction," 24 min., 1969. (Additional distributor: BAVI, CAFC, IU, NILL, OKSU, SCU, SYRCU, UIOWA, UKANS, UNEB.) Reviewed in *Sightlines* 4 (March/April 1971): 9. "*Julius Caesar*—An Introduction," 27.5 min., 1969. (Additional distributor: CAFC, OKSU, SCU, SYRCU, UARIZ, UCOL, UILL, UIOWA, UKANS, UMINN, UNEB.) "*King Lear*—An Introduction," 27.5 min., 1970. (Additional distributor: CAFC, OKSU, SCU, SYRCU, UARIZ, UILL, UKANS, UMINN, UNEB.) "*Macbeth*—An Introduction," 26 min., 1968. (Additional distributor: KENT, SYRCU, UARIZ, UCOL, UIOWA, UKANS, UMINN, UNEB, USC.) Reviewed in *EFLA* 71-7525. "*Midsummer Night's Dream*—An Introduction," 25.5 min., 1970. (Additional distributor: CAFC, OKSU, SCU, SYRCU, UARIZ, UILL, UKANS.) Reviewed in *EFLA* 71-7525. "*Twelfth Night*—An Introduction," 23 min., 1969. (Additional distributor: SCU, SYRCU, UARIZ, UMINN, UNEB.) Reviewed in *Sightlines* 4 (March/April 1971): 8; in *Visual Education* (January 1971): 40; and in *EFLA* 71-7537.

Abridged versions by English company with narration carrying the plots.

[*Taming of the Shrew*] Man and Woman. (H,C) 33 min., col. 1973. Distributor: BU, CAFC, KENT, LCA, MSP, QUAD, ROA, SILU, SYRCU, UARIZ, UILL, UMICH.

Excerpt from Zeffirelli's *Taming of the Shrew*. Petruchio (Richard Burton) woos Katharine (Elizabeth Taylor). Narrated by Orson Welles. Reviewed in *Booklist*, 15 May 1974, p. 1945; by D. Sticking in *English Journal* 63 (May 1975): 159.

The Tempest. Four parts. (H,C) 28.5 min., b/w. Producer: WEBC, 1964. Distributor: ASF, MACMIL. The Fair Adventure Series.

Frank Baxter discusses background and key passages.

The Tempest. (H,C) 27 min., b/w. 1960. Distributor: UARIZ, UILL, UNEB.

Presents John Barrymore in 1928 production with the Russian Revolution as background.

Tempest. (H,C) 27 min., col. 1970. Distributor: MACMIL.

Studies the methods of Peter Brook in a series of encounter group exercises with an international cast preparatory to rehearsals of *Tempest.* Reviewed in *Landers* 18 (February 1975): 173.

Twelfth Night. Three parts. (H,C) 28.5 min., b/w. Producer: WEBC, 1964. Distributor: ASF, MACMIL, OKSU.

Frank Baxter discusses background and key passages.

Twelfth Night. (H,C) 13 min., b/w. Producer: UEVA, 1957. Distributor: OKSU, UILL.

The Old Vic Repertory Company performs II. v.

Winter's Tale. (H,C) 13 min., b/w. Producer: UEVA, 1957. Distributor: UILL.

Old Vic Repertory Company performs V. iii.

The World of William Shakespeare. Seven parts. (H,C) col. Producer: NGES, 1978. Distributor: KAROL, NGES.

"*Hamlet,*" 35 min. Abridged performance. "The Time Is Out of Joint," 20 min. Documentary. "*Macbeth,*" 36 min. Abridged performance. "Fair Is Foul, and Foul is Fair," 20 min. Documentary. "*Romeo and Juliet,*" 36 min. Abridged performance. "Star-crossed Love," 20 min. Documentary. "Shakespeare of Stratford and London," 32 min. Introduction to the man and his environment.

A series of seven films (or video-cassettes) that provide an excellent introduction and discussion of Shakespeare's life and environment. Each play is covered by two films, one an abridged performance, the other documentary background. Worth using at any level.

World of William Shakespeare Series. Six parts. (H,C) 28.5 min. ea., b/w. Producer: WEBC, 1964. Distributor: ASF.

"How to Read a Shakespeare Play." "Life of William Shakespeare." "Printing of the Plays." "Shakespeare's Theater." "Shakespeare's World." "Shakespeare's London."

Shakespeare's Plays: Audio-cassette Tapes

Antony and Cleopatra: Politics, Myth and Theater/*Coriolanus*: Politics and Tragedy. Distributor: AL.

Lectures by J. Goode and T. Eagleton.

Cleopatra. 43 min. 1965. Distributor: JNP, LA, LISTEN.

Harrison shows how Shakespeare created one of his most complex characters. Includes readings from the play.

Approach to Shakespeare: A Series. Eighteen parts. (H,C) 60 min. ea. Distributor: BFA.

"*Antony and Cleopatra,*" A. R. Humphreys and R. A. Foakes. "*As You Like It,*" T. Hawkes and W. Moelwyn Merchant. "*Coriolanus,*" A. R. Humphreys and A. Nuttall. "*Hamlet,*" T. C. Knights and D. Daiches. "*Julius Caesar,*" N. Brooke and N. Alexander. "*King Henry IV, Part I,*" G. Lloyd Evans. "*King Henry IV, Part 2,*" G. Lloyd Evans and P. Hollandale. "*King Lear,*" G. Lloyd Evans and B. Morris. "*King Richard III,*" T. Hawkes and W. Moelwyn Merchant. "*Macbeth,*" K. Muir and R. A. Foakes. "*Measure for Measure,*" G. Lloyd Evans and B. Morris. "*Merchant of Venice,*" W. Moelwyn Merchant and B. Morris. "*Othello,*" K. Muir and R. A. Foakes. "*Richard II,*" W. Moelwyn Merchant and B. Morris. "*Romeo and Juliet,*" N. Brooke and N. Alexander. "*The Tempest,*" T. C. Knights and D. Daiches. "*Twelfth Night,*" E. A. J. Honigman and J. Dickson. "*The Winter's Tale,*" G. Lloyd Evans and B. Morris.

Discussions between academic critics include readings of key scenes.

As You Like It. Distributor: LISTEN.

By Folio Theatre Players.

As You Like It: The Pastoral World/The Play of Attitudes. Distributor: AL.

Lectures by K. Walker and I. Armstrong.

Aspects of Shakespearean Sonnets/Two Shakespearean Sonnets. Distributor: AL.

Lectures by B. Greenslade and B. Hardy.

Construction in Shakespeare. 27 min. Distributor: LA, LISTEN, JNP.

Ernest Schanzer analyzes the two-part structure of *Tim., Cor., Per.,* and *WT.*

Shakespeare's *Coriolanus*. 30 min. Distributor: CBCLS.

Points out that *Coriolanus* is one of the less familiar plays by Shakespeare but in recent years has been performed often.

Did Shakespeare Anticipate Erikson's Theory of Identity Diffusion? 30 min. Distributor: JNP, LISTEN.

H. M. Bell points out that *Coriolanus* presents various phases of personality in dynamic settings.

Critical Approaches to Shakespeare. 60 min. Distributor: CBCLS.

Discusses the meaning of meaning and attempts to find a more satisfactory vocabulary to express responses to drama.

The Elizabethan Age: A Series. Distributor: ERS.

Selected Sonnets of Shakespeare. Soliloquies from *Hamlet, Othello,* and *Lear.* Includes individual tapes on *Macbeth, JC, Rom, MV, AYL, Sounds and Sweet Airs; Song from Shakespeare.*

Hamlet. Distributor: EVED.

Lecture by Maynard Mack, Jr.

Hamlet. 29 min. Distributor: CCASS.

Features John Barrymore as Hamlet. A discussion of the questions, does the tragedy of Hamlet seem to be one of fate or of personal weakness, why is Barrymore's Hamlet deliberately naturalistic when he instructs the players, and why is Barrymore's Hamlet lyrical during the soliloquy.

Hamlet. Distributor: LISTEN.

Presents Michael MacLiammoir and the Dublin Gate Players recording their production.

Hamlet. Distributor: CU. Literary Classics Series.

Includes introduction, biography, plot summary, critical comment and bibliography.

Hamlet. Part 1, 37 min. Part 2, 41 min. Distributor: CCASS.

Sir John Gielgud's adaptation; addresses several critical questions.

Hamlet: **Book or Play?/***Hamlet* **and the Popular Dramatic Tradition.** Distributor: AL.

Lectures by T. Hawkes and M. Charney.

Hamlet: **Character and Theme.** 35 min. Distributor: EVED.

C. C. Colwell lectures.

Hamlet: Everyman's Passive Hero. 29 min. 1963. Distributor: PTL.

John Monteverdi declares that the melancholy Dane is found wanting only by our false conventional, short-sighted standards.

Hamlet: **Plot and Structure.** 35 min. Distributor: EVED.

C. C. Colwell lectures.

Hamlet: **A Series.** Four parts. Distributor: LISTEN.

Features the Shakespeare recording society with Paul Scofield, Zena Walker, Diana Wynyard and cast recording their production.

Hamlet **As A Play of Revenge/The "Play" of** *Hamlet.* Distributor: AL.

Lectures by M. Merchant and T. Hawkes.

Hamlet on the Stage. 21 min. Distributor: LA, LISTEN, JNP.

Thomas M. Parrott discusses famous portrayals of Hamlet by actors from Edwin Booth to Maurice Evans.

Hamlet Rethought. Distributor: LISTEN, JNP.

Salvador De Madariaga re-examines Hamlet, and rejects the view that Hamlet could not make up his mind.

Creative Madness: Shakespeare's *Hamlet* **and Pirandello's** *Henry IV.* Distributor: EVED.

Anne Paolucci lectures.

Shakespeare At Work/The Madness of *Hamlet.* (H,C) Distributor: JNP.

Gilbert Highet lectures on *Julius Caesar* to exemplify Shakespeare's sources and on *Hamlet.*

Henry IV. (H) 30 min. Distributor: CU. The Dialogues in Literature Series.

Henry IV: **Parts 1, 2, 3.** Distributor: LISTEN.

Presents Swan Theatre Players' production.

Henry IV Parts I and II: **Introduction of Falstaff's Debt/Necessity and Time.** Distributor: AL.

Lectures by R. Knowles and S. Wintle.

Shakespeare's *Henry IV*: **History and Kings/Character of Falstaff.** Distributor: AL.

Lectures by A. R. Humphreys and G. L. Evans.

The Structural Pattern of *Henry IV.* 20 min. Distributor: LA, LISTEN, JNP.

For Ernest Schanzer the play typifies Shakespeare's method of construction by making the play turn on a central theme and using parallels and contrasts between characters as silent commentators.

Henry V. Distributor: LISTEN.

Presents the Swan Theatre Players in their production.

The Hero's Self-Understanding in *Othello, Lear* **and** *Macbeth.* 33 min. Distributor: JNP, LISTEN.

Robert Heilman analyzes Shakespeare's exploration of man's mingled openness to self-knowledge and his resistance to it.

Julius Caesar. 55 min. Distributor: CCASS.

Includes a discussion of the questions, was Caesar a power hungry dictator, were the motives of the conspirators questionable, what is the turning point for the conspirators, and was Mark Antony motivated by personal ambitions when he roused the mob against the conspirators?

Julius Caesar. (J,H) 30 min. Distributor: CU. The Dialogues in Literature Series.

Julius Caesar. The Dublin Gate Players' production. Distributor: LISTEN.

Julius Caesar. Distributor: LA, LISTEN, JNP.

Gilbert Highet discusses whether Julius Caesar was a reformer and hero or a traitor.

Julius Caesar. (J,H) Distributor: VALINT. The Famous World Leaders Series.

Julius Caesar, **by William Shakespeare.** (J,H) 15 min. 1966. Distributor: NCAT. The Wonderful World of Books, 1 Series.

Julius Caesar: **A Series.** Three parts. Distributor: LISTEN.

Presents the Shakespeare recording society with Ralph Richardson, Anthony Quayle, and John Mills.

Julius Caesar—Macbeth—The Merchant of Venice. (J,H) Selections. Distributor: VALINT. The Shakespeare Series.

Shakespeare and the Roman Plays/*Julius Caesar.* Distributor: AL.

Lectures by R. A. Foakes and J. R. Mulryne.

King Lear. (J,H) Distributor: AL. Literary Classics Series.

Includes introduction, biography, plot summary, critical comment, and bibliography.

King Lear. Dublin Gate Theatre Cast. Four cassettes. Distributor: LISTEN.

King Lear. (H) 15 min. 1961. Distributor: NCAT. The World of Story Series.

King Lear. Distributor: EVED.

C. C. Colwell lectures.

King Lear: **Issues/Resolutions.** Distributor: AL.

Exploration of Evil: *Dr. Faustus, King Lear, The Changeling.* 59 min. Distributor: JNP.

John Simon lectures.

Shakespeare's Tragic Structure in *King Lear.* 40 min. Distributor: JNP, LA, LISTEN.

Love's Labours Lost. 57 min. Distributor: CCASS.

Discusses why King Ferdinand and his lords forswear worldly and social delights, their resolve, and the king's shabby treatment of the princess.

Macbeth. 29 min. Distributor: CCASS.

Features John Barrymore. Discusses if Macbeth is driven to his bloody deed by his wife, the causes of his anguish, and why *Macbeth* is considered Shakespeare's most perfect play.

Macbeth. 57 min. Distributor: CCASS.

Features Orson Welles. Discusses what propels Macbeth to murder, the purpose of the three witches, the theme of the play, and why Macbeth is a sympathetic character.

Macbeth. Distributor: LISTEN.

Presents a recording of play by Hilton Edwards and the Dublin Gate Players.

Macbeth. 30 min. Distributor: NCAT. The High School English Radio Dramatic Adaptations Series.

Features Judith Anderson and Maurice Evans.

Macbeth. Distributor: EVED.

C. C. Colwell lectures.

Macbeth. Distributor: EVED.

Maynard Mack, Jr. lectures.

Macbeth and His Wife. 50 min. Distributor: LA, LISTEN, JNP.

G. B. Harrison lectures on the meaning of the tragedy as worked out in the relationship between Macbeth and his wife. Gwen Olson plays Lady Macbeth and Nafe Katter plays Macbeth.

Macbeth **As a Tragedy/*Macbeth* As a Drama.** Distributor: AL.

Lectures by A. R. Humphreys and R. Warren.

Macbeth: **A Series.** Three parts. Distributor: LISTEN.

The Shakespeare Recording Society with Anthony Quayle, Gwen Ffrangcon-Davies, and Stanley Holloway.

Measure for Measure **as a Problem Play.** 35 min. Distributor: EVED.

C. C. Colwell lectures.

Performing Isabella in *Measure for Measure.* Distributor: FOLGER.

Lecture by Marth Henry.

Meet Mr. Shakespeare: A Series. (H) 15 min. ea. 1966. Distributor: NCAT.

"And Everything Handsome about Him." "Beauteous Ladies: The Ladies in Shakespeare's Plays." "Fellow of Infinite Jest." "Fight to the Last Gasp." "The Great Plays: *Hamlet.*" "The Great Plays: *Julius Caesar.*" "The Great Plays: *Midsummer Night's Dream.*" "The Great Plays: *Macbeth.*" "The Great Plays: *Romeo and Juliet.*" "Oh Villain, Villain: Shakespeare's Villains." "Rhapsody of Words: Shakespeare's Poetry." "Something More Than Natural." "That Loved Not Wisely, But Too Well." "What a Piece of Work Is Man." "What Fools These Mortals Be." "When Good Queen Bess Ruled England's State."
Presents the plays and poetry of Shakespeare.

The Merry Wives of Windsor. 57 min. Distributor: CCASS.

Discusses the questions, why did Shakespeare write the play, how did he pick the title, and was the play a sequel to *Henry IV*?

A Midsummer Night's Dream. Three cassettes. Distributor: LISTEN.

Dublin Gate Theatre Cast.

A Midsummer Night's Dream. 22 min. Distributor: JNP, LA.

Ernest Schanzer discusses play's unity, its central themes, and Shakespeare's treatment of the fairies.

A Midsummer Night's Dream. 58 min. Distributor: CCASS.

Dick Powell and Jean Muir discuss the questions, what is the reason for Oberon's dispute with Titania, how does Puck create the error that provides the comedy, why is Bottom given the head of an ass, and how does Shakespeare resolve all problems of the lovers?

Midsummer Night's Dream. 35 min. Distributor: EVED.

C. C. Colwell lectures.

Patterns and Character in *A Midsummer Night's Dream*/**Fantasy and Imagination in** *A Midsummer Night's Dream.* Distributor: AL.

Lectures by J. R. Brown and J. R. Multryne.

Shakespeare's Dreams and Dreamer/The Lady and the Poet. Distributor: JNP.

G. Highet lectures on *Midsummer Night's Dream.*

Much Ado About Nothing: **Plot and Characters/The Society and Its Problems.** Distributor: AL.

Lectures by M. Hattaway and J. Dusinberre.

The Myth and Ritual Approach to Shakespearean Tragedy. 55 min. Distributor: JNP, LISTEN.

Herbert Weisinger discusses the patterns of thought and feeling underlying Shakespearean tragedy.

Othello. 56 min. Distributor: CCASS.

Features Walter Hampden in *Othello.* Discusses the questions, what motivates Iago's deception, why is Othello taken in by Iago, how does Iago come by Desdemona's handkerchief, and was there a point in having Othello be a black man?

Othello. Two parts. 60 min. Distributor: APHB. The Dramatic Productions Series.

Performed by members of University of Minnesota Radio Guild.

Othello. 35 min. Distributor: EVED.

C. C. Colwell lectures.

Othello: **The Structure and Organisation of the Play/The Characters and**

Their Inter-Relationships. Distributor: AL.

Lectures by D. J. Palmer and F. W. Thompson.

Poetry of William Shakespeare. 31 min. 1961. Distributor: NCAT. The Words with Music Series.

Comments and readings with background music.

Richard II. 40 min. Distributor: LA, LISTEN, JNP.

Derek Traversi defines the play's tragedy as an acute and personal reading of historical events.

Richard III. 28 min. Distributor: CCASS.

Features John Barrymore as Richard III. Includes a discussion of the questions, was the play written to deplore the bloody succession of the British crown, does it show the weakness in hereditary monarchy, why is the play considered a challenging and exhausting role, and why is Barrymore's Richard a sympathetic tyrant?

Romeo and Juliet. Distributor: LISTEN.

The Dublin Gate Players with Hilton Edwards, Milo O'Shea and Christopher Casson.

Romeo and Juliet. Distributor: NCAT. The High School English Radio Dramatic Adaptations Series.

Romeo and Juliet. Distributor: CU. Literary Classics Series.

Includes introduction, biography, plot summary, critical comment and bibliography.

Romeo and Juliet. Distributor: EVED.

C. C. Colwell lectures.

Romeo and Juliet, **the Death of the Lovers.** 30 min. Distributor: UMICH. The Shakespeare and Music Series.

Romeo and Juliet **(Movie Version): A Series.** Two parts. Distributor: LISTEN.

Features the complete soundtrack of the movie starring Olivia Hussey and Leonard Whiting.

Scenes from Shakespeare: *Julius Caesar, Macbeth, Merchant of Venice.* Distributor: ERS.

The Secret of Shakespeare. 30 min. Distributor: LA, LISTEN, JNP.

C. B. Purdom analyzes nine Shakespearean plays to reveal the distinction between great drama and entertainment.

Shakespeare: A Series. 50 min ea. 1961. Distributor: NCAT.

"1 & 2 Henry IV," 6 parts. *"Henry V,"* 3 parts. "Introduction." "Introduction to Histories." *"King Lear." "Macbeth." "Measure for Measure,"* 3 parts. *"Merchant of Venice,"* 4 parts. *"Midsummer Night's Dream,"* 3 parts. *"Much Ado About Nothing,"* 2 parts. *"Othello,"* 3 parts. *"Richard II,"* 4 parts. *"The Tempest,"* 2 parts. *"Twelfth Night,"* 4 parts.

Lectures by Professor C. A. Aimansky.

Shakespeare at Work: A Series. Approx. 29 min. ea. 1961. Distributor: NCAT.

"How Shakespeare Uses Words." "Introduction to Shakespeare." *"Julius Caesar,* Act I–V." "The Shakespearean Atmosphere," 2 Parts. "The Shakespearean Character." "The Shakespearean Comedy." "Shakespearean Diction and Speech." "Shakespearean Plot."

G. B. Harrison illustrates Shakespeare's methods.

Shakespeare Cassettes. Eight parts. Distributor: LONDONTIMES.

"Henry V." "Julius Caesar." "Macbeth." "Merchant of Venice." "Midsummer Night's Dream." "Othello." "Romeo and Juliet." "Twelfth Night."

Shakespeare Library: A Series. Six parts. Distributor: SPA.

"Julius Caesar." "Life in Shakespeare's London." *"Macbeth." "Merchant of Venice." "Tempest." "Twelfth Night."*

Presents a collection of Shakespeare's plays at various performances.

Shakespeare, Master of Comedy/Shakespeare, Master of Tragedy. Distributor: CU.

The Shakespeare Plays. Six parts. (H,C) 30–40 min. Distributor: EVED.

"As You Like It," Martha Andresen-Thom. *"Julius Caesar,"* Robert Knoll. *"Romeo and Juliet,"* Maynard Mack. *"Richard II,"* Michael Mullin. *"Measure for Measure,"* Marjorie Garber. *"Henry VIII,"* John F. Andrews.

A series designed to coordinate with the PBS television broadcast of the BBC's productions over the next several years. These tapes, meant for students' use, apply to the 1979 telecast, but the series will expand each year. Part One introduces students to aspects of Shakespeare's language and meaning; Part Two provides a critical commentary on each play.

The Shakespearean Character. 28 min. 1961. Distributor: NCAT. The Shakespeare At Work Series.

Relates the three main ways in which Shakespeare creates and portrays character: having the character act and speak in a revealing manner, having others, both friend and foe, speak about the character, and putting the character in revealing situations.

Shakespearean Plot. 30 min. 1961. Distributor: NCAT.

Shakespeare's Comedies. 23 min. Distributor: JNP, LA, LISTEN.

Thomas Parrot compares and contrasts *MV* and *MND.*

Shakespeare Dramas. Nine parts. 35–49 min. ea. Distributor: LISTEN, EVED.

"*Hamlet*: Plot and Structure." "*Hamlet*: Character and Theme." "*Macbeth*." "*Measure for Measure* As a Problem Play." "*Midsummer Night's Dream*." "*King Lear*." "*Othello*." "*The Tempest*." "*Romeo and Juliet*."
C. C. Colwell analyzes some of Shakespeare's most important dramas.

Shakespeare's Living Library. Eleven parts. 30 min. ea. Distributor: CU.

"*Macbeth/Merchant of Venice*." "*Midsummer Night's Dream/Antony and Cleopatra*." "*Richard II/Romeo and Juliet*." "*Taming of the Shrew/The Tempest*." "*Twelfth Night/Othello*." "*Julius Caesar/Coriolanus*." "*All's Well That Ends Well/Winter's Tale*." "*Two Gentlemen of Verona/Hamlet*." "*As You Like It/Much Ado About Nothing*." "*King Lear/Comedy of Errors*." "*Henry IV/Henry V*."

Shakespeare's Romances and Chronicle Plays: A Series. Five parts. Distributor: SPA.

"*Henry IV, Part 1*." "*Henry IV, Part 2*." "*Henry V*." "*Midsummer Night's Dream*." "*Richard III*."

Shakespeare's Romantic Comedies: A Series. Six parts. Distributor: SPA.

"*As You Like It*." "*Comedy of Errors*." "*Merchant of Venice*." "*Taming of the Shrew*." "*Twelfth Night*." "*Two Gentlemen of Verona*."

Shakespeare's Second Historical Tetralogy: A Series. Six programs. Distributor: UMINN.

"Henry IV, Part 1—Program 1 and 2," 134 min. *"Henry IV, Part 2*—Program 1 and 2," 116 min. *"Richard II*—Program 1 and 2," 143 min. Based on University of Minnesota stage productions.

Shakespeare's Tragedies. Seven parts. Distributor: LA. Audio Classics Library No. 65.

"Julius Caesar." "King Lear." "Othello." "Romeo and Juliet," 2 cassettes. *"Macbeth,"* 2 cassettes.

Offers selections from the plays.

Shakespeare's Tragedies: A Series. Six parts. Distributor: SPA.

"Hamlet." "Julius Caesar." "King Lear." "Macbeth." "Othello." "Romeo and Juliet."

Shylock. 30 min. Distributor: LA, LISTEN, JNP.

G. B. Harrison presents various interpretations of the character Shylock. Includes readings of principal speeches.

Taming of the Shrew. 58 min. Distributor: CCASS.

Features Douglas Fairbanks and Mary Pickford. Discusses the questions, was Katherine truly tamed, why has Petruchio decided to tame Katherine, what is the method by which Petruchio decides to tame the shrew, and why does he want to leave directly after the wedding?

Taming of the Shrew. 30 min. Distributor: NCAT. The High School English Radio Dramatic Adaptations Series.

Features Burgess Meredith and Joyce Redmond.

The Tempest. 54 min. Distributor: CCASS.

Features Sir Cedric Hardwicke and Jessica Tandy. Includes a discussion of the questions, why does Prospero cause a storm that shipwrecks the King of Naples' boat, what fate has Prospero set for Ferdinand, why does Caliban want Prospero murdered, and what is Ariel's final reward?

The Tempest. 35 min. Distributor: EVED.

C. C. Colwell lectures.

The Tempest **from Lamb's Tales from Shakespeare.** 30 min. Distributor: JNP.

Dolly Podolsky reads.

The Unity of the Tempest/*The Tempest***: Elements and Occasions?** Distributor: AL.

Lectures by R. Knowles and J. Philling.

Twelfth Night. 29 min. Distributor: CCASS.

John Barrymore as Toby Belch and Malvolio. Discusses Barrymore in the minor roles, if his personality can be detected, and if he kept his characterizations pure.

William Shakespeare Character Interviews: A Series. Four parts. (J,H) Distributor: CU, EAV, LA.

"Macbeth." "Romeo and Juliet." "Julius Caesar." "Hamlet." Major characters are interviewed.

Women in Shakespeare: Classical Figures. Distributor: EVED.

Margaret Ranald lectures.

Women in Shakespeare's Comedies. Distributor: EVED.

Margaret Ranald lectures.

Women in Shakespeare Histories. Distributor: EVED.

Margaret Ranald lectures.

Women in Shakespeare's Last Plays. Distributor: EVED.

Margaret Ranald lectures.

Women in Shakespeare's Tragedies. Distributor: EVED.

Margaret Ranald lectures.

Shakespeare's Plays: Transparencies

***Hamlet*: Analysis and Interpretation.** 1965. Distributor: SVE.

Julius Caesar. Nineteen transparencies. Distributor: EAV.

"Shakespeare's England." "Julius Caesar's Rome." "Why Sophomores Should Read *Julius Caesar.*" "The Structure of the Play." "The Turning Point." "The Transition." "Cassius/Brutus Looks at Caesar." "The Conspiracy—Its Leaders/Brutus." "The Conspiracy—Its Leaders/Cassius." "The Triumvirate Formed after the Assassination." "Division among Leaders." "Division between Husband and Wife." "Divisions of Love." "The Whole Divided into Parts." "Other Structures." "Other Structures—The Signs." "Sub-Plots Summary." "Summing It Up." "Stage Direction in Shakespeare's Plays."

A series of transparencies with overlays analyzes aspects of the play.

Julius Caesar. Five parts. Distributor: CREATV.

Julius Caesar: **Series.** (J,H) col. Distributor: LA.

Act I: Five transparencies, manual (Sc. i, The Tribunes Disperse Mob; Sc. ii, Cassius Fears That Caesar Will Become Too Powerful, Sc. ii, Antony offers Crown to Caesar; Sc. iii, Plot to Assassinate Caesar). Act II: Four transparencies, manual (Sc. i, Conspirators Call Upon Brutus; Sc. ii, Caesar's Wife's Dream: A Warning; Sc. iii, Artemidorus Reads a Letter of Warning Which He Plans to Give to Caesar; Sc. iv, Portia Meets the Soothsayer). Act III: Six transparencies, manual (Sc. i, Artemidorus Offers His Letter to Caesar; Soothsayer Again Warns Caesar; Sc. i, Caesar Is Killed; Sc. i, Antony Vows Revenge against the Assassins; Sc. ii, Brutus Speaks: Reasons for Assassination of Caesar; Sc. ii, Antony's Funeral Oration; Sc. iii, Cinna Is Attacked and Killed by the Mob.) Act IV: Three transparencies, manual (Sc. i, Antony Plans Strategy for Coming Combat against Brutus and Cassius; Sc. ii & iii, Conspirators Make Plans for the Coming Battle; Sc. iii, Brutus Sees Caesar's Ghost). Act V: Four transparencies, manual (Sc. i & ii, The Enemy Forces meet; Sc. iii, Cassius Instructs One of His Slaves to Kill Him; Sc. iv, Brutus' Army Loses; Sc. v, Brutus Kills Himself).

Complete program of transparencies is meant to help students understand the plot and the time period of the play. Also available individually.

Macbeth. 1969. Distributor: TECN.

Series focuses on imagery and symbolism of Shakespeare's language.

Records

Ages of Man. Distributor: LISTEN.

J. Gielgud reads descriptive scenes as presented in his 1958 Broadway production.

All's Well That Ends Well. Argo. Distributor: LISTEN.

The Marlowe Society. M. Scott, P. Scales, P. Orr.

All's Well That Ends Well. Caedmon-SRS. Distributor: LISTEN.

E. Portman, F. Robson, and cast.

Antony and Cleopatra. Argo-ZPR. Distributor: LISTEN.

The Marlowe Society. J. R. Johnson and I. Worth.

Antony and Cleopatra. Caedmon-SRS. Distributor: ERS, LISTEN.

Scenes from *Antony and Cleopatra.* Caedmon. Distributor: LISTEN.
A. Quayle and P. Brown.

Cleopatra. Distributor: FOLK.
Read by C. Luce.

As You Like It. Distributor: LISTEN.
The Folio Theatre Players. An abridgement of the play presents major scenes in sequence.

As You Like It. Argo-ZPR. Distributor: LISTEN.
The Marlowe Society. C. Baker, D. Gibson, A. Jacobs.

As You Like It. Caedmon-SRS. Distributor: LISTEN, ERS.
V. Redgrave, K. Michell, M. Adrian.

Comedy of Errors. Argo-ZPR. Distributor: LISTEN.
The Marlowe Society. G. Rylands, M. Bates, J. Hart.

Comedy of Errors. Caedmon-SRS. Distributor: LISTEN, ERS.
A. McCowen and A. Massey.

Comedy of Errors. Distributor: LISTEN.
Folio Theatre Players present an abridgement.

Coriolanus. Argo-ZPR. Distributor: LISTEN.
The Marlowe Society. T. Church, A. Jacobs, I. Worth.

Coriolanus. Caedmon-SRS. Distributor: LISTEN.
R. Burton and J. Tandy.

Cymbeline. Argo. Distributor: LISTEN.
The Marlowe Society. M. Drabble, D. McCarthy, T. Hardiman.

Cymbeline. Caedmon-SRS. Distributor: LISTEN.
C. Bloom, P. Brown, B. Karloff. Text.

Cymbeline. Distributor: LISTEN.
The Folio Theatre Players present an abridgement of the play.

Great Shakespearean Actors. Distributor: LISTEN.
Voices of J. Barrymore, J. Marlowe, and other greats of the Shakespearean stage reading excerpts.

Hamlet. Distributor: LISTEN.

An abridgement with M. MacLiammoir and the Dublin Gate Players.

Hamlet. RCA Victor Redseal.

Excerpts from the sound track.

Hamlet. Columbia.

J. Gielgud's Broadway production with R. Burton.

Hamlet. Argo. Distributor: LISTEN.

The Marlowe Society. T. White, P. Wymark, M. Scott.

Hamlet. Caedmon-SRS. Distributor: LISTEN, ERS.

P. Scofield, Z. Walker, D. Wynyard.

Henry IV, Part 1. Argo. Distributor: LISTEN.

The Marlowe Society. B. Watson, D. Beves, A. Jacobs. Reviewed by J. L. Limbacher in *Previews* 3 (January 1975): 50.

Henry IV, Part 1. Caedmon-SRS. Distributor: LISTEN.

H. Andrews, P. Brown, A. Quayle, M. Redgrave.

Henry IV, Part 1. Distributor: LISTEN.

The Swan Theatre Players present an abridgement.

Henry IV, Part II. Argo. Distributor: LISTEN.

The Marlowe Society. B. Watson, D. Beves, A. Jacobs.

Henry IV, Part II. Caedmon-SRS. Distributor: LISTEN.

H. Andrews, P. Brown, A. Quayle, R. Johnson.

Henry IV, Part II. Distributor: LISTEN.

The Swan Theatre Players present an abridgement.

Henry V. Argo. Distributor: LISTEN.

The Marlowe Society. G. Watson, D. Jones, T. White.

Henry V. Caedmon-SRS. Distributor: LISTEN.

I. Holm, J. Gielgud, and cast.

Henry V. RCA Recordrama. Distributor: ERS.

Excerpts from text accompanied by Philharmonic Orchestra.

Henry V. Distributor: LISTEN.

The Swan Theatre Players present an abridgement.

Henry VI, Part I. Argo. Distributor: LISTEN.

The Marlowe Society. R. Marquand, M. Morris, W. Devlin.

Henry VI, Part II. Argo. Distributor: LISTEN.

The Marlowe Society. R. Marquand, M. Morris, P. Wimark.

Henry VI, Part III. Argo. Distributor: LISTEN.

The Marlowe Society. P. Orr and R. Wordsworth.

Henry VIII. Distributor: LISTEN.

The Folio Theatre Players present an abridgement.

Henry VIII. Argo. Distributor: LISTEN.

The Marlowe Society. F. Duncan, R. Speaight, M. Scott.

Highlights from Nine Plays. Distributor: LISTEN.

A. McMasters and Company in scenes from *Hamlet, Macbeth, Othello, Lear, Rom, MV, Shrew, AYL.*

Homage to Shakespeare. Columbia.

Reviewed in *Listening Post* 5:3 (March 1973): 30.

John Barrymore Reads Shakespeare. Audio Fidelity Records.

Readings from broadcasts shortly before Barrymore's death in 1942. Reviewed by R. Wayne in *Film News* 30 (December 1973): 32.

Julius Caesar. Distributor: LISTEN.

A Mercury Theatre Production; an abridgement starring O. Welles and cast.

Julius Caesar. Argo-ZPR. 1970.

I. Holm and R. Johnson.

Julius Caesar. Caedmon-SRS. Distributor: LISTEN, ERS.

R. Richardson, A. Quayle, J. Mills.

Julius Caesar. Distributor: EAV.

An abridgement produced in England by M. Bailey-Watson.

Julius Caesar. Argo. Distributor: LISTEN.

The Marlowe Society. J. Barton and A. Jacobs.

Julius Caesar. Distributor: LISTEN.

Dublin Gate Players with H. Edwards and M. MacLiammoir. Reviewed by J. L. Limbacher in *Previews* 3 (Feb. 1975): 34.

Julius Caesar. Distributor: LISTEN

An abridgement by the Dublin Gate Players.

King John. Argo. Distributor: LISTEN.

The Marlowe Society. M. Hordern and A. Jacobs.

King John. Caedmon-SRS. Distributor: LISTEN.

D. Wolfit, K. Hatch, R. Harris.

King Lear. Distributor: LISTEN.

D. Thomas reads excerpts. Also excerpts from *Duchess of Malfi.*

King Lear. Distributor: LISTEN.

The Dublin Gate Players present an abridgement.

King Lear. Distributor: SPA, LISTEN.

The Dublin Gate Players with H. Edwards and M. MacLiammoir. Reviewed by H. C. Verdun in *Listen Post* 6 (May 1975): 20; by J. L. Limbacher in *Previews* 3 (Feb. 1975): 34.

King Lear. Argo. Distributor: LISTEN.

The Marlowe Society. W. Devlin and J. Balcon.

King Lear. Caedmon-SRS. Distributor: LISTEN, ERS.

P. Scofield, R. Roberts, P. Brown, and cast.

Literature Units for High School, Volume I (Windows for Youth). Distributor: FOLK.

Includes discussion and readings from Shakespeare for grades 7–9.

Living Shakespeare Box Set. Distributor: LISTEN.

Ten plays in abridged form. Includes *Hamlet, Macbeth, Rom, MV, H5, Lear, JC, Othello, Shrew, MND.*

Love in Shakespeare. Distributor: SPA.

Love's Labour's Lost. Argo. Distributor: LISTEN.

The Marlowe Society. D. Godfrey, G. Watson, R. Eddison.

Love's Labour's Lost. Caedmon-SRS. Distributor: LISTEN.

G. McEvans, J. Brett, I. Richardson, I. Holm. Reviewed by H. C. Verdun in *Listen Post* 6 (Nov. 1975): 29.

Macbeth. Distributor: LISTEN, ERS.

H. Edwards and the Dublin Gate Players present an abridgement.

Macbeth. RCA-Victor. Distributor: ERS.

Old Vic Company.

Macbeth. Argo. Distributor: LISTEN.

The Marlowe Society. T. Church and I. Worth. Reviewed by J. L. Limbacher in *Previews* 3 (Jan. 1975): 50.

Macbeth. Caedmon-SRS. Distributor: LISTEN.

A. Quayle, G. Ffrangcon-Davies. S. Holloway.

Scenes from *Macbeth.* Caedmon. Distributor: LISTEN.

A. Quayle and G. Ffrangcon-Davies.

Measure for Measure. Argo. Distributor: LISTEN.

The Marlowe Society. G. Rylands, J. Richer, R. Marquand.

Measure for measure. Caedmon-SRS. Distributor: LISTEN.

J. Gielgud, M. Leighton, R. Richardson.

Mercant of Venice. Argo. Distributor: LISTEN.

The Marlowe Society. T. Church and M. Scott.

Merchant of Venice. Distributor: EAV.

An abridgement featuring P. Sparer, N. Marchand, J. Randolph.

Merchant of Venice. Caedmon-SRS. Distributor: LISTEN, ERS.

H. Griffith, D. Tutin, H. Andrews.

Merchant of Venice. Distributor: LISTEN, ERS.

The Dublin Gate Players present an abridgement.

Merchant of Venice. Caedmon. Distributor: LISTEN.

An abridgement featuring M. Redgrave.

Merry Wives of Windsor. Argo. Distributor: LISTEN.

The Marlowe Society. P. Wymark. G. McEwan, B. Lehmann.

Merry Wives of Windsor. Caedmon-SRS. Distributor: LISTEN.

A. Quayle, M. MacLiammoir, J. Recman.

A Midsummer Night's Dream. Distributor: LISTEN

Dublin Gate Theatre. H. Edwards and M. MacLiammoir. Reviewed by J. L. Limbacher in *Previews* 3 (February 1975): 34.

A Midsummer Night's Dream. Argo. Distributor: LISTEN.

The Marlowe Society. T. White, J. Balcon, R. Goolden.

A Midsummer Night's Dream. Caedmon-SRS. Distributor: LISTEN, ERS.

P. Scofield and J. Parker.

A Midsummer Night's Dream. Distributor: LISTEN.

The Folio Theatre Players present an abridgement.

A Midsummer Night's Dream. Distributor: FOLK.

Much Ado About Nothing. Argo-ZPR. Distributor: LISTEN.

The Marlowe Society. J. Gielgud and P. Ashcroft. Reviewed by J. L. Limbacher in *Previews* 3 (January 1975): 50.

Much Ado About Nothing. Caedmon-SRS. Distributor: LISTEN.

R. Harrison and R. Roberts.

Much Ado About Nothing. Distributor: LISTEN.

An abridgement by the Folio Theatre Players.

Olivier in Scenes from Shakespeare's *Hamlet* and *Henry V*. RCA Victor Redseal.

One Man in His Time. Distributor: LISTEN.

J. Gielgud reads from *JC, Macbeth, R2, H5.*

Othello. Distributor: LISTEN.

M. MacLiammoir. An abridgement by the Dublin Gate Theater.

Othello. RCA-Victor. Distributor: ERS.

L. Olivier.

Othello. Columbia-CSL.

P. Robeson, J. Ferrer, U. Hagen.

Othello. Argo. Distributor: LISTEN.

  The Marlowe Society. T. Church, D. Beves, W. Gifford.

Othello. Caedmon-SRS. Distributor: LISTEN.

  F. Silvera, A. Massey, C. Cusack, C. Johnson.

Pericles. Argo. Distributor: LISTEN.

  The Marlowe Society. W. Squire, P. Scales, F. Duncan.

Pericles. Caedmon-SRS. Distributor: LISTEN.

  P. Scofield.

Queen Elizabeth and the Spanish Armada/Mary, Queen of Scots. Distributor: SCHOLASTIC.

Rape of Lucrece. Caedmon.

  R. Burton, E. Evans, D. Wolfit.

Rape of Lucrece. Argo. Distributor: LISTEN.

  The Marlowe Society. T. Church and P. Ashcroft.

Richard II. Argo. Distributor: LISTEN.

  The Marlowe Society. G. Rylands and A. Jacobs.

Richard II. Caedmon-SRS. Distributor: LISTEN, ERS.

  J. Gielgud.

Richard II. Distributor: LISTEN.

  An abridgement by the Folio Theatre Players.

Richard II. RCA Victor.

Richard III. Argo. Distributor: LISTEN.

  The Marlowe Society. P. Wymark, R. Wordsworth, P. Garland.

Richard III. Caedmon-SRS. Distributor: LISTEN.

  C. Cusack and P. Ashcroft.

Richard III. Distributor: LISTEN.

  An abridgement by the Folio Theatre Players.

Romeo and Juliet. Distributor: LISTEN.

  An abridgement by the Swan Theatre Players.

Romeo and Juliet. Distributor: LISTEN, ERS.

  C. Bloom and A. Finney.

Romeo and Juliet. Distributor: LISTEN.

> Dublin Gate Players. Reviewed by J. L. Limbacher in *Previews* 3 (Feb. 1975): 34.

Romeo and Juliet. Argo. Distributor: LISTEN.

> The Marlowe Society. R. Marquand and J. Richer.

Scenes. Distributor: SPA.

> A. McMaster.

Scenes from Comedies. Distributor: LISTEN.

> The Marlowe Society in scenes from *MV* (Trial Scene), *MND* (Bottom's Rehearsal), *TN* (Viola Meets Olivia, Cakes and Ale).

Scenes from Histories. Distributor: LISTEN.

> The Marlowe Society presents *King John* (King John and Hubert), *R2* (Death of John of Gaunt, King's Dethronement), 1H4 (Falstaff and Justice Shallow), *H5* (First Prologue).

Scenes from Shakespeare. Distributor: SPA, LISTEN.

> P. Rogers reads famous soliloquies from seven plays.

Scenes from the Tragedies—Vol I. Distributor: LISTEN.

> The Marlowe Society presents *JC* (Funeral Speech), *Rom* (Balcony Scene), *Othello* (Murder of Desdemona), *Macbeth* (Murder of Duncan and Sleepwalking Scene).

Scenes from the Tragedies—Vol. II. Distributor: LISTEN.

> *Hamlet* (To Be or Not To Be, Claudius' Prayer, Hamlet and Gertrude, Final Scene), *Lear* (Division of Kingdom, Edmund's Soliloquy, Storm Scene, Recognition of Cordelia, Death of Cordelia).

Shakespeare for Actors—Vol. I. Distributor: LISTEN.

> M. MacLiammoir and H. Edwards demonstrate with scenes and soliloquies from *Hamlet, Othello,* and *Macbeth.*

Shakespeare for Actors—Vol II. Distributor: LISTEN.

> Scenes and soliloquies from *JC, Lear,* and *MV.*

Shakespeare for Everyone. Distributor: LISTEN.

> Includes biographical data, historical details, character analysis, and dramatic readings of two famous speeches. Teacher's guide.

Shakespeare's Library. Distributor: ERS.

Life in Shakespeare's London, vignettes from *MV, JC, Macbeth, TN, Temp.*

Shakespeare's Romances and Chronicle Plays. Distributor: ERS.

Includes *MND, Temp. 1H4, H5, R3.*

Shakespeare's Romantic Comedies. Distributor: ERS.

Includes *Err, TGV, AYL, MV, TN, Shrew.*

Shakespeare's Tragedies. Distributor: ERS.

Includes *Rom, JC, Macbeth, Othello, Hamlet, Lear.*

Soliloquies and Scenes from Shakespeare for Actors. Distributor: EAV, SPA.

M. MacLiammoir and H. Edwards of the Dublin Gate Theatre explain how they cope with the problems of a soliloquy or scene. (Scenes from *Hamlet, Macbeth, Othello, JC, Lear,* and *MV.*)

Songs from Shakespeare. Distributor: LISTEN.

Selected songs from his plays. K. John sings.

Songs from Shakespeare. Caedmon. Distributor: LISTEN, ERS.

Complete collection of songs sung by P. W. Jones and J. Vyvyan. Reviewed in *Listen Post* 4 (Sept. 1973): 18.

Songs from Shakespeare's Plays and Popular Songs of Shakespeare's Time. Distributor: SCHOLASTIC.

Harpsichord, recorder, cello accompaniment.

Popular Songs of Shakespeare's Time. Distributor: ERS.

J. Gielgud as King Richard.

Sonnets and Elizabethan Lyrics. Distributor: LISTEN.

A. Quayle reads twenty-three sonnets plus poetry of Donne, Marlowe, Spenser, Sidney, and others.

Sonnets of Shakespeare. Three LPs. Distributor: EAV.

Read by R. Speaight.

The Complete Sonnets. Distributor: LISTEN.

Read by R. Colman.

The Complete Sonnets. Caedmon. Distributor: LISTEN.

Read by J. Gielgud.

The Complete Sonnets. Argo. Distributor: LISTEN.

By the Marlowe Society.

Selected Sonnets. Distributor: LISTEN.

E. Evans reads.

Soul of an Age. Caedmon. Distributor: LISTEN.

R. Richardson and M. Redgrave read from thirteen plays. Original NBC documentary.

Sounds and Sweet Aires. Distributor: SPA, LISTEN.

C. Casson, B. McCaughey, and P. Mant in a program of poetry and song from *AYL, TN,* and *Hamlet.*

The Taming of the Shrew. Caedmon-SRS. Distributor: LISTEN, ERS.

T. Howard and M. Leighton.

The Taming of the Shrew. Argo. Distributor: LISTEN.

The Marlowe Society. D. Godfrey, P. Ashcroft, P. Orr.

The Taming of the Shrew. Distributor: LISTEN.

The Dublin Gate Theatre.

The Taming of the Shrew. Distributor: LISTEN.

Folio Theatre Players abridgement.

The Tempest. Distributor: LISTEN.

Dublin Gate Players. Reviewed by R. J. Behles in *Listen Post* 6 (April 1975): 7.

The Tempest. Argo-ZPR. Distributor: LISTEN.

The Marlowe Society. M. Hordern, N. Parry, M. Fieldhyde. Set also includes *The Phoenix and the Turtle.*

The Tempest. Caedmon-SRS. Distributor: LISTEN, ERS.

M. Redgrave, V. Redgrave, H. Griffith, A. Massey.

The Tempest. Distributor: LISTEN.

Folio Gate Players in an abridgement.

Timon of Athens. Argo. Distributor: LISTEN.
The Marlowe Society. W. Squire, J. Wood, C. Redgrave.

Titus Andronicus. Argo. Distributor: LISTEN.
The Marlowe Society. W. Devlin, P. Orr, J. Balcon.

Titus Andronicus. Caedmon-SRS. Distributor: LISTEN.
A. Quayle, M. Audley, M. Hordern.

Troilus and Cressida. Argo. Distributor: LISTEN.
The Marlowe Society. T. White, I. Worth, G. Rylands.

Troilus and Cressida. Caedmon-SRS. Distributor: LISTEN.
J. Brett, D. Cilento, C. Cusack.

Troilus and Cressida. Distributor: LISTEN.
An abridgement by the Folio Theatre Players.

Twelfth Night. Distributor: LISTEN.
Dublin Gate Players.

Twelfth Night. Argo. Distributor: LISTEN.
The Marlowe Society. C. Tutin, P. Wymark. T. Church.

Twelfth Night. Distributor: LISTEN, ERS.
S. McKenna, P. Scofield, J. Neville.

Twelfth Night. Distributor: LISTEN.
An abridgement by the Folio Theatre Players.

Two Gentlemen of Verona. Distributor: LISTEN.
An abridgement by the Folio Theatre Players.

Two Gentlemen of Verona. Caedmon-SRS. Distributor: LISTEN.
P. Wyngarde, E. de Souza, J. Dunham, J. Laurie.

Two Gentlemen of Verona: A Lover's Complaint. Argo. Distributor: LISTEN.
Marlowe Society. J. Barton, R. Marquand, G. Rylands.

Understanding and Appreciation of Shakespeare. Distributor: LISTEN.
Includes: Art of Shakespeare, Character Portrayal, Range and Depth, Great Themes, Style and Language, and Significance for Our Times.

Venus and Adonis. Argo. Distributor: FOLK, LISTEN.

Marlowe Society. I. Worth, G. Rylands, P. Orr.

Venus and Adonis. Caedmon. Distributor: LISTEN.

C. Bloom and M. Adrian read *Venus and Adonis* and *A Lover's Complaint.*

Sir William Walton: Music from Shakespeare Films. Angel.

Philharmonic Orchestra in excerpts from the scores of Olivier's three Shakespeare films.

Winter's Tale. Argo-ZPR. Distributor: LISTEN.

Marlowe Society. W. Squire, M. Scott, T. White.

Winter's Tale. Caedmon-SRS. Distributor: LISTEN.

J. Gielgud and P. Ashcroft.

Winter's Tale. Distributor: LISTEN.

An abridgement by the Folio Theatre Players.

Women in Shakespeare. Distributor: FOLK, LISTEN.

C. Luce gives a concert reading portraying female characters.

Feature Films Sources

As You Like It. (1936) d. Paul Czinner; s. Elizabeth Bergner, Laurence Olivier. Great Britain. 20th-British-Fox. b/w., 96 min. Available from: AUDB, BUD, JANUS, KIT PARKER, MSP, TWYMAN, WCF.

Chimes at Midnight or ***Falstaff.*** (1967) d. Orson Welles; s. John Gielgud, Orson Welles, Margaret Rutherford, Keith Baxter. Spain/Switzerland. International Films Espanola/Alpine. Germany. Available from: JANUS.

Hamlet. (1948). d. Laurence Olivier; s. Olivier, Jean Simmons, Basil Sidney, Eileen Herlie. Great Britain. Two Cities Films/Olivier/Rank. 152 min. Available from: ASF, AUDB, ROA, TWYMAN.

Hamlet. (1960). d. Franz Peter Wirth; s. Maximillian Schell, Dunja Movar. Atelier Gmb H. b/w., 127 min. Available from: AUDB, ASF, CW, ROA, SCU, UCEME, UCONN, UNITED, UWASH.

Hamlet. (1964). d. Grigori Kozintsev; s. Innokenti Smoktunovski, Anastasia Vertinskaya. USSR. Lenfilm. 148 min. Available from: AUDB.

Hamlet. (1969) d. Tony Richardson; s. Nicol Williamson, Marianne Faithfull. Great Britain. Woodfall. 114 min. Available from: AUDB, BU, BUD, KENT, LCA, MSP, OSU, ROA, WHOLESOME.

Henry V. (1944). d. Laurence Olivier; s. Olivier, Renee Asherson, Robert Newton. Great Britain. Two Cities Films. 137 min. Available from: ASF, AUDB, OSU, ROA, TWYMAN.

Julius Caesar. (1950). d. David Bradley; s. Bradley, Charleton Heston. USA. Avon Prod. b/w., 90 min. Available from: AUDB, SYRCU, TRANS WORLD, UWASH.

Julius Caesar. (1953). d. Joseph Mankiewicz; s. John Gielgud, Marlon Brando, James Mason. USA. MGM. 120 min. Available from: FI.

Julius Caesar. (1970) d. Stuart Burge; s. Charleton Heston, John Gielgud, Jason Robards, Jr. Great Britain. Commonwealth United Entertainment, Inc. 117 min. Available from: ASF, AUDB, BUD, MSP, ROA, WHOLESOME.

King Lear. (1969). d. Peter Brook; s. Paul Scofield, Irene Worth. Denmark. b/w., 134 min. Available from: ASF, AUDB.

King Lear. (1971). d. Grigori Kozintsev; s. Yori Jarvet, Elsa Radzin. USSR. 140 min. Available from: AUDB.

Macbeth. (1948) d. Orson Welles; s. Welles, Jeannette Nolan, Dan O'Herlihy. USA. Republic Pictures-Mercury Films. b/w., 85 min. Available from: ASF, AUDB, BUD, CHARARD, CINECRAFT, CW, FILM CENTER, IMAGES, ROA, SYRCU, TWYMAN.

[*Macbeth*] Kumonosu-Djo/The Throne of Blood. (1957) d. Akira Kurosawa; s. Toshiro Mifune. Japan. Toho Co. 105 min. Available from: AUDB.

Macbeth. (1960) d. Geo. Schaeffer; s. Maurice Evans, Judith Anderson. Great Britain. Grand Prize Films, Ltd. 107 min. Available from: ASF, AUDB, UWASH.

Macbeth. (1971) d. Roman Polanski; s. Jon Finch, Francesa Annis. Great Britain. Playboy Prod. 140 min. Available from: SWANK.

Merry Wives of Windsor. (1965). d. George Tressler. 97 min. Operatic version available from: AUDB.

Midsummer Night's Dream. (1935) d. Max Reinhardt; s. Mickey Rooney,

Olivia de Havilland, James Cagney. USA. Warner Bros. 117 min. Available from: UA.

A Midsummer Night's Dream. (1968) d. Peter Hall; s. Diana Rigg, David Warner. Great Britain. Royal Shakespeare Co./Filmways Prod. 124 min. Available from: ASF, AUDB, UWASH.

Othello. (1951) d. Orson Welles; s. Welles, Suzanne Cloutier, Michael MacLiammoir. Italy. Mogador Films (Mercury). b/w., 89 min. Available from: ROA.

Othello. (1955) d. Sergeo Yutkevich; s. Sergei Bondarchuk, Irina Skobzeva. USSR. Mosfilm. 108 min. Available from: AUDB.

Othello. (1965) d. Stuart Burge; s. Laurence Olivier, Maggie Smith, Frank Finlay. Great Britain. B.H.E. 166 min. Available from: WARNER.

Richard III. (1955) d. Laurence Olivier; s. Olivier, Claire Bloom, John Gielgud, Ralph Richardson. Great Britain. London Films. 155 min. Available from: JANUS.

Romeo and Juliet. (1936) d. George Cukor; s. Leslie Howard, Norma Shearer, John Barrymore. USA. MGM Pictures. 126 min. Available from: FI.

Romeo and Juliet. (1954) d. Renato Castellani; s. Laurence Harvey, Susan Shentall. Italy/Great Britain. Verona Prod./Universal Cine. 138 min. Available from: ASF, AUDB, ROA, TWYMAN, UCEMC.

Romeo and Juliet. (1956) Ballet. d. Paul Czinner; s. Margo Fonteyn, Rudolf Nureyev. Great Britain. Poetic Films. 126 min. Available from: AUDB.

Los Tarantos. (1963) d. Rovira-Beleta; s. Carmen Amaya, Sara Lezana, Daniel Martin. Spain. 81 min. Adaptation of *Romeo and Juliet.* Available from: AUDB.

Romeo and Juliet. (1965) d. Paul Lee and Val Drumm; s. Clive Francis, Angela Scoular. Great Britain. b/w., 105 min. Available from: CORNITH.

Romeo and Juliet. (1966) d. Rotha. Italy. Available from: SCHLOSS.

Romeo and Juliet. (1968) d. Franco Zeffirelli; s. Leonard Whiting, Olivia Hussey. Great Britain/Italy. B.H.E./Verona Prod. 150 min. Available from: FI.

The Taming of the Shrew. (1929) d. Sam Taylor; s. Mary Pickford,

Douglas Fairbanks. USA. Pickford Corp./Elton Corp. 70 min. Available from: MOMA (withdrawn from circulation).

The Taming of the Shrew. (1966) d. Franco Zefirelli; s. Elizabeth Taylor, Richard Burton. USA/Italy. Royal Films International. FAI Prod. 122 min. Available from: AUDB, CORNITH, MSP, SWANK.

Twelfth Night/Dwenatzataja. (1955) d. Yakov Fried; s. Klara Lutchko, Alla Larionoia. USSR. Lenfilm. 88 min. Available from: AUDB.

Winter's Tale. (1966) d. Frank Dunlop; s. Laurence Harvey, Moira Redmond, Jane Asher. Great Britain. Cressida/Hurst Park. 148 min. Available from: SCHLOSS.

Directory of Producers, Distributors, and Rental Sources

AAR Association of American Railroads, American Railroads Building, Washington, DC 20036

AL Audio Learning, Inc., 44 Parkway West, Mount Vernon, NY 10552

ANGEL Angel Records, 1750 N. Vine St., Los Angeles, CA 90028

APHB American Printing House for the Blind, Instructional Materials Reference Center, P. O. Box 6085, Louisville, KY 40206

ARGO Argo Sight & Sound, Ltd.—London Records, Inc., 539 W. 25th St., New York, NY 10001

ASF Association Films, 600 Grand Av., Ridgefield, NJ 07657

AUDB Audio Brandon Films, Inc., 34 MacQuesten Parkway South, Mount Vernon, NY 10550

BAVI Bureau of A-V Instruction, University of Wisconsin-Extension, 1327 University Avenue, P. O. Box 2093, Madison, WI 53701

BAYLU Baylor University, Baylor Theater, Waco, TX 76703

BFA BFA Educational Media, 2211 Michigan Avenue, P. O. Box 1795, Santa Monica, CA 90406

BU Boston University, A. Krasker Memorial Film Library, School of Education, 765 Commonwealth Avenue, Boston, MA 02215

BUD Budget Films, 4590 Santa Monica Blvd., Los Angeles, CA 90029

BYU Brigham Young University, Educational Media Services, 290 Herold R. Clark Building, Provo, UT 84601

CAEDMON Caedmon, 505 8th Ave., New York, NY 10018

CAFC Central Arizona Film Cooperative, Audiovisual Services, Arizona State University, Tempe, AZ 85281

CARMAN Carman Educational Association Inc., Box 205, Youngstown, NY 14174

CBCLS CBC Learning Systems, Box 500, Terminal A, Toronto, Ontario 116 Canada

CCASS Center for Cassette Studies, Inc., 8110 Webb Ave., North Hollywood, CA 91605

CHARARD Charard Motion Pictures, 2110 E. 24th St., Brooklyn, NY 11229

CINECRAFT Cine Craft, 611 SW 13th St., Portland, OR 97209

COLUMBIA Columbia Records, 51 W. 52nd St., New York, NY 10019

CONDS Contemporary Drama Services, Arthur Meriwether Educational Resources, 1131 Warren Ave., Downers Grove, IL 60516

CORF Coronet Instructional Films, 65 E. South Water St., Chicago, IL 60601

CORNITH Cornith Films, 410 E. 62nd St., New York, NY 10021

CREATV Creative Visuals Division/Gamco Industries Inc., P. O. Box 1911, Big Spring, TX 79720

CU Cassettes Unlimited, Roanoke, TX 76262

CW Clem Williams Films, 2240 Nobelstown Rd., Pittsburgh, PA 15205

DGC Denoyer-Geppert Company, 5235 Ravenswood Ave., Chicago, IL 60640

DOUBCO Doubleday and Company, Inc., Educational Systems Division, Garden City, NY 11530

DUFOUR Dufour Editions, Chester Springs, PA 19425

EALING Ealing Films, 2225 Massachusetts Ave., Cambridge, MA 02140

EASTIN Eastin-Phelan Distributing Corp., 1235 W. Fifth St., Davenport, IA 52808

EAV Educational Audio-Visual, 29 Marble Ave., Pleasantville, NY 10570

EBEC Encyclopaedia Britannica Educational Corp., 425 N. Michigan Ave., Chicago, IL 60611

EDUPRO Educational Productions, Inc., East Ardsley, Wakefield, Yorkshire, England

EDRS ERIC Document Reproduction Service, P. O. Box 190, Arlington, VA 22210

EFS Educational Filmstrips, 1401 19th St., Huntsville, TX 77340

EGH Eye Gate Media Inc., 146-01 Archer Ave., Jamaica, NY 11435

EMGEE Emgee Film Library, 16024 Ventura Blvd. Suite 211, Encino, CA 91436

ERS Educational Record Sales Inc., 157 Chambers St., New York, NY 10007

EVED Everett/Edwards Inc., P. O. Box 1060, DeLand, FL 32720

FI Films Inc., 1144 Wilmette Ave., Wilmette, IL 60091

FILMCENTER The Film Center, 938 K St. NW, Washington, DC 20001

FLU Florida State University, Instructional Support Center, Regional Film Library, Rm. 11 Seminole DH, Tallahassee, FL 32306

FOLGER Folger Shakespeare Library, 201 East Capitol St., SE, Washington, DC 20003

FOLK Folkways Records and Services Corp., 50 W. 44th St., New York, NY 10036

FOTH Films for the Humanities Inc., P. O. Box 2035, Princeton, NJ 08540

FSH Filmstrip House, 6633 W. Howard St., Niles, IL 60648

GEF Gateway Educational Films. See CORF.

HEP Hulton Educational Publications, Raans Rd., Amersham, Bucks., United Kingdom

HRAW Holt, Rinehart & Winston, School Dept., 383 Madison Ave., New York, NY 10017

IFB International Film Bureau Inc., 332 S. Michigan Ave., Chicago, IL 60604

IMAGES Images Motion Picture Rental Library, 2 Purdy Ave., Rye, NY 10560

IOWA Iowa State University, Media Resource Services, 121 Pearson Hall, Ames, IA 50010

ISU Indiana State University, Audio Visual Center, Stalker Hall, Terre Haute, IN 47807

IU Indiana University, Audio-Visual Center, Bloomington, IN 47401

JANUS Janus Films Inc., 745 Fifth Ave., New York, NY 10022

JNP Jeffrey Norton Publishers Inc., Tape Division, 145 E. 49th St., New York, NY 10017

KAROL Karol Media, E. 36A Midland Ave., Paramus, NJ 07652

KENT Kent State University, Audio Visual Services, 330 University Library, Kent, OH 44242

KIT PARKER Kit Parker Films, P. O. Box 227, Carmel Valley, CA 93924

LA Learning Arts, P. O. Box 917, Wichita, KS 67201

LCA Learning Corporation of America, 1350 Avenue of the Americas, New York, NY 10019

LISTEN Listening Library Inc., 1 Park Ave., Old Greenwich, CT 06870

LONDONTIMES London Times Design., Inc., 201 E. 42nd St., New York, NY 10017

MACMIL Macmillan Films Inc., 34 MacQuesten Parkway South, Mount Vernon, NY 10550

MFR Modern Film Rentals, 2323 New Hyde Park Rd., New Hyde Park, NY 11040

MGH McGraw-Hill Films, 1221 Avenue of the Americas, New York, NY 10020

MMAMC 3 M Company, Visual Products Division, 3 M Center, St. Paul, MN 55101

MOMA Museum of Modern Art, Film Library, 11 W. 53rd St., New York, NY 10019

MSP Modern Sound Pictures Inc., 1410 Howard St., Omaha, NB 68102

MSU Michigan State University, Instructional Media Center, Off-Campus Scheduling, East Lansing, MI 48824

NCAT National Center for Audio Tapes, Room 364, Stadium Bldg., University of Colorado, Boulder, CO 80309

NFBC National Film Board of Canada, 1251 Avenue of the Americas, 16th Floor, New York, NY 10020

NGES National Geographic Society, Educational Services, 17 and M Sts. NW, Washington, DC 20036

NILL Northern Illinois University, Media Distribution Dept., Dekalb, IL 60115

NU Northwestern University Film Library, P. O. Box 1665, Evanston, IL 60204

OKSU Oklahoma State University, Audio-Visual Center, Stillwater, OK 74074

OLESEN Olesen Films, 1535 Ivar Ave., Hollywood, CA 90028

OPRINT Out of Print

OPU Open University Educational Media Inc., 110 E. 59th St., New York, NY 10022

OSU Oregon State University, Film Library, IRAM Center, Corvallis, OR 97331

PATE Pathescope Educational Media Inc., 71 Weymay Ave., New Rochelle, NY 10802

PERF Perfection Form Company, 1000 N. 2nd Ave., Logan, IA 51546

PHM Prentice-Hall Media Inc., 150 White Plains Rd., Tarrytown, NY 10591

PSU Pennsylvania State University, Audio-Visual Services, Special Services Bldg., University Park, PA 16802

PTL Pacifica Tape Library, 5316 Venice Blvd., Los Angeles, CA 90019

PYF Pyramid Films, 2801 Colorado, Box 1048, Santa Monica, CA 90406

PURDUE Purdue University, Audio-Visual Center, Room 54 Stew, Lafayette, IN 47097

QUAD Quad Films, Inc., P. O. Box 2986, University City, MO 63130

RCA RCA Educational Service, Camden, NJ 08108

ROA ROA's Films, 1696 N. Astor St., Milwaukee, WI 53202

SCHLOAT Warren Schloat Productions, Inc. See PHM.

SCHLOSS Irwin Schloss, 165 W. 46th St., New York, NY 10036

SCNDRI John Secondari, 1560 Broadway, New York, NY 10036

SCU University of South Carolina, College of General Studies and Extension, Audio-Visual Division, Columbia, SC 29208

SILU Southern Illinois University, Learning Resources Service, Carbondale, IL 62901

SPA Spoken Arts Inc., 310 North Ave., New Rochelle, NY 10801

SUCB State University College at Buffalo, Media Library, Communication Center 102, 1300 Elmwood Ave., Buffalo, NY 14222

SVE Society for Visual Education Inc., Division of The Singer Co., 1345 Diversey Parkway, Chicago, IL 60614

SWANK Swank Motion Pictures Inc., 201 South Jefferson Ave., St. Louis, MO 63103

SYRCU Syracuse University, Film Library Collendale Campus, 1455 E. Colvin St., Syracuse, NY 13210

TECN Technifax Corp. See PHM.

TENMUS Tenth Muse, Inc., 300 Pine Ave., Goleta, CA 93017

TERF Teaching Resources Films, 110 S. Bedford, Mt. Kisco, NY 10549

TIMLIF Time Life Films, Multimedia Division, 43 W. 16th St., New York, NY 10011

TRANS WORLD Trans-World Films Inc., 332 S. Michigan Ave., Chicago, IL 60604

TWYMAN Twyman Films Inc., Box 605, 4700 Wadsworth Rd., Dayton, OH 45401

UA United Artists Corp., 729 7th Ave., New York, NY 10019

UARIZ University of Arizona, Bureau of Audiovisual Services, Tucson, AZ 85721

UCEMC University of California, Extension Media Center, Berkeley, CA 94720

UCOL University of Colorado, Bureau of Audiovisual Instruction, University Extension Division, Boulder, CO 80302

UCONN University of Connecticut, Center for Instructional Media and Technology, Storrs, CT 06268

UEVA Universal Education and Visual Arts, 100 Universal City Plaza, Universal City, CA 91608

UILL University of Illinois, Visual Aids Service, 1325 S. Oak St., Champaign, IL 61820

UIOWA University of Iowa, Audiovisual Center, Iowa City, IA 52240

UKANS University of Kansas, Audio-Visual Center, Film Rental Service, 746 Massachusetts St., Lawrence, KS 66044

UME University of Maine, Instructional Systems Center, 16 Shibles Hall, Orono, ME 04473

UMICH University of Michigan, Audio-Visual Education Center, 416 Fourth St., Ann Arbor, MI 48109

UMINN University of Minnesota, Audio-Visual Extension Services, General Extension Division, 2037 University Ave. SE, Minneapolis, MN 55455

UMISS University of Mississippi, Educational Film Library, School of Education, University, MS 38677

UMO University of Missouri, University Extension Division, 119 Whitten Hall, Columbia, MO 65201

UNC University of North Carolina, Bureau of Audio Visual Education, P. O. Box 2228, Chapel Hill, NC 27514

UNEB University of Nebraska, Instructional Media Center, Lincoln, NE 68508

UNITEDFILMS United Films, 1425 S. Main St., Tulsa, OK 74119

USC University of Southern California, Film Library-Division of Cinema, University Park, Los Angeles, CA 90007

USFL University of South Florida, Film Library, 4202 Fowler Ave., Tampa, FL 33620

USU Utah State University, Audio Visual Services, Logan, UT 84321

UTAH University of Utah, Educational Media Center, 207 Milton Bennion Hall, Salt Lake City, UT 84112

UTENN University of Tennessee, Teaching Materials Center, R-61 Communications, Knoxville, TN 37916

UTEX University of Texas, Visual Instruction Bureau, Division of Extension, Austin, TX 78712

UWASH University of Washington, Instructional Media Services, 23 Kane Hall DG-10, Seattle, WA 98195

UWLACROSSE University of Wisconsin-Lacrosse, AV Center, 1705 State, Lacrosse, WI 45601

UWYO University of Wyoming, Audio-Visual Services, P. O. Box 3237, University Station, Laramie, WY 82071

VALINT Valiant Instructional Materials Corporation, 195 Bon Hamme St., Hackensack, NJ 07602

WARNER Warner Bros. Inc., Non-Theatrical Division, 4000 Warner Blvd., Burbank, CA 91505

WASU Washington State University, Instructional Media Services, Pullman, WA 99164

WCF Westcoast Films, 25 Lusk St., San Francisco, CA 94107

WEBC Westinghouse Broadcast Co., 90 Park Ave., New York, NY 10016

WHOLESOME Wholesome Film Center Inc., 20 Melrose St., Boston, MA 02116

WSU Wayne State University, Systems Dist. and Utilization Division, 5448 Cass Ave., Detroit, MI 48202

Author

Andrew M. McLean is Associate Professor of English, University of Wisconsin—Parkside, where he teaches courses on various aspects of English Renaissance literature, including Shakespeare, Milton, Renaissance Drama, and a specialty course, Shakespeare on Film. He has published numerous articles and reviews in such journals as *Comparative Literature, CLIO, Southern Humanities Review, Renaissance Quarterly,* and *Literature/Film Quarterly.* His work has been supported by awards from the Wisconsin Humanities Committee, Catholic University of Louvain, and the American Philosophical Society. He also has served as Chair of the Executive Committee of the Literature and Science Division of the Modern Language Association.